THE
MARKETING
GURUS

Chris Murray is the former editor in-chief of Soundview Executive Book Summaries. he lives near Philadelphia, Pennsylvania, where he currently writes and edits business books.

THE
MARKETING
GURUS

LESSONS FROM THE BEST
MARKETING BOOKS OF ALL TIME

CHRIS MURRAY

AND THE EDITORS OF SOUNDVIEW
EXECUTIVE BOOK SUMMARIES

Atlantic Books
London

First published in the United States of America in 2006 by Portfolio,
a member of Penguin Group (USA) Inc., 375 Hudson Street, New York, New York, 10014.

First published in trade paperback in Great Britain in 2009 by Atlantic Books,
an imprint of Grove Atlantic Ltd.

The Summary of *Crossing the Chasm* by Geoffrey A. Moore is published
for the first time in this volume. The other summaries have been previously published
by Soundview Executive Book Summaries.

Permission acknowledgements appear on the last page of the respective selection.

PUBLISHER'S NOTE: This publication is designed to provide accurate
and authoritative information in regard to the subject matter covered.
It is sold with the understanding that the publisher is not engaged in rendering legal,
accounting, or other professional services. If you require legal advice or other expert
assistance, you should seek the services of a competent professional.

1 3 5 7 9 10 8 6 4 2

A CIP catalogue record for this book is available from the British Library.

Trade paperback ISBN: 978 1 84354 940 6
Designed by Stuart Polson.
Printed in Great Britain by CPI Mackays, Chatham ME5 8TD

Atlantic Books
An imprint of Grove Atlantic Ltd.
Ormond House
26-7 Boswell Street
London WC1N 3JZ

www.atlantic-books.co.uk

To my wife, Donna, and to our children, Samantha and Nick

Acknowledgments

There is nothing sadder than a great book that sinks in the marketplace with hardly a ripple. At Soundview Executive Book Summaries, our goal is to introduce and promote the best books on business to the widest audience possible. We want to thank all of the publisher and author partners featured in this book for helping us achieve our goal.

The summaries collected here—which present the key themes and case studies of two-hundred-and-fifty-page books in a little more than five thousand words each—were created thanks to the talent and efforts of Soundview's editors and contributing editors. Special thanks to Chris Lauer, who manages the day-to-day editorial operations at Soundview; to his team of contributing editors, including Robert Smith, Greer McPhaden, Anniken Davenport, and Kevin Gault; and to graphic designer extraordinaire Debra DePrinzio.

Special thanks also to former editor in chief Roger Griffith, former editor Jeff Olson, and former editor Anita Warren, who played vital roles in the selection and production of many of the summaries in this anthology.

Thank you also to Soundview vice president of business development Stan Kornaga; this book would not have happened without his hard work.

We at Soundview are very grateful to the team at Portfolio—Megan Casey, Adrienne Schultz, Nikil Saval, Sharon Gonzalez, and Bruce Sylvester—for their professionalism and guidance in this new adventure. Special thanks to Portfolio publisher Adrian Zackheim and associate publisher Will Weisser for their unwavering support of the project.

Finally, I wish to thank Soundview publisher George Clement and former publisher and co-founder Cynthia Folino for their leadership and guidance during the twelve years that I have been associated with Soundview. For more than two decades, Cindy Folino was the heart and soul of Soundview, the visionary pioneer of an industry that didn't even exist before Soundview. Thank you, Cindy.

Contents

INTRODUCTION

There is perhaps no discipline in the world of business more eclectic than marketing, as proven by the staggering variety of ideas, concepts, frameworks, and guidelines gathered in this collection from Soundview Executive Book Summaries. We have been providing busy readers with business book summaries for nearly thirty years; the following seventeen comprise some of the most interesting and influential among them. The authors of these books are marketing gurus—consultants, academics, and writers—who have created new thinking in the area of marketing over the past twenty-five years. Some of these authors, such as Jack Trout, Philip Kotler, and Seth Godin, have familiar names. Others may be new to you but bring to the collection insightful and innovative ideas. After all, we chose the books for this collection not because of blockbuster sales, but because they advanced and challenged accepted marketing theory and practice.

The collection begins with recent books by two world-renowned marketing thinkers. In *Differentiate or Die,* Jack Trout, collaborating with co-author Steve Rivkin, explores how companies can help their products stand above the crowd of competitors. Philip Kotler and Fernando Trias de Bes introduce the concept of lateral marketing in their book of the same name, which helps companies avoid the trap of creating new products that only further segment their current markets instead of developing new markets.

Then comes futurist Faith Popcorn's predictions for society and business in *The Popcorn Report,* which continues to provide grist for imagining new ideas and services.

The next summaries focus on connecting with the customer. Regis McKenna was one of the first to describe the changing role of the customer in the marketing equation in *Relationship Marketing.* Before scoring a bestseller with *The Millionaire Next Door,* Thomas Stanley was telling salespeople how to connect with those millionaires in *Networking with the Affluent.* In *Relentless,* Johny Johansson and Ikujiro Nonaka reveal the surprising attitudes of Japanese marketers toward market research.

One of the most important breakthroughs in marketing to the customer was the concept of one-to-one marketing, articulated memorably in *The One to One Future* by Don Peppers and Martha Rogers. Marketing consultants Murray Raphel and Neil

Raphel use many of their own experiences to describe the actions and attitudes of a business that make customers become loyal advocates of a company's products in *Up the Loyalty Ladder*. Then, in *Scoring Points*, Clive Humby and Terry Hunt with Tim Phillips present the inside story of one of the most successful customer loyalty programs in the world.

The next three summaries draw their inspiration from Silicon Valley. With typical enthusiasm, former Apple evangelist Guy Kawasaki urges companies to take on competitors with innovative and aggressive tactics in *How to Drive Your Competition Crazy*. *Crossing the Chasm* was the first of a string of bestsellers by Geoffrey Moore, one of the greatest gurus of marketing high technology products. The Internet finally makes an entrance in the collection with *Unleashing the Killer App* by Larry Downes and Chunka Mui.

The next summaries attack the issues and challenges of marketing in the twenty-first century. Emanuel Rosen dissects word-of-mouth marketing in *The Anatomy of Buzz*. In *Purple Cow,* the ever-inventive Seth Godin offers the perfect metaphor for the remarkable product. Lisa Johnson and Andrea Learned, two marketing consultants specializing in communicating with women, urge companies to become more modern in their marketing strategies in *Don't Think Pink. The Discipline of Market Leaders* by Michael Treacy and Fred Wiersema was a bestseller because of its simple but highly effective framework. Finally, *Renovate Before You Innovate* was written by Sergio Zyman, the former chief marketing officer of Coca-Cola. As the creator of New Coke, he knows all about the pitfalls of innovation for innovation's sake.

The Marketing Gurus includes some of the best thinking on marketing that has been published over the past twenty-five years. Because these summaries are presented as originally published, you will note some anachronisms in the examples; the underlying lessons, however, remain relevant and important. Whether you're a local retailer or a multinational manufacturer, whether you have fifteen employees or fifteen thousand, whether your company was founded in 1900 or last year, your marketing equation contains the same two variables: your product and services and your customers. Because this fundamental equation is universal to all businesses, we believe that each of these summaries will offer some insight or advice that you can bring to the workplace—wherever and whatever that workplace might be.

THE
MARKETING
GURUS

DIFFERENTIATE OR DIE
by Jack Trout with Steve Rivkin

In a series of *Advertising Age* articles published in 1972, two marketing consultants, Jack Trout and Al Ries, introduced a new P to marketing: positioning. Their concept was simple: the success of a new product depended on how consumers thought about that product or, in their terms, how the product was positioned in the consumer's mind.

Positioning was a response to what Trout and Ries saw as the overinformation age, or what they called the "overcommunicated society." Too much communication was being sent to consumers, Trout and Ries believed, so that one particular product's message had little chance of getting through. And this was before the Internet!

The best chance for companies in the overcommunication society was a targeted, focused approach to the consumer: choose one specific message that would drill through the noise and lodge in the consumer's mind.

A few years later, Jack Trout updated his ideas on positioning with *The New Positioning,* co-authored with Steve Rivkin. Trout also began talking about differentiation, in which the focus of the marketing effort is communicating how your product is unique compared to competitive products. Although he did not use the word specifically, the concept of differentiation existed in Trout's earlier books on positioning when he urged companies to look not only at their strengths but also at the competitors' weaknesses.

What follows is the summary of *Differentiate or Die,* in which Trout and Rivkin expand on their original thoughts of differentiation. *Differentiate or Die* is not a manifesto, however, but a nuts-and-bolts how-to guide that offers eight differentiation strategies in addition to a four-step process to differentiate your product from the competition.

Jack Trout is president of Trout & Partners, Ltd., a prestigious marketing firm with headquarters in Greenwich, Connecticut, and offices in thirteen countries. Trout and his partners have consulted for AT&T, IBM, Burger King, Merrill Lynch, Southwest Airlines, and many more Fortune 500 companies.

With Al Ries, his business partner for more than twenty-six years, Trout co-authored the industry classic *Positioning: The Battle for Your Mind,* published in

1980. Trout is the author or co-author of numerous other books, including *Marketing Warfare* and *The 22 Immutable Laws of Marketing*.

In addition to *Differentiate or Die,* Steve Rivkin co-authored *The New Positioning* and *The Power of Simplicity* with Trout. Rivkin heads his own communications firm, Rivkin & Associates, Inc., in Glen Rock, New Jersey. He was previously with Trout & Ries, Inc., for fourteen years. Rivkin's latest book is *The Making of a Name* (Oxford University Press, 2004).

DIFFERENTIATE OR DIE
Survival in Our Era of Killer Competition
by Jack Trout with Steve Rivkin

CONTENTS

THE SUMMARY IN BRIEF

What factors allow a company or product to stand out in an increasingly competitive (and global) marketplace? That's a question Jack Trout has been answering for thirty years as a consultant to Fortune 500 companies. It is a question that he (with co-author Steve Rivkin) uses in *Differentiate or Die* to help readers create solid strategies to get above the crowds of competitors and generate the business required to stay there.

What You'll Learn in This Summary

- *The tyranny of choice.* With nearly one million branded products available in the marketplace today, consumers have more choices than they know how to handle. Companies must thus give customers the tools they need in purchasing decisions to draw them to their products.
- *Losing and reinventing the USP.* In order to reinvent the idea of a unique selling proposition (USP) and differentiate their products from competitors', companies must

move away from differentiation based solely on product, and engage consumers in ways that truly reach them.

- *What differentiation is not.* Some differentiation strategies look appealing, but require more effort than is really necessary in order to make the case for a product or company over others.
- *The four steps to differentiation.* Trout lays out the basics of his differentiation strategy in four essential steps.
- *Eight successful differentiation strategies.* Differentiating your business actually has very little to do with creativity or imagination and everything to do with pursuing a logical approach to engaging customers. Trout lays out eight points of strategy that have proven to beget success.
- *Growth and sacrifice in differentiation.* Growth can kill differentiation by tempting companies to thin out their product lines in search of mass acceptance. Trout details why you should avoid the distractions growth poses.
- *Being different in different places.* What differentiation strategy will work abroad? This section presents some key considerations.

Your efforts to stand out in the marketplace begin now.

THE COMPLETE SUMMARY
1. THE TYRANNY OF CHOICE

Differentiating products today is more challenging than at any other time in history. When our earliest ancestors wondered, "What's for dinner?" the answer was clear: whatever the neighborhood could run down, kill, and bring back to the cave. Red meat? White meat? There was only one choice; it was a simpler time.

These days, the average supermarket stocks forty thousand brand items—or standard stocking units (SKUs)—an explosion of choice in just about every product category. That number is a mere fraction of the estimated one million SKUs available in America. The most interesting thing, though, is that the average family gets 80 to 85 percent of its needs from only 150 SKUs, which means there's a good chance the other 39,850 items in the store will be ignored.

What drives choice is the law of division, which states that a category starts off as a single entity and then breaks up into other segments. Computers, for instance, once were their own category; over time, however, this category segmented into mainframes, microcomputers, PCs, laptops, notebooks, and so forth. Television programming once meant network television programming; now it, too, is broken into segments: network, independent, cable, satellite, public, and now computer-based "streaming" video.

The explosion of choice has led to an entire industry dedicated to helping people with their choices, whether it be a guide to New York City restaurants or advice on which of eight thousand mutual funds to buy. The World Wide Web has expanded this industry past long-accepted structures and strictures, doling out advice on command and fulfilling needs—any need—instantly.

With so much competition, markets today are driven by choice; customers have so many choices that companies that don't address every whim of the marketplace will lose business and will not survive. Those that don't stand out will get lost in the pack. Indeed, companies must address differentiation in three key ways:

- If you ignore your uniqueness and try to be everything for everybody, you quickly undermine what makes you different.
- If you ignore changes in the market, your difference can become less important.
- If you stay in the shadow of your larger competitors and never establish your "differentness," you will always be weak.

It's an unforgiving world out there, and we haven't seen anything yet.

2. LOSING AND REINVENTING THE USP

In his 1960 book *Reality in Advertising*, Rosser Reeves defined the concept of the unique selling proposition (USP):

- Each advertisement must make a proposition to the consumer. Not just words, not just product "puffery," not just show-window advertising. Each advertisement must say to each reader, "Buy this product, and you will get this specific benefit."
- The proposition must be one that the competition either cannot or does not offer. It must be unique—either a uniqueness of the brand or a claim not otherwise made in that particular field of advertising.
- The proposition must be so strong that it can move the mass millions.

When Reeves wrote of being different, the world was an easier place. Global competition did not exist; in fact, real competition barely existed. Today, many companies have sales figures that dwarf the gross national product of some countries—the top five hundred global companies represent 70 percent of the world's trade. And the big keep getting bigger. Mergers and acquisitions are the rule of the day and competitors are tougher and smarter than ever before.

According to Reeves, in order to differentiate yourself from competitors, you must offer an option that the competition cannot or does not. To do so successfully, you should recognize how customers make decisions based on differentiation. Psychologists have come up with four functions that help people make these decisions: intuition, thinking, feeling, and sensing:

- *Differentiating with "intuitives."* This group uses intuition to concentrate on possibilities, avoiding details in favor of a "big picture" view. They are susceptible to a "next generation" strategy of differentiation. For example, when Advil positioned their ibuprofen tablets as "advanced medicine for pain," they perfectly differentiated themselves for the "big picture" crowd.
- *Differentiating with "thinkers."* This group is analytical, precise, and logical. They possess a lot of information, often ignoring the emotional or feeling aspects of a situation, and frequently act in response to the facts about a product. BMW's differentiating strategy of "the ultimate driving machine" and discussion of ergonomic design and maneuverability plays well with "thinkers."
- *Differentiating with "feelers."* This group dispenses with intellectual analysis in favor of following their own preferences, an ideal group for third-party endorsements from experts who look and sound real. Miracle-Gro's "choice of experts" campaign (nice people surrounded by flowers) is the perfect "feeler" strategy.
- *Differentiating with "sensors."* This group sees things as they are and has a great respect for facts, an enormous capacity for detail, and a knack for putting things into context. Hertz's differentiating strategy of leadership ("There's Hertz and there's Not Exactly") is a great program for "sensors," who accept it as common sense that the company is the best.

Reinventing the USP

Regardless of approach, it is more difficult for companies today to hang on to a USP or product difference or benefit, as the Reeves model suggests. There are three explanations for what has happened:

- A torrent of new products has washed over consumers, each product with conflicting claims and the smallest points of difference ("Now! Tartar control with the great taste of fresh mint gel!").
- The number-one response amongst competitors is "me-tooism." Technology enables competitors to tear apart and reconstruct knockoff products before companies even have the chance to establish their differences.
- The speed of technology has enabled companies to reinvent themselves as quickly and as often as they desire, making it difficult to differentiate on product differences alone. Intel, for example, increases data storage and performance each year at astounding rates. That said, it's not impossible to differentiate based on

product—just difficult. Gillette, for instance, reinvents shaving every few years: with two-bladed razors (Trac II), adjustable two-bladed razors (Atra), shock-absorbent razors (Sensor), and now with three-bladed razors (Mach 3). Mach 3, in particular, may seem like just a new product, but it is actually the result of $750 million in research, patents, testing, and all-around excruciating hard work.

Gillette's attention to detail and differentiation is spreading to its acquisitions. Oral-B, which Gillette acquired, hadn't introduced a new toothbrush in twenty-seven years. Gillette assigned a team of 150 people to research manual plaque removal and create new products to address their findings, resulting in a stream of new implements. By improving, upgrading, and reinventing their products, Gillette has become an excellent model in differentiation.

Will competitors get their arms around razors and toothbrushes? Most likely. "Me-tooism" remains a dominant force in competition, since being competitive so often means cashing in on a competitor's successes. Inventing and hanging on to a truly different product is hard work, but it can be done.

3. WHAT DIFFERENTIATION IS NOT

There are any number of ways to differentiate products; many of them have been proven successful (if executed properly). There are, conversely, several "yellow flags" to avoid—ideas that look appealing, but will rarely differentiate you.

Quality and Customer Orientation

The 1990s witnessed a war on quality. You couldn't walk into the business section of your local bookstore without seeing dozens of books on quality with acronym-strewn titles (TQM, SPC, QFD, CQL, etc.). While companies focused on quality improvement programs to meet the demands of their customers, customers simply got more demanding and not necessarily any more loyal to qualitycentric organizations. A Gallup survey done for the American Society for Quality Control found that only 28 percent of executives had achieved significant results (in profitability or market share) from their quality initiatives. That doesn't mean companies should (or can) abandon their quality improvement efforts. Customer expectations aren't going away, regardless of how much it costs companies to keep pace.

Indeed, "Do whatever it takes to satisfy customers" became every company's mantra in the 1980s and 1990s. Every complaint was a gift, a clue you needed in order to keep your customers "for life." Frequent buyer programs popped up, first in the airline industry (with American Airlines' AAdvantage program in 1983, then at nearly every airline). What airlines failed to do was to differentiate themselves for frequent travelers to the degree that justified the costs and drawbacks of the program; such programs were, and are, too easily imitated.

What airlines (and, indeed, many industries in the "Quality Decade") should have done was draw the line between operational effectiveness and strategic positioning. Operational effectiveness means performing better the same activities your competitors perform—a common short-term strategy. Positioning, however, dictates that you find unique and meaningful points of differentiation, and use them to competitive advantage.

Creativity

Rosser Reeves railed against "puffery" and ineffectual advertising—"the best taste ever," "incredibly smooth," and so on. While such bits of fluff were not up to Reeves's standards, at least they made the attempt to sell. Puffery has, today, been replaced with vagueness—"Start something," "People drive us," "Expanding possibilities." These slogans are creative, even entertaining, but it's sometimes hard to tell what companies are advertising.

One argument for such ads is the belief that advertising has lost its effectiveness in an age of overcommunication and cynicism. Ads that are emotional or bonding or "cool" connect with consumers, forming a bond with them. The more unconventional your ads, the more success you'll have at differentiating yourself from your competition.

Yet, one factor remains true: if people think you have an important message to convey, they will generally open their eyes and ears long enough to absorb what you have to say. The trick is not to bury that information in what some call creativity.

Price

Price is often the enemy of differentiation. When price becomes a focus of a message or a company's marketing, you begin to undermine your uniqueness. If you make price the main consideration for picking you over your competitors, you set yourself up to lose, since anyone can mark down a price. Cutting prices is insanity if the competition can go as low as you can.

There are, however, several methods you can employ to get around a price attack:

- *Do something special.* The leader can go to its biggest customers and do something special. Nike, for instance, offered the athletic shoe store chain Foot Locker the Tuned Air, a $130 shoe made exclusively for the chain. So far, so good: Foot Locker has ordered a million pairs thus far, and expects to sell $200 million worth.
- *Cause some confusion.* The leader wins when the market is confused about competing offers. AT&T countered MCI's "Friends and Family" discount program with an aggressive advertising campaign that challenged whether their competitor's program indeed saved consumers as much money as it claimed. The resulting confusion led the bulk of the market to simply stay with AT&T.
- *Shift the argument.* Introduce the concept of total cost as opposed to initial cost. In some categories, the costs you incur after you buy a product (an expensive car, for example) can be substantial. If your product performs better, you can build a cost-for-cost ownership versus cost-of-purchase comparison.
- *Differentiate with high price.* High prices tell the consumer that the product is worth a lot; in essence, the high price becomes an inherent benefit of the product itself. High quality should be more expensive; high-priced products offer more prestige.

Breadth of Line

People are overwhelmed by choice, causing confusion and making decisions difficult to come by. For some businesses, however, big selection works as a differentiator. Charles Lazarus, the founder of Toys "R" Us, noted, "When parents have no clear idea of what to buy, they go to the store with the biggest selection."

"Biggest selection" is a mantra in retailing, with superstores (or "category killers") becoming successful by using an everything-under-one-roof approach and deep discounts to cater to different niches.

But "big" can be too big, as such onetime kings of category killers as CompUSA, Sports Authority, and Party City have found out. You have to manage endless selections of SKU inventories; you alienate core consumer groups with endless mazes of aisles; you alienate older consumers with huge parking lots and massive floor space; you alienate parents who, with cranky kids in tow, don't have time to figure out your store layout.

What's really needed is guidance on what and where to buy, something the Web provides in spades. Breadth of line is nowhere near as strong a differentiator as leadership or preference or product difference. Breadth of line can be copied easily by a competitor, leaving you with only price (another easy copy) as a differentiator.

SOUTHWEST BUILDS A PRICE ADVANTAGE

One of the few success stories of using price as a differentiating factor is Southwest Airlines. By using one kind of airplane, they saved on training and maintenance costs. By offering no advanced seats, they avoided expensive reservation systems. By offering no food, they eliminated expense and time. By avoiding costly hub airports and using less expensive, smaller airports, they avoided high gate charges.

Southwest used the savings incurred from these efforts to construct a system with a lower cost per air mile than any other airline, then passed that savings on to their customers. They have differentiated themselves as a low-fare airline and have become big enough that they can't be forced out of a market by a bigger competitor that lowers their price. Many airlines have tried to use Southwest as a model for their own operation; most, if not all, have failed.

---

4. THE FOUR STEPS TO DIFFERENTIATION

Differentiating your business does not mean being cute or "creative" or imaginative. It has everything to do with logic—the science that deals with the rules and tests of sound thinking. Here is a four-step process you can follow to successfully differentiate yourself from competitors.

Step 1: Make Sense in Context

Arguments are never made in a vacuum; there are always competitors swimming around you, making arguments of their own. Your message must make sense in the context of the category; it must start with what the marketplace has heard and registered from your competitors.

You need a quick snapshot of the perceptions that exist in the market; from that snapshot, you can discern the perceptual strengths and weaknesses of you and your competitors as they exist in the minds of your target customers. You must also pay attention to what's happening in the market, to gauge whether the timing is right for your differentiating idea. For example, Nordstrom's idea of "better service" played perfectly into the context of a department store market that was reducing its people and service as a way of cutting costs.

Step 2: Find the Differentiating Idea

Your "differentness" does not have to be product-related. There are many ways to set your company apart; the trick is to find that difference and use it to set up a benefit for your customer.

Consider Hillsdale College, near Detroit—one of thousands of postsecondary institutions in the United States. Hillsdale has constructed a differentiation strategy based on the fact that it does not accept any federal aid for grants and student loans. The college's pitch is "We're free from government influence"—a successful argument that has positioned Hillsdale as a mecca for conservative thought.

Step 3: Have Credentials

To build a logical argument for your difference, you must have the credentials to support your differentiating idea, to make it real and believable. If you have a product difference, you should be able to demonstrate it; that demonstration, in turn, becomes your credentials.

Claims of difference without proof are simply empty claims. A "wide track" Pontiac must be wider than other cars. As the "world's favorite airline," British Airways should fly more people than any other airline. When it's "Hertz or Not Exactly," there should be some unique services that others don't offer.

Step 4: Communicate Your Difference

If you build a differentiated product, the world will not automatically beat a path to your door. Better products on their own don't win; you must build a strong perception in the marketplace to succeed. Every aspect of your communications should reflect your difference—your advertising, brochures, Web site, sales presentations, and so on. You cannot overcommunicate your difference.

A real differentiating idea can be a motivational bonanza. When Avis said, "We're only Number Two; we try harder," their employees were motivated to do just that. They were proud to be underdogs. You must give employees something they can latch on to and let them run with it. Come up with a differentiating idea and challenge them to bring it to life.

But there's more. Differentiating does not stop with a simple idea. You must have the resources to build a solid communications program to broadcast your idea. Indeed, an idea without money is worthless; if you don't have funding to put behind your idea, be prepared to give away a lot to get the funding. Steve Jobs and Steve Wozniak had a great idea, but it took Mike Markkula's $91,000 to put Apple on the map. For his investment, he got one-third of the company; he should have held out for half.

5. EIGHT SUCCESSFUL DIFFERENTIATION STRATEGIES

■ **Be First.** Getting into the mind with a new idea, product, or benefit is an enormous advantage. People tend to stick with what they've got, and if you're there first, any copycat measures by a competitor will just reinforce your idea. Being original translates into more knowledge, more expertise. Studies show that, in most cases, being first to the market provides a significant market share advantage over later entrants. It also forces those later entrants to find their own distinctive positioning strategy.

Being first is one thing; staying first is another. It takes hard work and enormous energy to stay on top with a new product or idea. Continued innovation is key; Gillette pioneered razor blades and remains the leader, thanks to their endless improvements in product and technology.

NOT-SO-GREAT FIRSTS

Successful firsts come from good ideas; unsuccessful firsts tend to stem from bad ideas:

• RJ Reynolds spent a fortune on the first smokeless cigarette, thinking that smokeless cigarettes would appeal to nonsmokers. Unfortunately, nonsmokers don't buy cigarettes.

• The makers of Frosty Paws (billed as "the first ice cream for dogs") never took into consideration the fact that Rover will eat anything you throw on the floor. Why would anyone buy premium-priced fake ice cream when dinner scraps will do?

Being first with a stupid idea will get you nowhere.

■ **Maintain Attribute Ownership.** An attribute is a characteristic, peculiarity, or distinctive feature of a person or thing; persons or things comprise a mixture of attributes. Each toothpaste, for example, is different from other toothpastes in terms of cavity prevention, plaque prevention, taste, and other attributes.

What makes a person or product unique is being known for one of these attributes. In fact, attribute ownership is probably the number-one way to differentiate a product or service. There is one caveat: you cannot own the same attribute or position that your competitor owns; you must seek out another attribute. Many companies attempt to emulate a leader, when it is much better to find an opposite attribute that will allow you to play off against the leader. To be most effective, attributes should be simple and benefit-oriented.

■ **Be a Leader.** Leadership is the most powerful way to differentiate a brand, because it's the most direct way to establish the credentials of a brand. Credentials are the collateral you put up to guarantee the performance of your brand.

GETTING CREDIT FOR ATTRIBUTES

Visa has dominated the credit card world by taking possession of the attribute of being "everywhere." It accounts for 53 percent of the $1.16 trillion annual credit card transactions, more than MasterCard by a two-to-one ratio. Master-Card, on the other hand, does not own an attribute of its own. It tries to act like Visa (a mistake), rather than staking out some other attribute for competitive advantage. Even American Express has seized upon a separate attribute, as an everyday usage card in grocery stores, gas stations, and the like. Not owning an attribute has been an expensive lesson for MasterCard.

Powerful leaders can take ownership of the words that stand for their category. When you think of computers, copiers, or chocolate bars, chances are you think of IBM, Xerox, and Hershey's. An astute leader will go one step further to solidify its position. Heinz, for example, owns the word ketchup, but it also owns the word that describes the ketchup's most important attribute: slow. Owning that one word helps Heinz maintain a 50 percent market share.

■ **Have a History.** Heritage has the power to make your product stand out. It can be a commanding differentiating idea because there appears to be a natural psychological importance to having a long history, one that makes people secure in their choices. Heritage also gives people the impression that they are dealing with an industry leader; if not the biggest, the company certainly is a leader in longevity.

Tradition isn't always enough, though. Companies must strike a balance in their marketing between consumer-comforting tradition and progressiveness that is crucial to continued success. A good example of this is Tabasco (the longtime leader in the pepper sauce business), which both honors its heritage and looks forward (through, for example, its trendy neckties, Cajun cooking festivals, and Tabasco-laced drinks that originated in Louisiana oyster bars).

■ **Specialize in Your Market.** People perceive those who concentrate on a specific activity or product as experts on that activity or product, giving them more knowledge and experience than they sometimes deserve. Conversely, the generalist is rarely associated with expertise in many fields of endeavor, regardless of how good he or she may be. Common sense dictates that a single person or company cannot be expert in everything.

Consider a big food name like Kraft, which, when taken out against specialist brand names (such as Hellman's in mayonnaise or French's in mustard), is trounced every time. In retail, the biggest names that are in trouble today are department stores like Macy's, Hills, and Gimbel's—all of which have ended up in bankruptcy court. The big successes are the specialists. Gap, Victoria's Secret, and Foot Locker have all succeeded by focusing on one thing.

■ **Be the Preferred Provider.** More often than not, people buy what they think they should have, like sheep following a herd. The main reason for this kind of behavior is insecurity. People are more likely to purchase a product that other people think is the correct one to buy. This is called "preference," and it is widely used by companies to differentiate their products from competitors'.

Tylenol, for example, has become the number-one pain reliever in America in part because Johnson & Johnson promotes its product as "the pain reliever hospitals prefer." Science Diet, a premium-priced dog and cat food, is "what vets feed their pets." The list goes on and on. Companies use the preferences of others to establish authenticity and to set themselves apart from the competition.

SCHWAB'S PREFERENCE STRATEGY

Charles Schwab unleashed the ultimate preference strategy by taking out a three-page ad in *The Wall Street Journal* and quoting six authorities (including *Money* magazine, *Smart Money,* and the Financial Net News) who named the company the number-one online broker in the field. That wasn't enough; they also noted that 2.5 million investors chose Schwab to help them invest online; that Schwab handles more online trades than any other broker; and that they handle more online assets than any other broker.

By the time Schwab was finished, there was no doubt that it was the most preferred online broker.

■ **Make Your Products in a Special Way.** Companies spend millions of dollars and thousands of man hours developing, producing, and testing new, innovative products, only to have their marketing departments hide all evidence of this work in their messages to consumers. Marketers dismiss such information as too complex, preferring to focus on the lifestyle experience associated with the product.

The problem with this strategy is that many competing products can provide the same lifestyle experience; focusing on the unique design or technology in the product, on the other hand, can help distinguish the product in the marketplace. Give the design element a name, and package it as the magic ingredient that differentiates the product from all others. If you've got it, flaunt it, as the following companies found out:

- Sony started its dominance in television by making a fuss over its "Trinitron." Did anyone know what it was? Nope, but it sounded impressive.
- When Crest introduced its fluoride cavity-prevention toothpaste, they made sure everyone knew it contained Fluoristan, though no one knew what that was. However, it sounded impressive.

■ **Be Hot.** When you're hot, the world should know you're hot: word of mouth is a powerful force in marketing. While people love underdogs, they usually bet on winners. It is surprising, then, that so many companies are shy when it comes to telling people about their success. While a few may carp that bragging is pushy, the real reason they're reluctant is the fear that they might not stay hot forever.

What they don't realize is that getting a product or company off the ground is a lot like getting a satellite into orbit: it takes a lot of thrust to get it off the ground, but once it's in orbit, it's a whole different ballgame. Being hot or experiencing tremendous growth can get your product or company some altitude; once you're there, you can figure out something else to keep you there.

6. GROWTH AND SACRIFICE IN DIFFERENTIATION

Brands often lose their uniqueness to the desire to be bigger. Indeed, the urge to grow seems almost like a reflex action, in part because that's how businesses tend to reward employees and management. The question of whether growth is indeed necessary is rarely brought up. In the words of economist Milton Friedman, "We don't have a desperate need to grow; we have a desperate desire to grow."

Negative Effects

Growth negatively affects differentiation in two key ways:

- The company becomes distracted. Rather than pouring on the resources and preempting a differentiating idea, companies in "growth mode" tend to focus efforts on growing their businesses. When they do this, they miss out on opportunities to improve their niche development, pursuing instead a broader (and, in most cases, less rewarding) line of growth.
- The company overextends its product lines. In an effort to pursue "endless" growth, companies fall into a line extension trap, trying to hang their brand in as many related or unrelated categories as possible. McDonald's, for instance, built a successful business on inexpensive, high-speed cheeseburgers. When the company decided

to branch out into pizzas, chicken, and kids' menu items, its growth slowed and its hold on the fast food market weakened.

Companies must recognize that maintaining focus on their basic business makes more sense in the long run than watering down their efforts in search of wider growth.

Conversely, giving up something can, on occasion, be good for your business. When you study categories over a long period of time, you can see that adding more can weaken growth, not help it. Philip Morris, for example, sought to maintain growth by adding products to its flagship brand, Marlboro. Soon, Marlboro Country was filled with Lights, Mediums, Menthol, and Ultra-Lights. Sales went down (real cowboys don't smoke Ultra-Lights), so Philip Morris returned to the tried-and-true red-and-white packaging, focusing once again on the main Marlboro brand.

The more you add, the more you risk undermining your basic differentiating idea.

7. BEING DIFFERENT IN DIFFERENT PLACES: FIVE RULES FOR THE ROAD

Making your brand a global brand is a tricky, though not impossible, proposition. Before deciding that one differentiating idea can take your brand around the world, consider the following:

1. *The current idea may be the wrong idea.* Coke inexplicably got rid of its powerful slogan "The Real Thing," only to bring it back in another form when it cracked the Russian market, where there's a rediscovery of roots and a respect for authenticity. "Drink the Legend" is Coke's slogan there.
2. *Attributes can change when you cross borders.* In Mexico, Corona is a low-rent, humble brand of beer; you can pick up a six-pack in Mexico City for about $2.50. In America, Corona has a spring-break, palm-trees, drink-it-with-a-lime image, and can usually be found for $6 to $8 a six-pack.
3. *Your market leadership may not translate.* Nescafé is Nestlé's top-selling coffee brand in the world, except in India where the company's specially made Sunrise coffee (made with chicory to give it a familiar flavor) outsells the flagship brand.
4. *Your heritage may not be respected.* Kellogg's is a proud old name for breakfast food, but the cereal giant got a cold shoulder in India, where hot food is preferred for breakfast. So much for heritage.
5. *Your specialty may get blurred.* What is Lux? In Indonesia, it's a soap; in China, Taiwan, and the Philippines, it's a shampoo; in Japan, it's both. It's difficult to

convince the world that you're a specialist when your expertise varies according to geography.

8. WHO'S IN CHARGE HERE?

Top management has to be in charge of making sure that differentiating strategy is generated, communicated, and maintained. They cannot leave those duties to marketing people and ad agencies in a hands-off capacity. The pages of business publications are littered with tales of CEOs who were misguided in their strategy or who pursued no strategy at all.

In contrast, when you study success, you tend to find that the best CEOs do their own strategy, in their own specific ways. Herb Kelleher of Southwest Airlines helps maintain his company's success by being intimately involved in all aspects of the business. Jack Welch of GE can't go to every meeting and be involved with strategy; instead, he trusts his top business unit leaders to figure out the best way to meet corporate goals.

In 1966, Peter Drucker defined leadership as "thinking through the organization's mission, defining it, and establishing it, clearly and visibly." In a new age of killer competition, the foundation of leadership could be redefined slightly as "thinking through the organization's *difference*, defining it, and establishing it, clearly and visibly."

Rosser Reeves would have agreed with that revision.

LATERAL MARKETING
by Philip Kotler and
Fernando Trias de Bes

E verything that can be invented has been invented," said U.S. Office of Patents Commissioner Charles H. Duell in 1899. While his assertion proved to be slightly off the mark, product developers and marketers today may sometimes feel as if, indeed, every product and variation of product possible *has* been invented!

Take a look at the one thousand varieties of cereal in a grocery store cereal aisle. Is there possibly a combination of cereal that has *not* been dreamed up, developed, and displayed? The problem, according to marketing *eminence grise* Philip Kotler, is that marketers are taking a *vertical* approach to product development. In other words, they take a product category and drill down into that category to find subcategories that can attract more customers.

The cereal category, for example, features dozens of subcategories for consumers who watch their weight, want fiber, want fruit in their cereal, prefer cereal with chocolate, want cereal in special shapes, and so on. This traditional vertical marketing, with its emphasis on market segmentation and brand proliferation, leads to markets that are fragmented and saturated.

In recent years, Kotler has been evangelizing a new approach called "lateral" marketing. As explained in the following summary, co-authored with marketing consultant Fernando Trias de Bes, the goal of lateral marketing is not to capture part of a market; it's to create an entirely new market.

The fact that the cereal market is extremely fragmented and saturated, for example, didn't prevent a European food company named Hero from inventing a completely new cereal product, thanks to some lateral thinking. Instead of developing another variety of cereal, the marketers at Hero asked themselves: Why should cereal be limited to breakfast? Why not turn cereal into a healthy snack that can be eaten at any time of the day?

The idea needed refining, of course. Carrying around cereal in bags and eating it with your hands wasn't the best solution. Eventually, the company decided to adopt the shape of another snack food, the chocolate bar. The result was the Hero

Muesli cereal bar, which is Europe's leading cereal bar and the inspiration for all cereal bars now sold around the world.

In the following summary, Kotler and Trias de Bes show how marketers can think laterally—and offer scores of examples that demonstrate the power of lateral thinking. Philip Kotler, the S. C. Johnson & Son distinguished professor of international marketing at Northwestern University's Kellogg School of Management, is considered the father of modern marketing. His seminal marketing text, *Marketing Management,* is now in its twelfth edition. He has written numerous other books including *Principles of Marketing, Marketing Models,* and *Kotler on Marketing.* He is also the author of more than one hundred articles in leading marketing journals.

Fernando Trias de Bes is a co-founder and partner of Salvetti & Llombart, an international marketing consultancy based in Spain, and a professor at ESADE, one of Spain's most respected business schools. His most recent book is *Good Luck: Creating the Conditions for Success in Life and Business.*

LATERAL MARKETING
New Techniques for Finding Breakthrough Ideas
by Philip Kotler and Fernando Trias de Bes

CONTENTS

THE SUMMARY IN BRIEF
In a consumer economy saturated with homogenous products and inhabited by customers who are more and more immune to advertising messages, traditional vertical marketing—with its emphasis on market segmentation and brand proliferation—is failing us. But there is a better way to reach consumers, to create innovative products and markets that don't yet exist, and to gain a real competitive advantage. This way is through an entirely different way of

thinking—through lateral marketing. Lateral marketing complements traditional marketing by providing an alternative route to generating fresh new ideas. Whereas vertical marketing helps us find increasingly smaller subgroups for which a product might be developed, lateral marketing lets marketers develop an entirely new product that finds a much wider audience. Instead of accepting that your product or service will have a small share of a saturated market, you will find yourself the leader in new markets.

THE COMPLETE SUMMARY

1. THE EVOLUTION OF MARKETS AND THE DYNAMICS OF COMPETITION

The last decades of the twentieth century were prosperous for most companies in the developed world. Population growth and longer life expectancy meant greater purchasing power. Increasingly sophisticated marketing efforts resulted in greater product trials, repeat purchases, and brand loyalty. But you can't expect to use twentieth-century marketing tactics in the twenty-first century to get the same result.

Nowadays, a strikingly high percentage of new products are doomed to fail. Only twenty years ago, the proportion of failures to successes was much lower. Why is it so difficult to succeed now? Because of the breadth of what's available and what it means. Take the cereal category, which features dozens of subcategories and varieties, each addressed to a very specific target market: those who watch their weight, who need fiber, who prefer cereal with fruit, who prefer cereal with chocolate, and so on. Among milk-based products there are over fifty yogurts competing for shelf space. In any developed country there are several dozen TV channels, leaving little room for one more.

Marketing today is not the same as it was in the 1960s and 1970s. Today there are products to satisfy almost every need. Customers' needs are more than satisfied. They are hypersatisfied.

Companies can continue to segment the market more finely, but the end result is markets too small to serve profitably.

Further complicating the picture are the facts that:

- Distribution of packaged goods is now largely in the hands of giant corporations and multinationals, such as Wal-Mart and Ikea. Distributors own shelf space and decide who gets it.
- There are more brands but fewer producers. Each segment and niche of the market got its own brand as producers discovered that by creating more brands it became more difficult for a competitor's attacks to make headway.

- Product life cycles have been dramatically shortened. A brand arms race has developed in which competitors quickly launch new brands, competitors respond with their own new brands, and the cycle repeats.
- It's cheaper to replace than repair. It's faster, easier, and cheaper to buy new, and people have accepted that products are disposable, encouraging more new product launches.
- Digital technology has led to a new range of products and services, including the Internet, global positioning systems, and computer and consumer products.
- Trademark and patent registrations are increasing.
- The number of varieties of products has increased radically.
- Markets are hyperfragmented. Companies, in their search for differentiation, have identified and created more and more segments and niches, resulting in highly fragmented markets.
- Advertising saturation is increasing and a fragmented media is complicating product launches, making it harder to reach consumers.
- Claiming consumer mind space is harder. Consumers have become selective, ignoring commercial communications. Novelty might be the only way to catch their attention.

The challenge in marketing today is to fight against fragmentation, saturation, and the storm of novelties that appear daily in the market. But recently new business concepts have appeared that are the result of a different creative process from the endless vertical segmentation of yesterday. This process is responsible for cereal bars that can be eaten as a snack or in the morning instead of with milk, grocery stores at gas stations, refrigerated pizza, and yogurt that busy women can carry in a purse.

The new priority must be to find ways to create and launch more successful products. This is the main objective of lateral marketing.

Traditional Marketing Thinking

To understand how lateral marketing will transform how you market, you must first understand the strength and weaknesses of the traditional approach to marketing. Marketing starts by studying consumer needs and figuring out how to satisfy them. Yet many manufacturers forget to focus on needs and instead focus only on selling their products.

Once needs have been identified, the next step is determining who is the market. The market is defined as the persons or companies who buy or might buy the product or services you produce in a given situation to cover a given need. For example, the market for yogurt might be any person older than one year old (age when children start eating yogurts) who is in a breakfast, dessert, or snacking occasion.

In turn, every product and service is included in a category and a subcategory. For example, the product "yogurt" belongs in the milk-based foods market and has subcategories such as fruit yogurt. Defining a category for your product is necessary if you want to develop a marketing strategy because you need to know where and against whom you are competing.

Defining needs and categories is important but can also cause problems. By defining needs and categories for your products, you necessarily exclude from consideration those you think don't need your product or service.

Imagine that we are in the first years when yogurts started to be commercially produced. Normally, markets are born with a first brand that creates the category. There is a current and potential market for the category. Competitors will appear if they sense an opportunity. The first two in the category typically capture 75 percent of the market, leaving just 25 percent for later arrivals.

If you are third or later, you typically choose a subgroup or persons/situations in the market and address your product directly to them. You usually do this by highlighting a concrete characteristic of the product to emphasize—this is your positioning. It allows you to divide and conquer. Instead of attacking the whole market and getting a tiny share, you segment the market and obtain a major share of that segment. And there is another benefit. By targeting specific needs, you fill the needs of a group of customers better and they may increase their consumption—they may eat more yogurt. Segmentation provokes a double effect: it fragments the market and at the same time makes it bigger.

Of course, as companies continue to segment the market, it becomes fragmented and saturated. Market fragmentation leaves little room for new products—which are the key components for companies that want to grow.

Another tactic you can use is "positioning." Positioning is linked to segmenting. In the case of yogurt, there are brands positioned as healthier or cheaper or fresher or more natural. Choosing a characteristic and accentuating it gives personality to your brand and makes it more noticeable. It helps you stand out in a crowded field. On the other hand, it may also blind you to innovative new concepts.

Innovations Originated from Inside a Given Market

Another way you can innovate is through modulation. Modulation-based innovations consist of variations in any basic characteristic of a given product or service by increasing or decreasing that characteristic. Examples include:

- Juices: with low sugar content, with more juice, not from concentrate, with vitamins.
- Detergents: with more bleach, with more soap concentration, fragrance-free, with less foam, with more foam.
- Banking: with monthly interest payment, without usage charges, with more offices, with better-trained staff.
- Couriers: faster delivery, higher maximum weight, better guarantee.

SLIDE RULE MARKETING

A classic example of focusing on selling the product and forgetting about need is the slide rule. The slide rule was a wood or plastic device on which many numbers were printed. By gliding the parts of the ruler, a user could carry out most arithmetic operations. In its heyday, every engineer and math student had one and used it to make calculations faster than the old paper-and-pencil process allowed. But sales started to decline when the electronic calculator arrived on the scene. The calculator was easier, faster, and more accurate even if at first it was much more expensive.

Could its manufacturers have saved the slide rule by using traditional strategies for segmentation, targeting, and positioning? Would it have helped to make separate slide rules for different groups in different colors or to advertise how they feel good to hold and use? Was there any way to segment the market to make room for newer and better slide rules? No!

Could the slide rule makers have thought of a new product such as electronic calculators to substitute for slide rules? Probably not since segmentation thinking and positioning would not lead to imagining an electronic calculator. They were stuck looking at what they already had and not able to imagine something entirely different. The problem was a lateral one. Someone had to think of the idea of slide rule + technology + a need to calculate to create a product that was more efficient than the slide rule.

Current marketing theories tend to work from the top down. They are not very effective in creating alternative or substitute products.

You can also innovate by size—such as by selling in large packs and individual serving size. In this case, you never change the product or service, just the volume, intensity, or frequency of the offer. Another possible innovation is through packaging such as chocolates marketed in an array of boxes from simple to extravagant.

Another variation is design-based. The product, container, or package and size sold are the same, but the design or look is modified. A car company may launch the same product with a different exterior design or a ski maker may change the color of the skis. The changes keep the product fresh and appealing. There are also innovations based on adding complementary ingredients. Cookies can be sprinkled with sugar or chocolate or cinnamon, for example.

All these innovations have a common factor. They consist of continued variations on what the product or service is, but do not intend to modify its essence. The innovations occur within the category in which they compete, since the methodologies for creating them assume a fixed market. These innovations do not create new categories or new markets. The innovation always occurs within the category where the idea originated. The end result is still fragmentation and a small share of the total market.

2. LATERAL MARKETING AS COMPLEMENT TO VERTICAL MARKETING

Lateral marketing involves taking a product and sufficiently transforming it in order to make it appropriate for satisfying new needs or new persons and situations not considered before. The big advantage is that instead of capturing part of a market, it creates an entirely new one.

THE CASE OF CEREAL BARS

Cereals have many advantages. They are nourishing, rich in nutrients, and healthy. Hero, a European company selling food sector products but having a low market share in the breakfast cereal category, needed to gain more market share. Since the cereal segment was highly fragmented and saturated with cereal choices, it didn't make much headway there. The solution was to redefine the utility of cereals. Hero decided to market them as a healthy snack at any time of day.

Hero adopted the form of another product—the candy bar. By combining cereal with chocolate and caramel, they created a cereal bar that could be carried and eaten any time. Today Hero is one of the European leaders in the cereal bar category. The innovation wasn't within the market "breakfast cereals." Instead, Hero used the positive attributes of cereal but embedded them in another concept, a candy bar, and created a new convenience and a new category. This lateral marketing process expanded the market for cereals into new occasions.

Vertical marketing and lateral marketing work side by side—both are necessary and complementary. In fact, lateral marketing cannot be fully developed without vertical marketing since the latter will produce more variations after a new category is discovered.

WHEN EACH TYPE OF MARKETING IS APPROPRIATE

Both lateral and vertical marketing are important. In understanding which is most appropriate in a given circumstance, remember that innovations that come from vertical marketing are easier for customers to assimilate and understand, while lateral marketing innovations need more time for assimilation.

Vertical marketing:
- works best in new markets
- works best to convert potential customers and to develop the market
- is less risky
- requires fewer resources
- doesn't depend on high volume
- fragments markets
- maintains business focus

Lateral marketing:
- works best for mature markets with no growth
- creates markets from scratch
- is riskier
- requires greater resources
- anticipates high volume
- may redefine mission and business focus

The vertical marketing process obliges you to first define the market. Vertical marketing uses the definition of the market to create competitive advantages. The innovation is done inside the definition. Lateral marketing is based on seeking an expansion by approaching one or more needs, uses, targets, or situations that we discarded earlier when we defined the market.

Lateral marketing requires you to make an important transformation to your product. When you engage in lateral marketing, you restructure the product by adding needs, uses, situations, or targets unreachable without the change. Put simply, lateral marketing uses a process that creates by opening up new directions, being provocative, and making leaps.

The innovations that come from lateral marketing create new categories or subcategories. It does this in one of four ways:

1. *A lateral product can restructure markets by creating new categories or subcategories.* For example, the launch of Walkman by Sony radically restructured the market for electronic goods since it converted millions of young potential customers into personal audio products consumers.
2. *It can reduce the volume of other products within the given market.* For example, Barbie dolls, a lateral product, have taken a huge percentage of the doll market. When Barbie was introduced, the doll market consisted of baby dolls, but a lateral thinker saw the potential for adult dolls to be played with by children. The result—an entirely new category—was the fashion doll. Barbie remains the leader in the category.
3. *A lateral product can sometimes generate volume without hurting other volume.* For example, cereal bars have not slowed the consumption of cereal but have instead expanded the occasions when cereal is consumed.
4. *A lateral product may take volume from several categories.* The cereal bar has affected the chocolate, salty snacks, and other snack categories by adding another alternative.

3. THE LATERAL MARKETING PROCESS

Lateral marketing is a work process that, when applied to existing products or services, produces innovative new products and services that cover needs, uses, situations, or targets not currently covered. As a result, lateral marketing leads to new categories or markets.

The lateral marketing process is a creative one. Creative thinking follows three simple steps:

- Select a focus. This will be a product or service.
- Make a lateral displacement for generating a stimulus. A lateral displacement is an interruption in the middle of a logical thought sequence.
- Make a connection.

Here is an example. Let's take "flowers" as our product focus. A logical thought sequence about flowers is the fact that "flowers die." A lateral displacement of that sequence is "flowers that never die." Then we make connections between the new concept and the original focus. In this case, that would involve asking ourselves under what circumstances will a flower never die? If a flower is made of cloth, silk, or plastic, then it would never die. We have found a new concept—"artificial flower." This is creativity. Innovations are a result of connecting two ideas that have no apparent or immediate connection.

How to Apply the Process

If you want to apply lateral marketing, it is essential that you understand each step. If you are thinking about the focus, you must be prepared to generate a displacement. If you are thinking about a possible displacement, you have to be aware that you are generating a stimulus for later use. And if you are working on a movement for making a connection, you have to be aware that you are working on changing your stimulus to make it logical.

Applying the process to real life, here is how it would work. First, choose a product or service you market. Creative thinking works from the bottom up, from the concrete to the general. It is inductive, not deductive. Make sure it is one where you have difficulty competing.

Once you have chosen a product or service, break it into pieces using the scheme of vertical marketing. You will then be able to see the whole picture.

The basis of lateral marketing is creating a gap. If there is no gap, there is no lateral marketing. A gap exists only if it requires you to jump. But this is hard to do, because we have been trained to think logically. You are thinking laterally if you are thinking about substituting, inverting, combining, exaggerating, eliminating, or reordering your product or service.

Take, for example the practice of sending roses to the beloved on Valentine's Day. Here are some possible lateral marketing ideas:

- *Substitute* it: Send lemons instead.
- *Invert* it: Send roses all the rest of the days of the year, but not on Valentine's Day.
- *Combine* it: Send roses and something else on Valentine's Day.
- *Exaggerate* it: Send either dozens of roses or one rose on Valentine's Day (upward and downward exaggeration).
- *Eliminate* it: Don't send roses on Valentine's Day.
- *Reorder* it: The beloved sends the roses on Valentine's Day.

Making Connections

The object of creating the gap is to find a way to fill it. Let's use an example. Someone has proposed that you sell popcorn in discos. When you consider a couple ordering popcorn in a disco, you realize that it will be hard to see. You get the idea that you might sprinkle fluorescent salt on it. You imagine them eating popcorn and getting thirsty. They order drinks. Now we have solved the gap. There is an opportunity for popcorn companies to convince discos to offer free popcorn: the profit margin of an additional drink compensates for nearly four and a half pounds of popcorn.

Of course, not every gap can be connected and not every idea will be a winner. But every idea doesn't have to be—just a few winners are all you need.

SIMILARITIES BETWEEN HUMOR AND CREATIVE THINKING

The logic of creativity is very similar to humor. A funny story consists of someone describing an initial situation (focus) and a displacement in order to generate a gap (change of perspective at the middle of the funny story). The listeners have to search for logic and will make a movement in order to connect both ideas. When they're connected, the result is laughter. Take as an example the famous remark by Groucho Marx, "I don't care to belong to any club that will accept me as a member." The first part of the sentence is the focus. (We think he is going to specify a certain type of club composed of people he does not like.) The lateral displacement is to talk of himself being accepted by the club. The gap is that Groucho would never accept membership in any club that would accept him. The sentence makes no sense at all until we force it to by seeing another perspective. Groucho is telling us that he realizes his personality is unacceptable to anyone, even himself.

---

4. LATERAL MARKETING AT THE MARKET LEVEL

It's time to apply what you have learned at the market level by using one simple technique: change one of the dimensions. The easiest and most efficient technique is substitution. A market level contains several dimensions where a product or service competes. These dimensions are need, target, and occasion. The last one is a combination of place, time, situation, and experience.

Substituting one dimension for another is easy. What you are doing is substituting one of the dimensions of the market for another that was discarded. Here are some examples:

- Red Bull opened the category today called energy drinks—soft drinks that stimulate one's energy. This serves the new need (besides the normal one of quenching thirst) and a new market (those interested in sports and energy replenishment).

• Bayer aspirin, seeing that there were lots of competitors for treating aches, began recommending an aspirin a day to recent heart attack sufferers after scientific evidence emerged that aspirin might prevent heart attacks.

You can also change the target of your product. These should be nonpotential
targets of your current product—not those who have a need for the present
product but who could buy it at any moment. Examples of products that have
been altered in order to reach nonpotential targets are:

• Gillette's sale of razors to women by introducing pink and feminine Venus
razors.
• Amusement parks and colleges that offer their locations off-season for busi-
ness conferences. Otherwise idle facilities remain in use.
• Classical music for babies, leading to the recent success of *Baby Mozart* and *Baby
Beethoven* videos in which the music is played with colorful images.

Other ideas include changing the time your product is used and moving
your product to a new setting. Occasions and events are often linked to specific
products. Champagne is for Christmas, end-of-year parties, and celebrations,
while white wine is for special dinners; candy is for Halloween, while cake is
for birthdays. You can also choose activities or experiences where other products are strongly positioned and move in. For example, an important radio station created a new program of thirty minutes of news designed for commuters
who might otherwise listen to music. Others who have moved into the com-
muting experience are developers of books and language courses on tape.

In most cases, you will have to refine some characteristic of the product. You
will identify elements to be removed, generally those elements that are anchoring
the product to its natural dimension. Do this by eliminating it or changing it. For
example, a French company that produced cheese wanted to get kids to eat more
of it. The anchor was that kids did not find cheese sweet or fun to eat. The cheese
producer sweetened the cheese and put it on a stick, which kids loved.

5. LATERAL MARKETING AT THE PRODUCT LEVEL

To apply lateral marketing at the product level, you must use one of six techniques for making lateral displacements. This is how each could be applied:

• *Substitution.* Substitution consists of removing one or several elements of the product and changing it. For example, you could substitute "students teach students"

for "professors teach students." Students, one by one, prepare a class. Every day, one explains a lesson to the rest while the professors act as moderators. Or consider what happened when someone added batteries to watches or when hard candies were put on a stick to make lollipops.

- *Combination.* Combination consists of adding one or several elements to the product or service, maintaining the rest. For example, a "Pedelec" was the result of the idea of powering a bicycle with electric batteries that are recharged when it is ridden. Result: one million units already sold in China. Or consider what happened when someone added the attribute "funny" to ties—the subcategory of funny ties with Disney and Looney Tunes characters was born.
- *Inversion.* Inversion consists of saying the contrary or adding "no" to an element of the product or service. For example, just-cooked pizza inverted into noncooked pizza, a staple now in freezers and refrigerators around the world.
- *Elimination.* Elimination consists of removing an element of the product or service. For example, a telephone without a wire led to wireless phones, and perfume without a bottle led to home fragrances in wax. In some parts of the world, the idea of a motorbike that couldn't be parked led to folding bikes that can be stored in apartments. And the idea of not waiting for film to be processed led to Polaroid prints and now digital cameras.
- *Exaggeration.* Exaggeration consists of exaggerating upward or downward one or more elements of a product or service or imagining a perfect product or service. Tandem bikes are one example as are tiny cars for congested areas. Disposable contact lenses were made possible from the idea that contacts could be discarded every day.
- *Reordering.* Reordering consists of changing the order or sequence of one or more product or service elements. For example, the idea that people could request that ads be sent to them led to permission marketing. Other examples include popcorn packaged before being cooked (leading to microwave popcorn) and soap foam dispensers in restrooms. (Ordinarily people have to handle the soap first to create foam.)

Each of these examples involves finding a new possible setting (a small car for a congested, urban area) or extracting a positive thing (disposable lenses eliminating the old fear of losing a contact).

6. LATERAL MARKETING AT THE MARKETING MIX LEVEL

Making a lateral displacement using as a focus the rest of the marketing mix elements (price, place, and promotion) implies moving away from the current way of presenting the product or service to the customer. But here you are modifying neither the essence of the product or service nor the need, target, or situation that the product or service covers.

In most cases, the lateral marketing displacement made at the mix level will result in a subcategory or an innovative commercial formula for the product or service, rather than a completely new business or category.

You can use lateral marketing to diversify your marketing mix by applying existing pricing, distribution, or communications formulas that correspond to other existing products or services and that are not naturally associated with the category you compete in.

For example, coffee vending machines have applied the credit card concept to selling coffee. You can "charge up" a coffee card in a machine by depositing money and then use the card as cash in the machines. Toll roads allow you to use an electronic device to pass through toll gates without having to fumble for change—your account is simply charged for the amount of the toll. Note that in each case, the payment system isn't new, nor is the product. What's new is using the existing method to pay for an existing product that was paid for differently before.

Examples of changes to distribution are all around too. For example, real estate companies have started to sell houses and apartments in shops located in malls or other urban shopping areas, and booksellers such as Amazon.com are selling books on the Internet. Finally, companies are using communication to sell existing products. Telecom giants are advertising on television to reach more small business prospects, for example.

7. IMPLEMENTING LATERAL MARKETING

To successfully implement lateral marketing, you must understand the underlying principles, summarized here:

- Companies need to innovate if they are to grow and prosper.
- An excessively high percentage of new products fail (80 percent of consumer goods and 40 percent of business goods) in spite of careful market research and planning. The reasons for the innovation crisis lie in the traditional innovation process.
- Most new products offer just a specialized version of something already on the market, such as a new flavor, size, or package. This is segmentation or vertical thinking.
- Repeated application of vertical thinking results in a hyperfragmented market so that few niches remain that are big enough to yield profit.
- Marketers need a complementary way of thinking up new products or services

that will lead to new categories or markets. This strategy is lateral thinking, and although it carries greater risks, the rewards are also greater.

- Lateral marketing thinking uses a distinct framework and processes that can be taught to anyone and can become a part of an innovative company's culture used in conjunction with vertical marketing.
- Lateral marketing thinking might occur spontaneously or consciously. It requires putting together ideas such as food + fast or cellular phone + camera. If you can get everyone to think laterally, you will create a company full of innovative market creators. Innovative companies like Sony and 3M have created corporate cultures that allow lateral thinkers to flourish. Yours can, too.

An innovative company does not have a few wildly creative individuals who spontaneously think up new ideas. Rather, it is characterized by several systems: an idea market, a capital market, and a talent market.

Companies have an idea market if they have a system for actively soliciting, collecting, and evaluating new ideas. Such a company appoints a high-level executive to manage an idea committee made up of high-level representatives from different departments. The committee meets regularly and evaluates ideas that have flowed in from employees, suppliers, dealers, and distributors. They arrange funding for evaluating the most attractive ideas.

To make lateral marketing really work, you need to have a system in place that takes ideas and puts them through the lateral marketing process. For example, if a brainstorming session nets ideas, the next step is to connect proposals through concrete and shared displacement techniques like those presented earlier in this summary. Using this lateral marketing framework will make idea generation a normal activity. Funding must be set aside to support idea evaluation as well as to train employees in thinking laterally. And the company will have to hire people with the talent to develop the best ideas.

The first part of the lateral marketing process, "doing a lateral displacement," can be done individually. Pick one of the three levels and apply any or several of the six techniques to it.

Next, a lateral marketing meeting should be dedicated to listening to displacements and thinking about possible ways to connect them. This is a working session where a group applies analytical and vertical thinking. After the session, you should have some discarded ideas and some valid ones. Discarded ones should be stored away as they may prove valuable in the future. The ideas should be readily available for recycling and to avoid the wasted effort of later considering an idea already discarded.

Take the valid ideas and put them through the normal product development process—from initial idea to concept testing to prototype testing to market testing and finally to market launch. By doing so, you position yourself as the leader in a new category or market rather than a bit player in an already saturated one.

THE POPCORN REPORT
by Faith Popcorn

B y laying out scenarios and anticipating the trends that might govern consumer behavior in the future, futurists offer an important service to marketers and corporate strategists. Faith Popcorn has been an innovative and creative futurist for a number of years, not only finding a way to foresee what might happen, but also capturing that future in memorable and evocative phrases.

One of her most compelling predictions, and the first trend featured in her eponymous 1991 book *The Popcorn Report,* is cocooning, which states that consumers will react to the growing dangers of the world by withdrawing into their own private worlds. While most people would reject the idea that they are going through life with a "bunker" mentality, the truth is that their worlds are more insular now than in the past. The dangers of today's world inspire parents to keep their children in a cocoon—albeit a creative and fun cocoon.

Popcorn also foresaw the growing concern about the environment. And, true to her prediction, the environment is no longer just a concern of the political left, but of Americans of all political persuasions.

In *The Popcorn Report,* Popcorn also talks about hot-branding—style with a vengeance. While her phrase did not stick, it is now universally recognized that consumers are blanded out and want creative styling in even the most mundane products. The importance of design and aesthetics that Popcorn wrote about in 1991 has since been explored in a number of books, including two—*A Whole New Mind* by Daniel Pink and *The Design of Things to Come* by Craig Vogel, Jonathan Cagan, and Peter Boatright—that were published fifteen years after *The Popcorn Report.*

While not every prediction panned out in detail in the 1990s, and cocooning especially was overstated, *The Popcorn Report* and its sequel, *Clicking,* continue to inspire creative thinking about future consumer behavior and trends that might lead to new markets and new products.

A graduate of New York's famous High School for the Performing Arts and New York University, Popcorn was creative director at a New York advertising agency before starting her consulting company BrainReserve. In addition to lecturing and writing, Popcorn—whom *Fortune* magazine called "the Nostradamus of marketing"—is an adviser to Fortune 500 companies and businesses around the world.

Besides *The Popcorn Report* and *Clicking,* co-authored with fellow futurist Liz Marigold, Popcorn is the author of *EVEolution,* a book on marketing to women.

THE POPCORN REPORT
How We'll Live, What We'll Buy, Where We'll Work
by Faith Popcorn

CONTENTS
1. Ten Trends to Shape the 1990s
2. Getting On-Trend
3. Capitalizing on the Trends

THE SUMMARY IN BRIEF

There's a consumer-driven shakeup coming in America that will change what we buy and how and why we buy it.

Faith Popcorn—the "Nostradamus of American marketing"—believes these changes are more total than any she has seen in her fifteen years of predicting consumer behavior for Fortune 500 clients.

The Popcorn Report identifies ten trends that form a portrait of tomorrow's consumer. It's not a bright picture. Consumers feel frightened and helpless in the face of society's problems. They're stressed out by the pressures of their lives, worried about their health and the planet. They're cynical about the products they buy and the companies they buy from.

That doesn't mean they won't buy. As you'll see, there are markets for products and services that make Americans feel safe, and for those that let them escape through risk-free "fantasy adventures." And the more, more, more of the 1980s is over; they want "small indulgences"—quality purchases that won't overburden them with debt or guilt. There's also a growing desire to drop out of the rat race or at least buy the trappings of a more down-to-earth lifestyle. Other opportunities exist for niche marketers: fitness and health concerns remain high, and people are searching for ways to streamline life and "buy" more time.

None of these angles alone, though, will make it easy to sell. In what Popcorn calls the "decency decade," companies will have to sell what they are as well as what they make. Businesses will have to prove they're "human," that their products are not harmful, that they are doing their part for the Earth and the people who live on it. Moreover, business will really have to listen to consumers and cater to their individual needs—and their need to be seen as individuals.

In this summary, Popcorn explains how to use the trends as a guide for developing, updating, and fine-tuning your product or service. The future won't wait until you're ready, but *The Popcorn Report* can help you get there in time.

THE COMPLETE SUMMARY

We're a consumer culture and when we change what we buy and how we buy it, we change who we are. There's a "socioquake" coming that will penetrate every household and company in America, bringing more changes than ever before. Those who see the shakeup coming in time will survive it. But if your customers reach the future before you, they'll leave you behind.

1. TEN TRENDS TO SHAPE THE 1990S

Simple demographic figures aren't enough for marketers to go on anymore. Suppose you sell to young, urban college graduates who make at least $75,000. You may think you know them—materialistic and acquisitive, right? Wrong. Many are restless and overburdened and would rather move to the country and earn $15,000. And they won't respond to your efforts unless you acknowledge their beliefs and yearnings.

Faith Popcorn's business is tracking and predicting trends, and today's trends reveal radically shifting assumptions about our past, present, and future.

The ten trends that follow are a map to the next decade, a database of consumer moods in the years to come: how buyers will feel, the impulses that will motivate their product choices, and the kinds of strategies, products, and services they'll accept or reject.

Each trend is a fraction of the whole. Viewed together, they're a portrait of the future that shows what directions businesses must take to reach consumers in the 1990s and beyond.

Trend 1: Cocooning in a New Decade

Cocooning began in the 1980s, as Americans turned homeward for a haven against the world's dangers and harassments. This self-preservation need continues in the 1990s, with a growing bunker mentality that incorporates three subtrends:

1. *The Armored Cocoon*. The desire for a private club that keeps more people out than it lets in will create major growth in "paranoia" industries—home security systems, bodyguards to rent by the hour. Marketers will increasingly have to reach the consumer in the cocoon itself.
2. *The Wandering Cocoon*. Cocooning is about controlling the environment, and there's a bonanza for marketers who can make drive time in the traveling cocoon, on the road or in the air, more pleasurable. (A microwave in the glove compartment? You can get it in Japan.)
3. *The Socialized Cocoon*. Instead of entertaining for social and business advancement or even extended family events, we'll invite in a few people we like and feel comfortable with—congenial friends with whom we'll wait out the storm. How about a return to the cocktail hour at someone's home instead of the local bar as people set aside time between work and home for cocoon hopping?

Trend 2: Fantasy Adventure

Adventure by association is all our overloaded sensory systems need when there's so much real danger outside. Most of us want to be transported out of our lives—safely. Fantasy adventure is vicarious emotional escape through consumerism.

This risk-free risk-taking can involve video rentals and aggressively foreign cuisines. It's watering the lawn wearing rafting gear. It's decorating that transports you to Santa Fe or to the country.

Offer the safe and familiar with an adventurous or exotic twist. By adding sensory value—taste, texture, sound, smell, color—you can make any product more "sensational." What about Scent-a-Rama movies or escapist rooms that project scenes and sounds on the wall?

Trend 3: Small Indulgences

Consumer culture has always been motivated by want rather than need. Now we've added another motivation: "I deserve it." However, we want the ego expression or sensory lift without worrying that the price may be too high—or that we're being too greedy.

The key is *Small* Indulgences. We buy a little red chair instead of a little red car, have lobster at home instead of out at a fancy restaurant. Desserts such as superpremium ice creams are pure Small Indulgence. Häagen-Dazs's experimental ice cream cafés in Europe could, if comfy and cocoony enough, be gangbusters here.

Crucial to this trend is quality—value and intrinsic worth rather than image and "name." You can't small-indulge yourself on junk. It may mean buying the best in one small category, such as food or shoes.

The good news for marketers: the worse it gets, the more we need these little life-enhancing lifts. More good news: expect an upturn in our spirits, culture, and economy. In that case, our appetite for indulgence will only get bigger.

Trend 4: Egonomics

Egonomics, a sister trend to Small Indulgences, is a nicer version of the "me-ness" of the 1970s and 1980s. It is niche marketing in the extreme, a product or service for me. People will pay for personalized product concept or design, "customability," and personal service.

Krause's Sofa Factory lets you choose this arm, that back, and that fabric to custom design your sofa. Matsushita in Japan custom builds bicycles to individual measurements. You wear the Belgian Shoes shop's soft-soled shoes (one basic style, many colors and fabrics) for a week, then come back for permanent soles once they're "custom fit" to your feet.

Think of the possibilities. How about jeans that actually look and fit just the way you want them? You pick the fit, fabric, pockets, get measured by a compu-tailor, and pick them up an hour later. Or how about cars with custom seats for people with bad backs, or custom cargo areas for grocery shoppers or gardeners? Flexible manufacturing systems make it all possible.

Trend 5: Cashing Out

In the 1970s, we worked to live. In the 1980s, we lived to work. Now we are asking, "Is this all there is?" We simply want to live—long and well. Cashing out is trading in the rewards of traditional success for a slower pace and greater quality of life. In 1989, three-quarters of the nation wanted less emphasis on money, according to Research Alert, up from 50 percent in 1983.

A number of factors contribute to the Cashing Out trend. Foremost is the stress of modern life. Also, our corporations have reneged on their promises of security in exchange for loyalty and hard work. The government has let us down. At the same time, technology enables more of us, both self-employed and corporate employees, to work at home, in the cocoon—in the "hoffice."

We now want the promise of safety, comfort, and old-fashioned values. We want life to be folksy and explainable. While some of us are actually cashing out to the country life, most of us cash out in other ways. Smart marketers are noticing that we're camping, gardening, and bird watching in record numbers. We wear flannel shirts and listen to country music. We decorate our homes like homesteaders or English country gentry.

Cashing out will signal the economic decentralization of America—for the better. Nobody works harder, more happily, or more productively than people working for themselves.

Trend 6: Down-Aging

The first baby boomers, a full third of our population, turned forty in 1986. Given courage, even arrogance, by their numbers, baby boomers insist that whatever age they are is the only age to be. So older is becoming better.

And we're down-aging: forty is what used to be thirty, sixty-five the beginning of the second half of life. We're redefining what's age-appropriate. More first-time brides and mothers are over forty. The age forty-plus Rolling Stones and Grateful Dead are still rocking. People magazine named sixtyish Sean Connery "the Sexiest Man Alive."

The baby boomers will not apologize for the changes that come with aging—or suffer them lightly. We'll still want to look terrific (we already spend $2 billion a year on products to ward off aging), so the skin-care market will surge. Look for big growth in at-home dental care and products that correct hearing and sight or aid dexterity and increase manual skills.

Down-aging is also the bridge that connects adults of all ages with their carefree childhoods. It's Dr. Seuss on the bestseller list, three movies in one season in which a kid and an adult switch bodies, advertising that tells you how Oreos and Frosted Flakes connect you back to the kid inside.

Marketers will find opportunities in almost anything that makes us laugh and have fun, that makes us feel like kids. Adults go on their own to Disney World, the movies, adult fun camps. We spend more money on recreation than clothing.

The sure thing for marketers is that this generation will grow old stylishly, expending more energy against growing old and the way growing old makes us feel than any generation before. And spending more money than ever doing it.

Trend 7: Staying Alive

We're sure that someone somewhere somehow can prevent disease, age, even death itself, if only we buckle down, find the right expert, do the right thing.

This superpositivism masks a supernegativism—about the conflicting advice of experts, the revelations that our food and water may be poisoned, and the growing belief that health-care providers and scientists don't have our best interests at heart. We're starting to believe that the way we choose to live our lives can make us sick, and that we're the only ones we can count on to take care of ourselves.

Self–health care is the future. Sales of self-diagnostic tests and preventive health-care products are expected to reach $2.2 billion by 1995. We'll pursue medical alternatives such as homeopathy, holistic medicine, acupressure, and biofeedback. We'll also look at what we eat, going beyond organic foods to hydroponically grown produce in clinically controlled conditions. We'll want fish grown on farms; feeding standards for livestock; and meat, fish, and poultry tagged with their growing history.

The market opportunities are endless. Personal nutrition advisers can customize our diets by the day, week, mood needs, or symptoms. We can take "foodaceuticals," prescribed doses of food, as preventive medicine. Health- and longevity-oriented entertainment and travel will boom. Light consultants can prescribe light environments to optimize energy, mood, and health.

The liquor industry can again sell "spirits": a shot of rum for PMS, brandy for a cold. Big food companies can offer modular meals and 900 numbers that give you options for lunch and dinner based on what you had for breakfast and your particular health/mood goals—with delivery in an hour. Products will be sold as service.

We may not yet be ready to admit out loud that our goal is truly to live forever. But we will pay anything to Stay Alive.

Trend 8: The Vigilante Consumer

The Protest Generation, confronted with shabby product quality, irresponsibility, and false claims, now protests marketing "immorality" and emerges as the Vigilante Consumer.

We wonder why every product isn't as good as promised, and why we're sold toys that cause injuries or food tainted by pesticides. We've moved beyond quality to ethics; consumers are saying to companies, "Don't lie, don't cheat, don't steal." Exxon's handling of the Alaska oil spill made it synonymous with irresponsible destruction—and it lost ten thousand credit card customers as a result.

The Vigilante Consumer is less concerned with mistakes than with whether the company responds to them quickly, responsibly, and honestly. (It's best if the company makes the discovery.) And consumers don't like to feel fooled or ignored. Audi lost sales and reputation for ignoring consumer complaints about sudden involuntary acceleration. But when canned tuna was boycotted to protest the accidental trapping of dolphins in drift nets, tuna companies listened. Now consumers willingly pay more for tuna "guaranteed safe for dolphins."

We want corporations with human faces, with people we can hold account-able and trust. Tell consumers what they need to know when they need to know it. Listen to their concerns and desires.

Labels will have to tell us the product's biography and the maker's ethics—the company's stand on the environment, animal testing, human rights—all with an 800 number connecting consumers to the corporation.

Give buyers interactive warranties for appliances and home office equip-ment; check on their satisfaction within days of purchase. Expect to expand guarantees to fix things faster; the "loaner car" concept should become basic for such essentials as phones and computers.

No corporation can afford to ignore the Vigilante Consumer.

Trend 9: Ninety-nine Lives

We ran through the 1980s in a frenzy, trying to be as many people as we could possibly be. We have never been busier or lived faster—fulfilling all our roles, chasing all our dreams, processing all our data bytes, living our ninety-nine lives.

What used to be one job per family, one marriage, one house, one commu-nity for a lifetime, one crop of kids, has multiplied. We move, divorce, remarry, jobhop, or even take on two jobs. We frantically pursue lifestyle as high con-cept. We crusade to stay young, fit, and healthy, achieve self-fulfillment, win friends and influence people, get rich, save the planet, save ourselves. We try to process a never-ending stream of data.

Even time itself has become faster. Technology makes information constantly and instantly accessible. Portable phones and call forwarding mean we're al-ways accessible. Faxes have taken away the little "grace notes of time" we used to have waiting for news to get from here to there.

Now we wonder if all ninety-nine lives are really worth the stress. We don't want more anything except more time.

The antidote (besides cocooning and cashing out): streamlining. For in-stance, we have instinctively streamlined one time-intensive necessity, eating, by "grazing," microwaving, and taking out meals.

The future is multifunction products and services, cluster marketing. Espresso Dental in Seattle combines dentist, espresso bar, and massage parlor. VideoTown Laundrette in New York has a tanning room, exercise bike, copying and fax machines, video rentals, popcorn—and laundry facilities.

Why not bring services to our offices? Consider coffee carts that bring us take-home meals at five o'clock or rooms for lunchtime hairdresser and tailor appointments. (Remember, office gyms once seemed unlikely.) And what about home services that can help us "delegate" a few of those ninety-nine lives, like services that not only walk dogs but train and groom them?

We also need information editors to edit down all the information that assaults us daily. How about a computer to scan selected publications and give us information to match our tastes, needs, and inclinations? Or that sorts and edits mail?

We want to buy back time and live more slowly again. Marketers that help us do that will win big.

Trend 10: S.O.S. (Save Our Society)

The S.O.S. trend describes any effort that contributes to making the 1990s the first socially responsible Decency Decade. This decade is dedicated to the three critical Es: environment, education, and ethics.

Doing good is no longer an option—it's a must. Our problems are too big to be solved by individuals alone. Our big power structures must lead us to moral transformation through marketing. The current early stages of the S.O.S. trend indicate that we can and will do what we have to do. Here are some signposts:

* Awareness of the need to save our society is at an all-time high. There are no "we didn't know" excuses anymore.
* Our aging nation is looking more at the long term and considering how to start giving back.

CULTURE SCANNING FOR TRENDS

You can anticipate and create new realities by scanning today's culture for signs of the future.

Say a new TV show takes off. What audience needs does it satisfy? The Cosby Show's family values, for instance, reflect a retreat from glitz and the sexual revolution.

Check lists of bestselling books, movies, and products at least monthly and ask, "Why this? Why now?" (No diet books? Are people tired of dieting? Did Oprah prove diets don't work?)

Once a month, pick up a magazine you've never seen. Read another industry's trade reports. Talk to cabdrivers and people in airports about what you're working on.

The future is out there in the world. The one place you won't find it is where most people look for it. It's not in your office.

• Nearly half of Americans took some kind of environmental consumer action in 1990. Environmental "seals of approval" (already used in some countries) will soon help educate and guide consumers in their purchases.

There's also growing recognition that decency can be profitable. Companies like Ben & Jerry's, The Body Shop, and Patagonia have helped set the tone, but more traditional firms have followed.

HOT-BRANDING

Consumers are blanded out: white chicken, fish, and wine; boring, boxy, indistinguishable cars. Maybe we've gained quality, but we've lost style.

The next wave will be style with a vengeance—hot-branding. Not designer initials, but character, personality, color, spirit, fun. How do you achieve it? Look back to the stylish 1940s, 1950s, and 1960s—the old T-Bird or the large-finned Cadillac.

There's room for at least one hot-branded product in every category. Hot-branding is the Mazda Miata—a wandering cocoon in the small indulgences price range; a safe fantasy adventure for the vigilante consumer with high standards. It's the variety of the Gap, the casual elegance of Ralph Lauren's Country Store, the tasty Amazon Basin nuts in Ben & Jerry's Rainforest Crunch (with profits going back into the rainforests), or Nike's "Just Do It" campaign.

Wal-Mart stores ask vendors for more environmentally friendly products, tag "green" products on shelves, and have recycling centers in their parking lots. Canada's Loblaw supermarket chain sold $5 million worth of recycled paper bathroom tissue, phosphate-free laundry detergent, and so on in its "green" line's first week. Rubbermaid has initiated a program dedicated to "helping the Earth bounce back."

In addition to helping the environment, large organizations will begin to reflect our desire to start taking care of each other again. Cornell University's School of Hotel Administration offers a course on housing and feeding the homeless. Coca-Cola has given over $50 million to educational charities. Nearly half of Americans are volunteers; about six hundred American corporations have employee volunteer programs, up from three hundred only ten years ago. Charitable giving rose 92.2 percent between 1980 and 1987.

The S.O.S. maxim: let the nation's concerns become the corporation's concerns. IBM gives computers to classrooms, Apple gives to ecological groups. We should also see soup companies run free soup kitchens, clothing companies donate clothes to the poor, publishers plant trees, and car companies provide transportation for the old and disabled.

Consumers will demand and search for products that not only work the best but offer some "just benefits." They'll respond to cause marketing in which each purchase includes money that goes to support an admirable crusade.

Expect a new American ethic of self-sacrifice, and more corporate moves toward decency. It isn't enough anymore just to "do no wrong." Be ethical. Do good. Do right.

THE CURRENT DECESSION

Just before consumers stop doing something, they do it with a vengeance—like binge eating before starting a diet. Companies that made money from the hedonism of the 1980s have cause to worry.

America has entered a decession, which is recessionary spending with a new twist—depressionary thinking. Consumers are not making impulse buys, even at sale prices.

How do you restructure a business that depends on consumer spending? Reorient yourselves from the company-convenient to the consumer-convenient. Win customers, for instance, through service. Estée Lauder offers more convenience and more service through its Origins stores than a department store ever could.

And if consumers aren't coming out, you have to learn how to get in—to the cocoon. One adaptable idea: Dishwasher retailers could institute a program of preventive care—washer "tune-ups" every nine months or so. They'd create loyal customers, presell them on the need for a new machine sooner, and get insights into what people want in future dishwashers.

---

2. GETTING ON-TREND

Too many marketers assume the future will wait until they're ready for it. It won't. Trends take off our blinders so we can see the future coming—and respond. Here are some techniques you can use to make sure your business is on-trend.

Discontinuity Trend Analysis

Big successes may be driven by one trend but are supported by at least four. Discontinuity trend analysis can help you determine if your business/product/concept is continuous or discontinuous with trends. If you're on-trend, look for ways to accentuate the positive; if you're off-trend, look for ways to correct the situation.

Here's a superficial discontinuity trend analysis of supermarkets—an industry that has changed little for decades:

Cocooning: Size, lights, atmosphere are the opposite of the cocoon. Off-trend.

Fantasy Adventure: Food is a fantasy adventure, but supermarkets are mundane. Off-trend.

Small Indulgences: It may sell indulgences, but "Do you deserve a trip to the supermarket today?" Hardly. Off-trend.

Egonomics: What's personal about a supermarket? It says volume, not customization. Off-trend.

Cashing Out: Supermarkets equal stress, which is what people cash out from. Off-trend.

Down-Aging: Maybe. Since supermarkets never change, they could be viewed as nostalgia. Minimally on-trend.

Staying Alive: There's no real information on what's healthy or not. Besides, supermarkets don't feel like "staying alive" places. Off-trend.

The Vigilante Consumer: Consumers feel supermarkets are in cahoots with manufacturers to pull the wool over our eyes and make a buck. That's off-trend.

99 Lives: Nothing streamlined here. Supermarket shopping is a hassle. Off-trend.

S.O.S.: Lots of packaging to throw away and little information on the implications of our purchases. Off-trend.

Supermarkets aren't doing well now, and trend observers can see them headed for catastrophe. As department stores are learning, consumers always find someplace else to go when what they're offered is out of sync with their lives and discontinuous with trends.

Universal Screen Test

The universal screen test, a culture-scanning technique, helps you screen seemingly irrelevant information—from ads or the news, for example—and channel it into trend-true directions.

Say you own a small chain of CD and tape stores known for a broad backlist and willingness to place special orders. You see a full-page Waldenbooks newspaper ad that introduces a new Preferred Reader Program with savings for members, an 800 number for ordering, and other services for those willing to pay a nominal fee each year. You turn the page—and miss an opportunity.

If you filter the ad through the universal screen, you see that it enhances the core business and lifts it into the future by expressing five trends. You order from home (cocooning); gain access to your fantasy adventures; pay a small fee for special privileges (small indulgences); become a member of a club that caters to your personal tastes and needs (egonomics); and streamline access to and acquisition of information (ninety-nine lives).

If you're smart, you'll be the first audio store chain to become a service/information business with a preferred listener program, special member savings, twenty-four-hour 800-number ordering, instant delivery, maybe even special fantasy adventure memberships.

Extremism Exercise

Here's another method to help you get on-trend: push a problem to its extreme worst future possibility, then let the trends help you work back to a solution.

Say you're an American car maker whose sales are down. The extreme: nobody will buy your cars. The solution: let trends guide you to a salable model. For example, create a fantasy adventure car that's a small indulgence for people who have cashed out and don't need to travel too far. It has panache, it's inexpensive, and it runs on electricity.

You're an attorney in a community with an excess of expensive, able attorneys. The extreme: no one hires you or can afford you. You could become a kind of legal midwife, charging less for standard problems (cashing out/egonomics). Or you could initiate an even less expensive service that gives uncomplicated advice by phone (ninety-nine lives).

Twisting the Familiar

Twisting the familiar turns something comfortable into something new—novelty without threat. Think of McDonald's Chicken McNuggets (much-loved fried chicken, only bite-sized and especially easy to eat). Or Nabisco's Teddy Grahams (with the teddy bears' charm and graham cracker taste enhancing each other). Or exaggerate the norm: giant sizes (plate-sized cookies), miniatures (bite-sized pizzas), new and different colors (ink-black pasta), new packaging (juice paks or squeeze bottles for ketchup).

Challenge assumptions and change the ground rules. What could be reshaped for the coming decade and a better world? Question everything:

- Why does shampoo come in bottles instead of bars, like soap?
- Why does cereal come with an inner bag and an outer box? Why not just the bag (like Pepperidge Farm cookies)? Or a refillable box?
- Do all products need packaging?

CONSUMERSPEAK

L istening to consumers is as important as ever to marketers. But you have to know how to listen to them.

Consumers use ConsumerSpeak, a special language, when they talk with market researchers. They say what they think you want to hear or what they think fits their role. Your job: To translate what is often not the absolute truth. For example:
- "That would make a great gift" means "I wouldn't have it in my house."
- "My sister would love it" means "I hate it."
- "It would be great for entertaining" means "This has nothing to do with my real life."
- "It would be great to keep on hand" is a way of pushing the product away with both hands.
- Enthusiasm for products that demonstrate "good mother" behavior or natural goodness is usually provoked by guilt rather than buying intentions.
- Is it action or intention? Does she really floss three times a day or just want to?

---

3. CAPITALIZING ON THE TRENDS

There's still plenty of time to take action to provide future consumers with what they want—at a healthy profit. Here are some ways to do it.

Marketing the Corporate Soul

It's no longer enough to make and market a good product. You've got to have a corporate soul. Before we buy, we'll want to know your environmental policy, stance on health and child care, what other brands you market, and so on. Like children, we won't open the door (to our cocoons) to strangers.

To win the consumer's heart in the decency decade you must reveal your corporate soul with a loud-and-clear four-part message:

1. *Acknowledgment.* Our industry hasn't always done everything in its power to make the world a better place.
2. *Disclosure.* This is who we were. And this is the company we're trying, with your help, to become.

3. *Accountability.* Here is how we define our arena of responsibility and who can be held accountable.

4. *Presentation.* Here is what we pledge to you, the consumer: You'll find our corporate soul in all our products.

The End of Shopping

Today's shopping experience is cumbersome, inefficient, and a violation of the trends. Even mail order is obsolete: too much wasted paper, an expensive and inefficient postal service.

The next revolution will be direct shopping, from the producer to your cocoon, with no middle men. Home delivery will become a way of life. One truck delivering to one hundred customers uses resources more efficiently than a hundred customers driving to stores. You'll have refrigerated tanks for milk and soda, bins for laundry soap and dog kibble—all delivered like home heating oil.

Portable showrooms, Good Humor trucks for grownups, will carry new or novelty or impulse items. Sales reps will come to the home for big-ticket items. We'll "try on" clothes by superimposing our image on the computer screen. The computer will also print out customized newspapers, with the news and ads we select. We pay only for what's printed and advertisers pay only for the number of people who print out their ads (they'll get our names and addresses, too).

TREND-ACTIVATING BRAND NAMES

You can't make it on tradition in the 1990s, but you can use the trends to bring back known brands, reposition them for the future, or create new products altogether. For instance:

Ford: Bring back the '57 T-Bird with 1990s technology and leverage America's desire to buy American.

Haig & Haig Pinch: This fabled Scotch, with the pinched bottle that reflects the glamour drinking of the 1950s, may be just right if we want to drink less but better.

Tupperware: Out of the kitchen and into the garden with a line of guaranteed tools?

Levi's: How about a national chain of rough-and-tough dude ranch hotels?

Buster Brown: Update the X-ray fittings of our childhood and use sonograms to custom-fit children's shoes.

McDonald's: Think about a chain of child-care centers.

Shopping outside the cocoon won't end completely—we'll still go out to shop a few times a month at small specialty boutiques with personality and style, and we'll go to huge emporiums where shopping becomes entertainment.

Keep Your Eyes Open

Trends never end and the future is never here. Sharpen your trend perception skills. Pay close attention to signals in the news, especially articles about food, new products, family structure transformations, workplace shifts, the environment, the economy, and the overall cultural mood (anxious? hopeful?).

Look away from your own office and your own world. Use the current trends as a reference point and you'll learn to interpret and make trend connections on your own.

RELATIONSHIP MARKETING
by Regis McKenna

One of the great transformations in the 1970, 1980s, and 1990s was the switch from a company-driven economy to a customer-driven economy. The prosperity of the post–World War II era in America was driven by companies developing products for consumers starved for products. This push economy made many companies complacent. All they had to do, these companies believed, was put products on the shelves and the consumer would buy. The automotive industry is the poster child industry for this kind of complacency. While seeking to differentiate themselves based on styling, the car companies never looked closely at the needs of their customers—until the Japanese car companies came along and started thinking not about what cars they could produce, but about what cars consumers wanted to buy.

In essence, the Japanese car companies recognized that this was, indeed, the age of the customer, a phrase that is reflected in the subtitle of *Relationship Marketing: Strategies for the Age of the Customer* by Regis McKenna.

A Silicon Valley marketing consultant, McKenna showed that a marketplace in which technology fuels a proliferation of products requires new marketing approaches.

The first step is to depend less on advertising to "sucker" customers. McKenna was one of the first to recognize that for most products, successful marketers cannot depend on slick ads to reel in customers.

Specifically, McKenna urged companies to become market-driven, not marketing-driven—succinctly stating the solution that has become standard for successful businesses: let the customers drive. Letting customers drive means letting customers guide your decision making. When customers started driving the car companies, the result was small, quality cars with high gas mileage.

As McKenna explains in *Relationship Marketing,* starting with the customer will guide a company's product, market, and corporate positioning decisions—and the strategies to implement those decisions.

Regis McKenna earned an undergraduate degree from Duquesne University in his hometown of Pittsburgh, Pennsylvania, before moving to Silicon Valley in 1962. McKenna worked in the marketing departments of several technology firms (including a stint as marketing services manager for National Semiconductor) before launching his own firm, The McKenna Group, in 1970. Over the past thirty years, the companies for whom McKenna has worked, especially in their early, formative years, read like a who's who of high technology: Apple Computer, Intel Corporation, Genentech, America Online, Lotus, and Microsoft.

Relationship Marketing was McKenna's third book, after *The Regis Touch* and *Who's Afraid of Big Blue?* McKenna also wrote *Real Time* and, most recently, *We Got Fired and It's the Best Thing That Happened to Us!*

RELATIONSHIP MARKETING
Strategies for the Age of the Customer
by Regis McKenna

CONTENTS:
1. New Marketing Themes
2. Start with the Customer
3. Product Positioning
4. Market Positioning
5. Corporate Positioning
6. Strategy

THE SUMMARY IN BRIEF

The old marketing methods don't work anymore. Gone are the days when you could invent a product, do market research, then run advertisements to snag consumers.

Unfortunately, most companies don't realize how the marketplace has changed. The advance of technology is fueling a proliferation of products, which makes it harder and harder for yours to stand out no matter how many ads you run.

Regis McKenna, one of Silicon Valley's marketing luminaries, offers a better way. Marketing is not a function, he says, it's a way to do business. Its job is not to fool customers into buying, but to integrate them into the product development process to give them exactly what they need, and to provide top-notch service throughout the relationship.

McKenna tells of two high tech firms, Gluco and Pumpco, that react differently to requests for help in dealing with the repair of products.

Pumpco's receptionist doesn't know how to handle a repair request, so the customer waits while she finds out. When she gets back on the line, she says the customer will have to pay for the repair as well as $15 for a temporary replacement.

The customer gets the loaner a few days later with no instructions for installation. Weeks later, the repaired part arrives but with no mention of sending the temporary item back. Then the customer gets an angry letter looking for money; apparently someone should have sent the part COD.

Gluco, where pleasing customers is a way of life, conducts business differently. The receptionist handles the repair request with care, and Gluco delivers a replacement to the customer in twenty-four hours—at no charge. What's more, the box contains instructions for sending the old part back and even includes a mailing label and tape.

To Pumpco, marketing means selling things and collecting money. Gluco sees business as an opportunity to solve customers' problems by providing excellent service and superb products—which customers have had a hand in creating.

With whom would you rather do business? This summary shows how to become like Gluco—the kind of firm that will own the Age of the Customer.

THE COMPLETE SUMMARY

The 1990s brings a marketplace transformed and driven by technology. That affects us all—with microprocessors in thousands of products in both the home and office, and a computer on every office desk, *every* company is a technology company.

A marketplace driven by technology, of course, means it changes rapidly. It also means consumers have greater choice. Between 1985 and 1989, for instance, the number of new products introduced into drugstores and supermarkets increased by an astonishing 60 percent. Everybody in this crowded and ever-changing market is finding it harder to make a sale.

That's why the old school of marketing—getting an idea, conducting market research, developing a product, testing the market, and, finally, going to market—won't work anymore. It's too slow, it's unresponsive to customers' needs, and it doesn't do a good enough job differentiating your product from the mass of others in the market.

Those who will prevail in the coming years will practice market-driven strategies—they'll become attuned to what their customers need from them to succeed. Here's how to do just that.

1. NEW MARKETING THEMES

Yesterday's rules don't hold anymore—managers are faced with new and ever-changing business circumstances out of their control.

For instance, products proliferate even in narrow niches; global competitors enter every niche; distinctions among industries blur; product life cycles accelerate; distribution channels are in flux; the sheer quantity of advertising messages creates confusion for consumers; and traditional forecasting methods don't point out a direction for action. How can anyone succeed?

The way to achieve a superior market position is to build relationships with customers based on trust, responsiveness, and quality. The following five themes comprise a new definition of marketing for the 1990s.

Marketing Is Like Going to the Moon

Marketing in fast-changing industries is like trying to guide a rocket from the Earth to the moon. The target is always moving—just as the market never stands still. Like astronauts, marketers have to keep tracking the environment and adjusting and altering their course. Missing the market, like missing the moon, means you may sail past it into oblivion.

Let's take the analogy one step farther. Just as the moon and the Earth exert gravitational forces on the rocket, so do your company and the market influence the course a product takes. The company can control some forces; the market controls others that must be watched and adapted to. The company can control:

The product. Is it competitive? Can you back it with great service?

Technology. Do you have all the leading-edge technology you need to develop the product?

Financial resources. Do you have enough money to develop and launch the product?

Timing. The door of opportunity opens and closes fast. Can you bring the product to market at the right time?

Service and support. These are no longer "fix-it" operations—service excellence is an aspect of marketing. Does yours support your product?

People. This is the most important ingredient for success. Do you have top talent in engineering, marketing, sales, and management?

The market's gravitational forces also affect your product; they help draw it in and position it in the minds of customers. Here are the most important forces:

Strategic customer relationships. Can customers help you define new products and services? Can big customers even help you launch your new products? Microsoft, for instance, got its start when IBM picked DOS as the operating system for its PC.

Market infrastructure. Support from the infrastructure—retailers, distributors, financial analysts, vendors, trade journalists, and so on—is critical for success. IBM spent $100 million advertising the PCjr., but the product failed because IBM failed to win over the infrastructure. The same was true for Apple's Lisa, Lotus's Symphony, and New Coke.

Fear, uncertainty, and doubt. If customers fear that you won't be around long, or that you won't or can't support the product line, you'll fail.

Competition. A competitor's new product can make yours obsolete overnight.

Social trends. The social environment can establish momentum for a product. The need for an AIDS cure, for instance, will supercharge the company that finally comes up with one.

These gravitational forces are always changing. Successful marketers evaluate external forces all the time to better react to changes.

Creating a Market

The real goal of marketing is to own the market. Most marketing people, however, have a market share attitude—they identify an established market, then develop advertising, marketing, pricing, and distribution strategies to gain a piece of that market.

Managers using a market-creating strategy think like entrepreneurs—they break new ground and take risks. Take Apple Computer. It realized that attacking IBM for a share of the business market was futile, so it decided to develop a different kind of computer—one easier to use. It ignored industry standards and came up with a new operating system whose destiny it could control instead of being at the mercy of IBM. The Macintosh achieved its goal of inventing and serving a new market, and Apple remains one of the industry's most profitable companies.

Process, not Promotional Tactics

As IBM's PCjr. fiasco shows, advertising and promotion are only part of the marketing equation. Advertising can reinforce a market position, but it can't create one.

Companies that build strong relationships with customers, suppliers, distributors, and anyone who has influence build lasting positions. That means companies, especially technology companies, must be market-driven, not marketing-driven. Marketing-driven companies use tricks, gimmicks, and promotions to capture customers. Market-driven companies initiate a dialogue with the customer and with the market itself.

The Texas put-down "he's all hat and no cattle" is particularly analogous to business. It means you have to concentrate on substance before image or else you won't survive. If you produce solid products and build relationships, image takes care of itself.

Marketing Is Qualitative, Not Quantitative

Businesspeople love numbers. In new markets, though, numbers aren't reliable. Those who rely on numbers alone rarely succeed.

Mitch Kapor, developer of Lotus 1-2-3, wrote a business plan for the product while at MIT's Sloan School of Management. He got a B for the project, instead of an A, because he didn't do any statistical surveys.

Mitch was smarter than his professor in this case. What would statistics have shown him? Probably that no one wanted his product. After all, hardly any corporations had personal computers in the late 1970s. Kapor figured, rightly, that eventually businesses would buy small computers, making his software useful.

Kapor's method was qualitative. He talked to people in the marketplace and tried to understand their needs. He explored trends and perceptions. Like all good marketing people, Kapor understood the market environment and all its forces.

Quantitative approaches, on the other hand, often ignore forces like social trends and business relationships. For instance, half a dozen research firms in 1978 each figured the total market for personal computers in 1985 would be $2 billion. The market actually exceeded $25 billion that year. If Steve Jobs of Apple or Rod Canion and Ben Rosen of Compaq had listened to prognosticators, they wouldn't have acted. Instead, they saw a need and made the market happen.

Marketing Is Everyone's Job

Marketing is about creating and sustaining relationships with customers and those in the industry's infrastructure. That means everyone, from salespeople to engineers and production workers, must see themselves as marketers.

Radius, a graphics-system company, won a big account solely on the basis of a plant tour. Its entire operation, which is focused on ensuring quality, reliability, and fast delivery, so impressed a potential client that it changed suppliers. Even manufacturing, then, is part of marketing.

WORKING THE INFRASTRUCTURE

Every industry has an infrastructure that includes all the people between the manufacturer and the customer who can influence buyers. Without support of the infrastructure, a product, service, or firm is bound to fail.

Here's how it works. Say influential people write well of your new computer. That means more software companies will write programs for it. Other notables then notice that your computer is useful, and they write and talk about it, which influences distributors and retailers positively. Then they talk it up to consumers, who buy it—and then talk to their friends.

Each part of the infrastructure helps build credibility for you.

If any segment of the infrastructure isn't in place, your marketing efforts fall apart. National Semiconductor has an excellent, technically superior thirty-two-bit microprocessor. That particular processor, however, has few peripheral chips and little software written for it, so it hasn't been used much. And people aren't talking or writing about it.

Besides a great product, then, you need to cultivate all the segments of the infrastructure through word-of-mouth campaigns (see Part 4, "Market Positioning").

2. START WITH THE CUSTOMER

Positioning your product or service begins with the customer. What matters most is how customers think about you in relation to your competitors.

Differentiating yourself used to be easier. Traditionally, a company might have decided it wanted to be perceived as a low-price alternative or as a premium-quality company. Then it came up with a slogan that summarized the message. Finally, it spent money on ads and promotions until people began to recognize the slogan and hence the company.

The old Avis-Hertz rental-car rivalry is a good case of traditional positioning. Avis decided it wanted customers to view it as the industry's hardworking runner-up. Its slogan, "We try harder," reinforced by advertising (and discounts and free gifts), caught on and Avis flourished.

But in today's changing markets, and in really dynamic ones like technology, such company-centered campaigns can't work. Unisys launched a campaign ("The Power of 2") that cost millions of dollars but did not stem the deterioration of its market base.

Because being number one today is no guarantee of being number one tomorrow, a customer-centered approach—dynamic positioning—is better. Dynamic positioning has three interlocking stages:

Product positioning. A company first determines how it wants its product to fit in the market. Should it emphasize low cost, high quality, or advanced technology? How should it segment its markets? Technology leadership and product quality are important intangible factors to consider, because these—not product specifications—fuel customer perceptions.

Market positioning. The product has to gain credibility, which is helped along by having good relations with all in the infrastructure. Ten percent of the people in any industry influence the other 90 percent, so it pays to win over those few arbiters of taste.

Corporate positioning. Companies need to position themselves as well as their products. The best way to do so is through financial success. If a company is profitable, its past mistakes are forgiven, and its weaker products are tolerated.

Let's explore each stage in detail.

3. PRODUCT POSITIONING

Thousands of new products enter the market each year. The U.S. alone boasts more than twenty thousand firms creating software. It would be simple to figure out what to say about a product, run some ads, and wait for the revenue to roll in. But that doesn't work in a crowded market, so a company must work to differentiate its product from all the others. To gain a strong position, pay attention to these central concepts:

1. *Understand trends and dynamics.* Remember the "gravitational" forces the company can't control. They suggest something revolutionary to many marketers: A company can't position a product by itself. The market positions the product.
2. *Focus on intangible factors.* Companies that sell products on the basis of specifications have trouble; those that sell on the basis of quality, reliability, technological leadership, and financial health do much better.
3. *Target the product to a specific audience.* Don't try to be all things to all people. Find a niche. Then serve that niche better than anyone else in the market.
4. *Understand success and failure.* Most companies never analyze why their products fail. (See "Why Products Fail," p. 59.)
5. *Understand the difference between being marketing-driven and market-driven.* Here's an illustration of the difference: Two product-line managers at a semiconductor company approached their jobs in radically different ways. One spent 80 percent of his time in the field calling on customers and getting useful feedback. The other sat at his desk and produced memos and brochures

and devised promotions that he then sent *out* to the field. The first manager—the market-driven one—was highly successful, while the second, the marketing-driven one, watched the sales of his line fall to the lowest in the firm.

6. *Be willing to experiment.* It's hard to determine in advance the market's reaction to your positioning efforts. In addition, no leading-edge products are perfectly in tune with the market. That's why you have to pay attention to it and modify your strategy as needed.

Specsmanship vs. the Intangibles

Basing your sales efforts on "specsmanship" (promoting a product's superior technical specifications) has limitations. A technology company will have trouble sustaining a technical superiority for more than six months. Besides, consumers won't care that computer A is five nanoseconds faster than computer B. They'll take the slower computer that comes with better support.

You must build other factors—like quality, reliability, and service—into the company's position. Such intangibles may not fit onto a product comparison chart, but they are more powerful as positioning levers than mere specs.

4. MARKET POSITIONING

In this, the second phase of the positioning process, the market responds to your product. While you can't control market forces directly, you can learn to use the market's leverage to create a good position for the product.

Credibility is the key to market positioning. Technology companies, especially, must concern themselves with credibility. Technology is a link to the future, so customers need to be reassured that you'll be there when they need you.

To offset buyers' fears, you must offer a security blanket along with terrific products. How? By building an image of stability and leadership through credibility.

Building Credibility

Traditional marketers try to build credibility through advertising. But people, nowadays, are inundated with ads. They distrust them. They are much more likely to favor your product or service based on what they hear from friends, experts, or knowledgeable salespeople.

Advertising should be the last portion of the marketing effort, not the first. Use it to reinforce a product's position, not to create it.

You build credibility by:

- *Inference.* Link up with an established leader for instant credibility. MIPS Computer was nobody until Digital Equipment chose MIPS's RISC processor for its workstations. Similarly, Tandem sold one of its first computers to Citibank. Potential customers then concluded, "If Citibank trusts Tandem, we can too."
- *Reference.* People often buy based on advice from a credible source. Anyone who comes in contact with the company or its products can act as a reference for you—if your company and product deliver—which is why it's important to court analysts, retailers, journalists, and, of course, customers.
- *Evidence.* People will look for evidence that you are doing well. If your market share rises, if your profits climb, if more retailers carry your products, if you start new ventures or ally with other strong companies, people will begin to respect your staying power and savvy. Positioning is hollow without such evidence.

Using Word of Mouth

Using word-of-mouth campaigns can help you achieve reference capability. Word-of-mouth testimonials are more believable than any advertising or marketing ploy you can dream up. Best of all, it's in your power to get the talk started. Here are a few good places to start:

■ **Customers.** Reach customers at user-group meetings, trade shows, technical conferences, training programs, and association meetings. Carefully select users at beta sites—places where you test your product, get the bugs out, and get early customer feedback—before a major launch. If you win over these and other early users, they'll carry your message far.

■ **The selling chain.** Training and educating the people who meet with customers pays handsomely. These include sales reps, distributors, and others who bring your product to market. As Harvard's Ted Levitt says, "Get to the customer last"—after you've enlisted the aid of all the intermediaries who can toot your horn.

■ **Industry watchers.** All industries, especially rapidly growing ones, are filled with analysts, consultants, soothsayers, futurists, and others who sort out and publish information or speak at conferences. They gain their information by word of mouth—they visit plants, attend analysts' meetings, and talk to people in any way connected with the industry.

Apple Computer gained the support of the industry watchers, who were attracted by Apple's countercultural attitudes, early in its life. People wrote honest and constructive articles about its products, and they called with advice when the company seemed to falter. They had become fans of Apple and didn't want to see it fail.

■ **The press.** More than 90 percent of major news stories in the business and technical press come from conversations with insiders. Journalists rarely write stories based on press releases, so it's up to you to engage them directly. Your goal: to gain allegiance from journalists and other tastemakers for your products.

If you want journalists on your side, help them achieve one of their goals—creating order out of chaos for their readers. Educate them not just about your product or company but about the industry itself. Treat journalists as well as you would treat your best customers.

WHY PRODUCTS FAIL

There were 13,244 new products introduced in the U.S. in 1990. It's estimated that 70 to 80 percent of them will fail. The following list tells why.

1. The product doesn't create or expand the market, so it ends up competing with existing successful products.
2. The product reflects indecision. Management can't decide whether to improve an old product, displace it with something entirely new, link two products, or go up or down in terms of price or performance.
3. Those who developed a first successful product have moved on or can no longer judge the role an improved second product might have in the market.
4. After the success of the first product, management becomes arrogant and blind to the possibility of failure.
5. The idea for a product occurs in a market environment that is no longer present.
6. Democracy decides how to produce and present the product. Everyone has a say.
7. The company ignores or does not cultivate the guiding influence of customers.
8. Promotional marketing techniques replace relationship marketing.

---

5. CORPORATE POSITIONING

Just as you want to achieve a strong position for your product in the market, so must you try to create a unique presence for your company in it.

If you're successful in product and market positioning, corporate positioning comes naturally, because its most important aspect is financial success. Without it, everything else is meaningless. Nobody will make a long-term commitment to a company with a hazy future.

This is true even for big firms. One manufacturing manager, for example, recently asked the president of a $1 billion company that supplied him to come in and explain a quarterly loss. His concern? That any loss means a cut in staff, product lines, and service.

The Silver Bullet

Sometimes you can create an excellent corporate position on the basis of just one or two key products—"silver bullets." If you can gain high (and visible) acceptance for them, you can create a reputation that extends to weaker products.

The strongest corporations develop a product mix of silver bullets and the "plain vanilla" products that bring in most of the revenue. Xerox, for instance, makes most of its money selling copiers. But its new Docutech Production Publisher, a very sophisticated piece of equipment, has received widespread praise from the media and customers. Though it won't bring in much money for some time, it has helped Xerox continue to build and maintain its image as a leader in technology, a reputation that envelops all its products.

Here's what a top corporate image means for you:

- Faster market penetration;
- Better access to market and technology information;
- Lower cost of sales;
- Higher prices;
- Better recruiting;
- More employee loyalty;
- A higher price–earnings ratio.

6. STRATEGY

Developing a positioning strategy begins with two important steps: understanding your company and understanding the market. Such knowledge, however, doesn't lead to a cut-and-dried, formulaic competitive strategy; it starts you on a unique path to success.

Knowledge Marketing

Want to stump your friends? Ask a simple question: "What business are you in?" Somebody once asked that of seven people at a Silicon Valley start-up and got seven different answers. One saw the firm in terms of product applications. Another saw it in terms of technology. Yet another viewed its place in the market. And so on.

Semiconductor companies Texas Instruments, Intel, and National Semiconductor all entered the consumer electronics business in the early 1970s. Each of them failed in that field, because none was suited to making watches, calculators, and games. When Hewlett-Packard entered the calculator business, it succeeded because its calculators served engineers, its traditional customer base. HP, unlike the others, knew what business it was in.

Conducting an "internal audit" is the best way to understand your company. Answer these questions:

1. What business are you in?
2. What are your company's fundamentals?
3. Describe your market. What makes it tick? Who are the key players?
4. Describe your company's technical, financial, and cultural strengths and weaknesses. How do your customers perceive you?
5. Who are your competitors? What are their strengths and weaknesses?
6. How competitive are your products? What would you change to make them more so?
7. What key milestones and timetables must be met in the next two years?
8. How do you segment your markets? What are the key factors for success in each of your market segments?
9. What are the significant trends in each of these market segments?
10. What is your pricing strategy?
11. What is your distribution strategy? How do you support each market segment?
12. How important is service to your company? What is your service strategy?
13. What must you change in order to become or remain the leader in your marketplace?
14. What percentage of the company's resources will be devoted to each market segment? Are the resources adequate?

These questions go beyond simple facts and statistics. They get to perceptions and feelings that can expose important information and insights about the firm. When answered by a wide range of top people in your firm, they may uncover conflicts between departments or people.

Experience Marketing

You can't develop a position strategy in a vacuum, which is why the "external audit" is so important. And traditional market research, with its statistical analyses, is a bad way to go.

For one thing, researching future products is impossible. For another, statistics don't help you understand customers better than actually talking to them. Moreover, statistics only reflect history—they don't chart trends. Last, opinions can change on a daily basis.

As John Scully of Apple has said, "No great marketing decisions have ever been made on quantitative data."

So what do you do? Get out into the marketplace. In this age of electronic communications, face-to-face communication is, ironically, more important than ever. That's why getting managers out of the plant and into the field is the best research method a company can use.

A manufacturer of digitally controlled equipment discovered—through field research—that workers were uneasy using its new equipment. Why? They were used to twiddling dials instead of pushing buttons. The manufacturer started replacing buttons with knobs, which kept workers happy and its place as a prime vendor secure. Could numerical data have uncovered this problem?

Besides observing, you need to interview people with industry expertise. These may include customers, distributors, experts, financial analysts, and journalists. Ask questions like:

1. Of the products now available, which do you like the best? Why?
2. Where do you think the market is headed? What are the most important trends?
3. What do you think of XYZ technology? What are its advantages or disadvantages compared with ABC?
4. Which companies do you consider the rising stars of the industry? Why?
5. When you buy this sort of product, what influences your buying decision? What about cost or ease of use?
6. What do you see as the major limitations to growth in this market?
7. Whom do you see as key opinion leaders in the industry?
8. Does our company provide the technology, support, and service you require?

Such audits aren't a one-shot deal—companies must constantly monitor the business environment to uncover changes in attitude. Engineers and top executives, as well as marketing people, should plan to meet regularly with customers and others prominent in the industry.

MONOLOGUES VS. DIALOGUES

Most companies still have monologues with customers—they create products, then sell them via direct mail, advertising, and promotional gimmicks. A reader won't nod yes or no to an advertisement, however, or ask it a question. There is no dialogue.

It is only through two-way conversation that you can build relationships or adapt products. American automobile producers got into trouble mainly because they thought the sale was complete once the dealer bought the car. The distribution channel, they learned, isn't the end of the sales chain.

You must begin to think about how to hold constructive conversations—the kind that create positive relationships—with customers. Tandem Computers, for instance, invites customers to brainstorming sessions. This helps the company create new uses for its computers that help customers succeed.

Deciding Upon a Strategy

After you've unearthed all you can about your company and your market, it's time to decide on a strategy for positioning your products. That doesn't mean writing a marketing plan—they usually sit on a shelf and collect dust. Instead, meet regularly to plan strategy, to make sure the strategy is implemented, and to analyze its impact and modify it as necessary.

The purpose of the positioning meetings is to identify a position and then decide how to get there. There's more to positioning, remember, than coming up with a new slogan. You may choose such radical moves as changing your overall direction, targeting a new market segment, or even changing products themselves.

Plan to meet with six to ten people representing different areas in the company. These freewheeling meetings will cover three stages, each of which can last an hour or a day.

In the first stage, input, people share their analyses of the company (from the internal audit). Look for patterns and connections, encourage outrageous ideas, and explore whether there's a better way of doing things.

Consider, too, all types of relationships. How does sales relate to engineering? How does the product relate to future products? How does the software program relate to the operating system? How does the company relate to suppliers? Here you can discover ways relationships can be used for advantage. Be patient for results.

In stage two, *analysis*, write your ideas on a board. List obstacles, competitors, and environmental factors. Consider your strengths and weaknesses in products and in the market. What are your product's specs compared to another's? How does your sales force compare to a competitor's? What's your company's reputation? Again, relate one item to another to see how you can best exploit your strengths or others' weaknesses.

The last stage, *synthesis*, is devoted to manipulating ideas. No graphs, no numbers. You try to integrate all the ideas people have brought up and link your strengths into a coherent plan. Battle back and forth until all the elements click. Don't be surprised if you have an "Aha!" experience—that's usually what happens. Out of the murky mess of these meetings, a clear vision of the future emerges.

Convex Computer worked through this process and came out a winner. It planned for its new high-quality computer to fit into the "superminicomputer" niche occupied by Digital Equipment's VAX and computers by fifty other makers. Convex knew it would be hard to stand out in the market no matter how good its machine.

The company began an external audit and discovered an interesting fact. There was still a huge demand for superminis like the VAX, but people were becoming dissatisfied with their speed and ability to handle very complex problems. On the other hand, people weren't yet ready to pop $5 million for a Cray supercomputer. Besides, supercomputers can't run much software.

The positioning session exposed that huge gap in the market, which Convex decided to fill. Its computer is twenty times faster than a VAX, runs all the same software, but costs only a quarter of the price of a supercomputer.

Convex decided to position its computer not as a superVAX, but as a "baby" supercomputer. Thus, instead of competing against fifty other suppliers, it competes against three or four.

See what a positioning meeting can do? Convex's technology hadn't changed at all, but the meeting transformed its marketing campaign.

There's no special magic in what Convex did—the same approach can work for any company.

NETWORKING WITH THE AFFLUENT

by Thomas Stanley

In *The Millionaire Next Door* and his sequels *The Millionairess Next Door* and *The Millionaire Mind,* Thomas Stanley demystified the rich, showing that most lead normal, suburban lives as opposed to the yacht-owning, globe-trotting wealthy covered in popular magazines and on TV. In fact, the only difference between the millionaire next door and you, Stanley told his readers, was that they know how to manage money—they are not making the same mistakes you are. The theme that anyone can be a millionaire if they just manage their money a little better—backed by the specific stories of actual millionaires next door— hit a chord with the American public, and Stanley's books on this theme became bestsellers.

Stanley's earlier books had been less ambitious; instead of proposing that anyone could *become* a millionaire, he had proposed that anyone could *sell* to a millionaire. Although sales books, these early titles from Stanley, including *Selling to the Wealthy* and *Networking with the Affluent,* revealed the accessibility of millionaires (if you knew how to go about it); thus, Stanley's career in demystifying the very rich had begun.

In *Networking with the Affluent,* the book summarized in this collection, Stanley argues that professionals and salespeople should make an active, planned effort to network with the wealthy. The goal is not to be introduced to affluent clients, but to become indispensable to them by fulfilling a number of their needs. One accountant featured in the summary not only crunches numbers for the wealthy members of his network. He'll also handle big-ticket purchases for them, screen suppliers of products and services, help get them free publicity in newspapers and trade publications, refer them to other members of his network who might be able to help them, and write unsolicited letters of support for their causes.

This summary also features an interview with Stanley.

Thomas Stanley began studying the affluent in 1973. His 1996 book, *The Millionaire Next Door,* has sold more than two million copies. His 1999 follow-up, *The Millionaire Mind,* has sold 750,000 copies. In addition to writing bestselling books,

Stanley is the head of the Affluent Market Institute and a marketing consultant to major corporations. He holds a doctorate in business administration from the University of Georgia and was a marketing professor at Georgia State University.

NETWORKING WITH THE AFFLUENT
Attract and Retain Wealthy Consumers
By Thomas J. Stanley

CONTENTS

1. Influence the Influential
2. How Successful Networkers Operate
3. Give Information; Get Clients
4. Increase Your Customers' Income
5. Put Yourself on Your Clients' Side
6. Turn Customer Problems into Opportunities for You Both
7. Stanley Says Networking Always Pays Off

THE SUMMARY IN BRIEF

In the early 1980s, a young accountant opened a small office, put an advertisement in the newspaper, made a few phone calls, and waited for clients to walk in. After several discouraging months, he knew he had to do something different or go out of business.

Today his firm has over fifty employees and over eight hundred clients.

How did he achieve this turnaround? He targeted prospects who could easily afford his services—and then learned how to win their business through networking.

As the accountant realized, most affluent prospects are members of trade associations, professional societies, and other affinity groups. When he started doing extraordinary things for the group members and their influential friends and acquaintances—such as helping them increase their revenues and save money—endorsements, referrals, and new clients followed.

If you'd like to sell more products or services to the wealthy, this summary is for you. Here you'll discover the eight forms of networking that can help you attract affluent clients and impress their friends and associates. Among the proven ways you'll find to reach the affluent:

- Refer them to high-quality suppliers.
- Write unsolicited letters of support for their causes.
- Help to publicize their achievements by notifying trade journals.
- Offer assistance in negotiating a loan or major purchase.

This summary offers all the tools you need to bring wealthy clients to your door. Whether you sell insurance, legal services, luxury cars, antiques, accounting services—or any other high-ticket product or service—you'll sell more when you network with the affluent.

THE COMPLETE SUMMARY

1. INFLUENCE THE INFLUENTIAL

It's simple logic: People with big incomes buy big-ticket products and services. These products and services give you the highest revenues in return for your sales efforts. It makes sense to market to the affluent. But to do it successfully, you have to learn how to follow their rules, understand their views, and speak their language.

You probably know how to influence middle-income prospects. They generally respond well to mass-market advertising, limited-time offers, and appeals to their craving for status symbols. In contrast, the affluent lean toward caution. One reason they're wealthy is that they save their money. They're long-range planners rather than impulse buyers. Before they agree to buy an expensive product or service, they must be convinced that it's worthwhile.

Tap the Power of a Network

Although the affluent often ignore sales messages, they listen attentively to the advice of trusted friends and colleagues. For instance, Dr. Smith, the distinguished plastic surgeon, may accept your glossy brochures and toss them unread into the wastebasket. However, if his colleague, Dr. Green, raves about your extraordinary service, Dr. Smith will be impressed. And if Dr. Jackson, the head of the plastic surgery association, endorses your firm, you may get a call from Smith the next day.

Networking: The Basics

Networking is a way to increase your revenues by sharing information, referrals, endorsements, and assistance with other people. It's based on a simple principle: when you delight people by doing more for them than providing your core product or service, they feel grateful and go out of their way to return the favor.

The more networking you do, the more referrals, endorsements, and clients you'll gain. When you network with the friends and colleagues of affluent people, your list of wealthy prospects and clients can grow rapidly.

Who are the best candidates for your influence network? Consider including people from these groups:

- Friends, acquaintances, and colleagues who are wealthy, know wealthy people, or know the friends and colleagues of wealthy people.
- Reporters and editors from newspapers and trade journals.
- People who sell products and services that appeal to the affluent.
- Leaders of trade associations, professional societies, alumni associations, and other groups with affluent members.

CONCENTRATE YOUR EFFORTS

If the names in your Rolodex file represent a wide variety of industries and professions, you need to narrow your focus. Target only a few centers of affluence.

Perhaps the electronics industry is a major producer of sales revenues and personal wealth in your region. If so, consider concentrating your efforts there.

Contact the heads of electronics companies, the presidents of electronic industry associations, and the leaders of companies that supply products and services to the electronics industry. Offer them free, unexpected help in solving problems, finding information, or meeting responsibilities. They'll thank you with endorsements, referrals, and business.

2. HOW SUCCESSFUL NETWORKERS OPERATE

Art Gifford is an accountant who knows there's more to his business than number crunching. He spends much of his time looking for opportunities to attract affluent clients. As a result, his firm's revenues are growing dramatically.

During his eleven years in business, Art hasn't made a cold call or knocked on a door. All of his clients have been referred to him by members of his network. In one recent month, network members referred thirty-seven affluent businesspeople and professionals to Art. Of those, thirty-four became his clients.

Who's in Art's Rolodex?

Some members of Art's network are friends and current clients. The rest are opinion leaders: prominent people with high credibility in the community.

These leaders include attorneys, physicians, bank officers, business brokers, securities brokers, financial planners, insurance agents, building contractors, and owners of automobile dealerships. In all, Art's network includes eighty categories of opinion leaders.

How did Art acquire such a large network of prominent people? He learned how to please his business contacts by providing far more than his core service.

How to Please the Wealthy

Art Gifford earns endorsements and referrals from his contacts because he's not just an accountant to them. He's also a problem solver, information provider, and wealth generator. Among the hats he wears are:

1. *Purchasing agent.* Art, a skilled negotiator, will handle the purchase of homes, automobiles, and other expensive items for members of his network.
2. *Revenue producer.* Art endorses and helps to sell the products and services of network members and prospective members.
3. *Loan broker.* Some people dread asking for a loan. Not Art. He enjoys finding credit sources for the members of his network.
4. *Talent scout.* Business owners and professionals need reliable, high-quality suppliers of products and services. Art screens suppliers and offers network members a list of the best ones.
5. *Publicist.* Affluent people often wish their accomplishments were better known to colleagues, competitors, and the general public. If they're members of Art's network, he'll help them get free publicity in newspapers and trade publications.
6. *Mentor.* When a network member has career or business problems, Art is more than willing to offer advice or refer the member to a specialist.
7. *Advocate.* Art Gifford enjoys writing letters—especially if they're unsolicited letters of support for his network members' causes.
8. *Family adviser.* Any accountant can tell you how much it costs to send your children to college. Art can also tell you what to do when they don't have the grades they need to get into college.

"What's the Catch?"

You've just offered to help your prospect find new clients. She looks at you, smiles nervously, and says, "I thought you sold office supplies. Why would you do that for me?"

Respond with two questions of your own: "With whom are you dealing now?" and "What is that person doing to increase your revenues?"

The typical answer will be, "I deal with Mr. Smith at ABC Supply. He offers fair prices, but that's all he does."

Now you can reply, "I'm willing to do more to earn your business. I'll give you products and prices that are at least as good as Mr. Smith's. Plus, I will help you where you really need help."

ART GIFFORD'S TIPS ON NETWORKING

*T*arget the business and professional groups whose members you want as clients. Then network with people who have connections with the members of those groups. Perhaps you want to sell your product to surgeons. Try to network with accountants, lawyers, and other professionals whose clients include surgeons.

It's easy to find these professionals, by the way. Just call the surgeons you wish to serve, and ask them for the names of their service providers.

Align yourself with those who will make you part of their networks. Some people may be delighted to accept your referrals and have you as a client—but reluctant to include you in their influence networks. Ask about their intentions before you start doing business with them. If you can't become at least a conditional member, look elsewhere.

Be patient. It can take years to develop an influence network or reap the benefits of such a network. If you see little progress, keep smiling and doing your part. In time, the referrals will come.

Spend more time with the key members of your influence network than with your colleagues and competitors. Similarly, read the literature of the industry you're targeting rather than that of your own industry. If you want to sell your legal services to retailers, for example, you need to know about the latest developments in retailing.

Act as an intelligence officer for the members of your network. To increase your visibility to network members, clip and send articles that may be of interest to them. Include personal notes with the articles.

---

3. GIVE INFORMATION; GET CLIENTS

Imagine that you're an accountant looking for affluent clients. Here's a step-by-step way to find them, approach them, and make them an offer they won't want to refuse:

■ **1. Focus.** Ask your local Chamber of Commerce or Industry and Trade Bureau to identify your region's top ten or twenty industries in terms of sales revenue. Although this ranking may not correspond precisely to the top millionaire-producing businesses in your area, it probably will be a reasonably good match.

■ **2. Enhance your credibility within an industry.** Perhaps you've learned that the processed-food industry is one of the top ten in your area. Contact an executive at a processed-food business, and ask for the names of the industry's leading trade publications.

Find copies of these journals and newsletters, and see if they include articles on bookkeeping, taxes, inventories, and other matters that would interest the owners of processed-food businesses. If not, call the editors and offer to submit a few articles. They probably will be delighted.

After a few of your articles appear in the trade publications, offer to become a regular contributor. Each time your name appears, your reputation as someone interested in the accounting needs of the food industry will improve.

■ **3. Target the leaders of the affluent group.** Go to the library, and look for an industry directory. In this case, you might find *Who's Who in the Food Industry*. Look up the names and addresses of the leaders of your area's local and regional trade associations.

You're going to present yourself as an industry talent scout, but don't worry. This isn't as difficult as it sounds.

Write to the association leaders, and tell them you're forming the Processed-Food Industry Advisory Council. Here's what your letter might say:

For some time I have provided investment advice to people within the food industry. Also, my articles on investments and corporate taxes have appeared in *Processed Food* magazine.

Based on my conversations with members of the industry, I believe that your association's meetings and conventions could benefit from a steady source of well-qualified speakers. For this reason, I have developed the Processed-Food Industry Advisory Council.

Members of the council will include CPAs who can speak on the subject of tax management, insurance executives who are authorities on estate and property protection, money managers familiar with the needs of individuals in the food industry, financial planners who can provide advice on retirement and 401(k) plans, and others.

Please consider having one or more of these speakers address your future meetings. Their services are available to your association at no charge.

■ **4. Recruit top professionals as speakers and network contacts.** Ask CPAs, insurance executives, financial planners, lawyers, and other professionals whether they'd like to address large audiences of wealthy prospects. They'll probably jump at the chance.

Also, offer referrals to members of the food industry. (When you call, you can introduce yourself as the head of the Industry Advisory Council.) If the CEO of a food-processing plant is moving his factory across town, for example, he may need the services of a packing-and-shipping firm, real estate agent, or sign painter. Search your network for qualified suppliers, or find new suppliers and ask if they'd like to join the network.

Read Your Way to Customers

Trade journals offer plenty of valuable information on affluent groups. To make the best use of these publications, however, you have to know which ones to read and where to find them. Here's how:

1. Find listings of affinity groups in the Yellow Pages. Look under headings such as "Clubs," "Associations," and "Fraternal Organizations." Don't look only for trade and professional groups. One networker discovered that the highest concentration of millionaires in his region was the membership of the Garden Club.

2. Call the groups and request back issues of their journals and newsletters. In most cases, the groups will provide these publications at no charge.

3. Weigh the value of each periodical. Subscribe to those that provide data on prospects and money. For example, look for listings of recently sold businesses.

4. React immediately to information about euphoric prospects. Perhaps Mr. Jones gained a windfall by selling his store. If so, he may be a hot prospect for your financial planning services.

5. Call or visit Mr. Jones and say, "I read about your business in the trade journal. Congratulations. A few of my current clients recently sold their businesses, and I thought you might want to talk with them. Sometimes it's not easy to walk away from your pride and joy." This tells Mr. Jones that you follow his industry and that you empathize with him.

The most important thing you can do to convert a prospect into a client is to say, "Give me a stack of your business cards. I have many clients who are likely to buy from you."

4. INCREASE YOUR CUSTOMERS' INCOME

If you're looking for the single most powerful way to turn prospects into clients—and turn their colleagues into supporters—look no further. The number-one need of business owners and professionals is revenue. Even the most successful, affluent people welcome new clients and additional income.

Consider the example of Fred Peterbaum. Ordinary construction equipment dealers offer only construction equipment. Fred, an extraordinary dealer, finds work for his customers. As he often says, "You can't sell equipment to contractors who have no contracts."

Networking and revenue enhancement are Fred's main business strategies. They account for a major portion of his own revenue, and they bring in most of his customers.

Most of Fred Peterbaum's clients are subcontractors. On their behalf, he talks to contractors about upcoming jobs. When he learns that a new building project is about to begin, he spreads the word to customers and prospects. Upon request, he also provides the contractors with the names of talented subcontractors who are looking for work.

As a result of his efforts, Fred earns the loyalty of current and future customers. At the same time, he enhances the demand for his own equipment.

There are thousands of construction equipment dealers in America, but only a few Fred Peterbaums. If you needed equipment, which type of dealer would you seek?

Make Deals for Clients

Many high-income people hate to shop for expensive items. They find price negotiations unpleasant, and they are reluctant to ask for any concessions.

Why not do the shopping for them? If you're even moderately successful at selling a product or service, you know how to negotiate. Use your knowledge to help clients cut good deals on homes, automobiles, or real estate. You could save them thousands of dollars.

Art Gifford, the networking champ, makes a specialty of his purchasing services. He provides his clients with a list of luxury-car dealers who are willing to offer discounts. He also negotiates purchase and lease arrangements with the dealers. In one case, Art saved a client $8,000 on the purchase of two new Mercedes-Benz cars.

Don't imagine that the dealers resent Art's intervention. Most of them are also his clients, and they are delighted to be included on his approved-dealer list. To them, Art's purchasing service is a highly effective customer-referral service.

Help Your Customers Boost Their Sales

It's easy to earn gratitude and endorsements from other people by helping them sell their products and services. Just ask these questions whenever you speak to a business owner or professional:

- What do you sell?
- What do you buy?
- What types of customers do you want?
- What types of suppliers do you seek?

As you go along, keep a list of each person's answers. Soon you'll be able to act as an intermediary between potential sellers and prospective buyers.

NEED A LOAN? HE LENDS ASSISTANCE

Bob Williams is both an attorney and an accomplished networker. He's always on the lookout for ways to help clients and prospects.

Recently Bob wrote an article on estate planning and offered it to a small magazine published for family businesses. Before he discussed the article, however, Bob asked the editor about the problems and opportunities facing the magazine.

Bob learned that the publication was suffering from growing pains. It had the potential to make considerable profits, but it was in dire need of a short-term credit infusion.

Two local banks had turned down the magazine's loan applications. A third had agreed to lend the money, but it wanted to charge an interest rate that the editor considered far too high.

Bob offered his assistance in obtaining a loan at a competitive rate. He knew over a dozen enlightened bank officers to whom he'd sent a lot of business. They owed him favors.

Thanks to Bob's loan brokering, several financial institutions competed against one another to grant the loan. The editor filled out an application and got his money four days later.

Bob Williams didn't walk away empty-handed, either. The editor sang Bob's praises to printers, office equipment dealers, and other suppliers. He also asked Bob to write a series of articles for the magazine.

Finally, the editor invited Bob to share his booth at the national family-business trade association meeting. Under a banner that read "ASK THE EXPERT ABOUT YOUR ESTATE PLANNING NEEDS," Bob introduced himself to hundreds of affluent family-business owners.

5. PUT YOURSELF ON YOUR CLIENTS' SIDE

"There are many well-qualified professionals who can supply me with basic services, but few of them have demonstrated any interest in the causes that are really important to me."

Most of your affluent clients would agree with this statement. They'd be glad to deal with businesspeople and professionals who had their interests at heart. But few lawyers, accountants, financial planners, or car dealers are willing to serve as advocates for their clients' causes.

Dan is an exception. He's a life insurance agent who looks for opportunities to protect the interests of his clients.

Consider the time that Dan visited a local garden supply company. He wanted to buy the Egan-brand grass seed that one of his clients produced.

When Dan requested Egan seed, the sales clerk tried to switch him to another brand. Dan refused to switch. He also gave the sales clerk a lecture on the differences in quality among grass seed brands.

The Size of the Problem

The garden supply store was one of more than thirty in a chain. If sales clerks throughout the chain had been told to steer customers away from the Egan brand, Dan realized, his client faced a serious competitive disadvantage.

When a client's livelihood is threatened, Dan takes it personally. That day, Dan wrote a letter to the owner of the garden supply company. He also mailed a copy to Mr. Egan.

Dan's letter said that Mr. Egan had spent a lot of time, money, and effort to provide a high-quality product and superior service; that a salesperson had tried to get Dan to buy a different brand; and that Dan believed Mr. Egan had earned the company's support.

Dan's letter cost him only half an hour and two stamps. But how many other insurance agents would have taken the simple step that won Mr. Egan's thanks and loyalty?

Every Customer Has a Cause

Your clients will thank you when you write a letter or circulate a petition on their behalf. And it's easy to guess what they care about. Almost without exception, businesspeople and professionals are concerned about paperwork, taxes, government policies, and red tape.

Within these general categories, a particular client's biggest concerns probably are specific to his or her industry. To identify them, read the relevant trade journals, or ask an industry spokesperson. For example, snack-food manufacturers recently grappled with some states' proposed legislation to reclassify snack foods as nonfood items.

In states such as New York, food was not taxed. But if those states redefined snack foods as nonfood items, the products would be taxed. A tax could raise prices and significantly reduce demand for snack foods.

If you have clients and prospects who own, work for, supply to, or distribute for snack-food businesses, you could become their advocate. Among the steps you could take:

- Petition state governments to classify snack foods as nontaxable food items.
- Write letters to the newspapers in those states.
- Send copies of your letters, along with cover notes, to members of the snack-food industry. Your note might say, "I hope the enclosed letter will help your cause. If I can be of any further assistance to you and your colleagues, please let me know. I'm a strong supporter of the snack-food industry, and I appreciate your comments and suggestions. Please call or write me."

PUT CLIENTS IN THE SPOTLIGHT

If business were nothing but a series of problems and setbacks, no one would stay in business. Fortunately, your clients and prospects often have good news that's worth spreading. Help them get the word out, and you'll help yourself as well.

Todd, a young financial consultant, used this strategy to demolish a networking roadblock. Early in his career, Todd had asked several accountants to network with him. Each one had turned him down because he had no affluent clients to share.

The problem, Todd realized, was that he had been focusing on his own needs and not theirs. He had to give something before he could receive.

Todd went back to the accountants and said, "If you refer your clients to me, I will have articles published about you and your firm. These articles will appear in the trade and professional journals that your clients read, and they'll enhance your reputation."

Todd had little aptitude for writing, but this wasn't a problem. He contacted the publicity director at a small college and hired her as a moonlighter.

Her first assignment involved Todd's top prospect, the senior partner at a large accounting firm. She interviewed the prospect, wrote articles based on what he told her, and credited him as the author.

The ghostwritten articles accomplished what Todd's sales pitches never could: they turned the prospect into a client.

6. TURN CUSTOMER PROBLEMS INTO OPPORTUNITIES FOR YOU BOTH

Who wouldn't want to know how to make their business more profitable and productive? Networkers who play the role of mentor offer this knowledge to clients, prospects, and network members. And they can end up getting as much as they give.

Mr. Gregory, for example, brings a welcome message to the luxury-car dealerships he visits: "I'll teach you to enhance your revenue before you enhance mine. I can offer you free seminars, books, and tapes that will help you sell cars to the affluent."

Mr. Gregory's approach may seem unusual, but it's a logical outgrowth of his normal job responsibilities. As the vice president at a brokerage firm, he teaches new brokers to find wealthy prospects and sell to them. This same mentoring, when offered to sales professionals in a noncompeting industry, allows him to enhance his company's revenues—and those of the car dealers.

Most auto dealers are eager to have Mr. Gregory's help. They sense his intelligence and integrity, and they appreciate his thorough understanding of the automobile business. Because he speaks their language and knows the problems they face, he quickly becomes the logical choice to handle their money.

One dealer took only two days to hand Mr. Gregory a $150,000 IRA account. He explained his decision this way: "Even basic quality service is rare, but enhancing the selling skills of my people is a divine form of service."

Good Advice Is Good Business

Mr. Wolfe, a financial planner, uses mentoring to generate new business. He recently found an ingenious way to reach affluent professors who write successful books.

At first, Mr. Wolfe had considered approaching professors by knocking on their doors. Then he discovered that local faculty members had written over four hundred books. To Mr. Wolfe, this represented a lot of door knocking and appointment making.

While interviewing several authors, Mr. Wolfe realized that they had one thing in common: a need to negotiate better publishing contracts.

Though Mr. Wolfe knew little about contracts, one of his clients—the senior partner in a law firm—was an expert. Mr. Wolfe offered him the chance to "speak to a large audience of outstanding professors, many of whom have written highly successful books."

The lawyer accepted the offer and chose as his topic "Publishing Contracts:

Factors That Favor the Author." Then, Mr. Wolfe arranged for other professionals to speak.

A literary agent talked about negotiating with publishers. A textbook writer spoke on the problems and opportunities in textbook publishing. Finally, Mr. Wolfe discussed ways of investing royalty dollars.

Mr. Wolfe considered the program a complete success. As he noted recently, "Now lawyers and authors I've never met are calling me up and asking for my advice on how to reach their financial goals."

WHAT'S YOUR ADVICE?

Affluence and business success don't immunize people from personal and family problems. You can help influential clients and prospects solve their problems—to your benefit as well as theirs—by referring them to skilled specialists.

Barbara, a financial planner, used this technique to turn her failing business into a success. At first, she had assumed incorrectly that her expertise and top-notch education would be enough to attract clients.

Barbara's business was declining because she'd concentrated only on her core service. Instead of continuing to study financial planning, she needed to develop a strong marketing system.

Following a consultant's suggestion, Barbara looked at financial planning from her clients' point of view. She realized that many affluent prospects had children who were poor or marginal students. Unless these students could be turned into "college material," their parents would have no use for Barbara's tuition-planning services.

Instead of ignoring the parents' problem, Barbara decided to capitalize on it. She began to network with the educational consultants, psychologists, and guidance counselors in her area. In addition, she contacted the directors of college preparatory programs that help underachieving high school students qualify for college.

Barbara told her contacts that she wanted to refer affluent clients to them. She mentioned that these referrals could bring them additional revenues. She also mentioned that she would appreciate the contacts' endorsements and patronage.

Barbara's strategy worked. Many of the underachieving students benefited from the coaching and counseling they received. Their grateful parents came to Barbara for tuition planning services. And the members of Barbara's network referred clients to her and came to her for their own financial planning needs.

7. STANLEY SAYS NETWORKING ALWAYS PAYS OFF

Soundview wanted to know more about who the affluent are and how to network with them. Here's what author Thomas Stanley told us:

SOUNDVIEW: How do you define affluence?

STANLEY: That's an interesting question. Many people have a misconception about the true meaning of affluence. It's not owning a Mercedes-Benz or living in a big house. Instead, it's simply a matter of whether or not you have a substantial net worth. Many people pretend to be wealthy when they're not.

SOUNDVIEW: Then how do you tell whether someone is affluent?

STANLEY: Two of the best indicators are self-employment and business ownership.

SOUNDVIEW: Why is word-of-mouth advertising so effective in persuading the wealthy?

STANLEY: I think that one of the reasons they're wealthy is that they're wise. They plan carefully before they spend money, and they often ignore commercial messages that aren't endorsed by some credible person or organization.

One other point: Most affluent people are older than the average population. Many are in their fifties and sixties. People who are older are less susceptible to promotional messages.

SOUNDVIEW: What else have you learned about affluent people?

STANLEY: We've found that people who acquire wealth early in life are unlikely to buy status products. They tend to live in smaller homes and drive American sedans. In fact, one of the strongest traits we've seen in them is discipline. They discipline their consumption of food, alcohol, and what might be called the swinging lifestyle. Also, they're less likely than the average population to move or get divorced.

At the other end of the continuum are affluent people who get a later start on accumulating wealth. These late starters may go to graduate school or business school and then enter a profession or start a company. They are more prone than the long-term affluent to move frequently, get divorced, and buy expensive foreign cars.

SOUNDVIEW: What can you do if you refer an affluent client to a member of your network, and that member makes your client unhappy?

STANLEY: Well, that happens. What you do is call the network member and say that the client is unhappy. Then the member has two choices: find a way to make the client happy, or be expelled from the network.

SOUNDVIEW: Is there a danger that the members of a network will accept referrals and endorsements without returning the favor?

STANLEY: Some beginning networkers imagine that they'll keep records on the network members and grade everyone on their performance. But the best net-workers don't do that. They're very unselfish.

Of course, there comes a time when networkers no longer give referrals to members who aren't giving something to the group. The same is true of members who lack credibility or can't provide a quality product or service. Eventually they'll be excluded from the network.

SOUNDVIEW: In some ways, networking seems to require a profound shift of attitude.

STANLEY: It's true. You have to think about other people's needs before your own. For example, networkers who act as publicists for their clients are able to stop saying, "How can I make myself look good?" and say instead, "How can I make them look good?"

Great networkers don't mind standing in the shadows because they have no problem with their egos. You can see this in their firms' employee newsletters. There may be a few blurbs about awards they've gotten or new people they've hired. But 90 percent of the space is devoted to praising their clients.

I agree, though, that this isn't the usual attitude in business. In fact, I remember talking to the sponsor of a family-business forum. (By the way, most affluent people are family-business owners.) His organization sent out twenty-five thousand letters to its state's attorneys and accountants, asking them to nominate the Family-Business Owner of the Year. They received only 123 replies. Isn't that extraordinary?

When I write about networking, I get letters telling me that it's the most remarkable idea in the world. I always reply, "No, it's not. It's just the Golden Rule. But some people have forgotten about it."

All you have to do is ask what you can do for others. I've never seen a good networker who wasn't paid back many times over.

RELENTLESS
by Johny K. Johansson
and Ikujiro Nonaka

Although this period is only a dim memory now, there was a time when America viewed Japan as a major competitor to be feared, defeated—and, as is typical in the if-you-can't-beat-them-join-them world of business, emulated. Americans were still reeling over the unexpected and unmitigated success of Japanese companies selling their small foreign cars in Peoria and every other part of Detroit's backyard.

Business books of the 1980s and, to a lesser extent, the 1990s reflected this schizophrenic response to Japan. Some books focused on how to defeat Japan while others focused on how to imitate it.

In Johny Johansson and Ikujiro Nonaka's *Relentless,* published in 1997, the authors focus on how the Japanese market their products. They reveal the Japanese emphasis on common sense and intuition, as opposed to American companies' preference for complex, statistic-laden market research.

Another fascinating insight is the power of what the authors call synergistic churning. Churning refers to the swift cycle of innovation and imitation among Japanese companies. When one company puts an innovation on the market, the other companies are adept at almost immediately copying and benefiting from the innovation. This innovation/imitation cycle spins like a tornado. The synergistic part of the equation comes from the fact that instead of competitors' defeating each other, the churning actually helps all competitors. The summary gives an example of a new design that requires new parts. If only one company has the new design, parts suppliers are not going to be too interested in investing in machine tools for the parts needed for that design. Since new designs are quickly copied, however, parts are not a problem.

Although the Japanese are no longer viewed as the behemoth on the horizon, the lessons in this summary are still valid for their contrarian and nontraditionalist approach to marketing, at least as far as American companies are concerned.

Johny K. Johansson is the McCrane/Shaker Chairholder in International Business and Marketing at Georgetown University. Johansson has published more than seventy academic articles and book chapters, as well as the textbook *Global Marketing* (Wiley, 1996, revised periodically).

Ikujiro Nonaka is a professor at the Graduate School of International Corporate Strategy at Hitotsubashi University in Tokyo and was the first Xerox Distinguished Professor in Knowledge at the Haas School of Business (University of California at Berkeley). With co-author Hirotaka Takeuchi, Nonaka wrote the influential book *The Knowledge-Creating Company* (Oxford University Press, 1995).

RELENTLESS

The Japanese Way of Marketing

By Johny K. Johansson and Ikujiro Nonaka

CONTENTS

PART 1: THE JAPANESE MINDSET

1. The Japanese Marketer as Egoless Servant
2. Quality for the Customer

PART 2: MARKET RESEARCH

3. Research People, Not Numbers

PART 3: INTUITIVE MARKETING STRATEGIES

4. Trial-and-Error Marketing: Why It Works
5. The Power of Imitation and Churning

PART 4: GETTING IT DONE

6. Developing "New and Improved" Products

PART 5: THE MARKETING MIX

7. The Four Decisions of Marketing
8. Price: Positioning Products from the Start
9. Distribution: Stay Close to the Customer

PART 6: FINAL THOUGHTS

10. Lessons for the West

THE SUMMARY IN BRIEF

In 1988, General Motors introduced an upscale sports car called the Buick Reatta. Before the launch, GM conducted seventeen studies between 1981 and 1987 to determine how to market the new car.

The Reatta had some initial success—until the Mazda Miata came on the scene soon afterward with a better price/value offering.

In contrast to GM, Mazda's decision to build an upscale sports car was based on intuition more than market research. The idea had been suggested to them by a California designer who wished someone would build a traditional British sports car but with Japanese functionality and quality. Mazda thought it was a good idea and built it.

The story of the Miata and the Reatta highlights the clash of styles between Japanese and Western marketing.

In the West, marketing is a professional specialty, a science involving complex statistical and research techniques. In Japan, marketing means applying common sense and intuition, not complex formulas. And marketing is not the domain of specialists but of every employee. Most firms in Japan still do not have marketing managers or marketing professionals.

And yet Japanese firms continue to chart victory after victory in foreign markets. (The successful entry of Japanese automakers into the luxury car market is but one recent example.) Superior product quality continues to play a large role in this impressive track record. But clearly, the Japanese are also superior marketers.

This summary examines why the intuitive Japanese way of marketing is so successful around the world.

You'll learn how the Japanese view customers and customer satisfaction differently from marketers in the West. You'll learn why trial-and-error marketing strategies work, and how cutthroat imitation, for which the Japanese are notorious, helps all competitors. Finally, you will see how Japanese companies make the fundamental decisions about the four Ps of marketing: product, pricing, place (distribution), and promotion.

The Japanese way of marketing works. Here's how they do it.

THE COMPLETE SUMMARY
Part I: The Japanese Mindset
1. THE JAPANESE MARKETER AS EGOLESS SERVANT

The differences between Japanese and Western marketing are rooted in radically different mindsets regarding customers.

Buyer Beware

In the West, there is an assumed equality between buyers and sellers. The sales process is an exchange, a negotiation in which both sides have power. No party can be forced into the transaction; each party is free to walk away.

A negotiation between equals is a zero-sum game, not a win-win situation. In a zero-sum game, when somebody wins, the other person loses.

In this kind of relationship, marketers try to "win" the sale, even if the customer loses. Marketers try to manipulate and exploit customers so that they will buy their products.

Customers, in return, distrust marketers. They have a "buyer beware" attitude that says, "We better watch out because marketers are trying to put one over on us."

MIKOSHI MARKETING

To better understand how Japanese marketers view their relationships with customers, let's use a metaphor taken from Japanese culture.

At Shinto shrine festivals, young men carry around a traditional ornamental litter called a *mikoshi*. The *kamisama*, or god of the shrine, is seated on the *mikoshi*.

The *mikoshi* is very ornamental, featuring plenty of gold and brass. It is also decorated with silk, colorful fans and streamers, and paper dolls. The beautiful ornamentation and decoration on the *mikoshi* give status to the *kamisama*.

To Japanese marketers, a customer is the *kamisama* carried on their shoulders. The *mikoshi* is the product or service supporting the customer. The ornamentation and decoration are the advertising, brand name, and promotion that make the product look good.

The job of the marketer is to decorate and carry the most impressive *mikoshi*, or product, so that the *kamisama*, or customer, looks good. Making the customer look good will, in turn, attract other customers to the product.

The Buyer Is the Master

In Japan, the buyer/seller relationship is not seen as a battle of equals. To Japanese marketers, the buyer is the master; the seller, or marketer, is only a servant.

The reason seems obvious to the Japanese: While the seller is always ready to sell, the buyer is not always ready to buy. A sale will occur only at the mercy of the buyer.

Once the seller or marketer gives up trying to be an equal, however, a new mindset emerges: The buyer readily cedes power to the seller and lets the seller's superior knowledge about a product guide the choices.

The servant mentality remains intact. The seller is not superior to the buyer. He or she is only an adviser, the customer's trusted aide.

The goal of a Japanese marketer, therefore, is to build a relationship of trust and support with his or her customers. This contrasts sharply with the battle-of-wits approach of most Western marketers.

About People

The Japanese concern with relationships emphasizes that marketing is first and foremost about people. It is about what people want or might want. It is about human behavior.

Understanding human behavior requires more than the scientific techniques of Western marketers. It requires an intuitive understanding of people and their actions.

The following pages will show how intuition is the constant thread that runs through all of Japanese marketing.

2. QUALITY FOR THE CUSTOMER

To satisfy customers, Western companies use quality programs learned from the Japanese. Many Western programs, however, focus on internal measures or processes that don't necessarily increase customer satisfaction. The following cases demonstrate the difference between Japanese customer-focused quality and Western ego-driven quality.

Redesigning the Walkman

Customers using the new Sony Walkman while jogging often dropped and broke them. Sony completely redesigned the Walkman to make them more re-silient.

Customers, however, were now using the Walkman not only while jogging but also while doing aerobics and other sports activities, leading to costly (for the company) warranty claims for breakage.

Having redesigned the Walkman once already, Sony could have chosen to limit warranty coverage to the uses for which the Walkman was made. But for the Japanese, a product that limits customers is not a quality product. So Sony went back to the drawing board a third time and designed an even stronger product.

Ignoring the Customer

Stereo speakers made by NBD, a Canadian manufacturer of high-quality stereo amplifiers and tuners, include an automatic-muting feature to protect speakers from sudden soundbursts.

Most users don't want this feature so they must switch it off every time they turn on their unit. In addition, modern speakers no longer need this technology for protection.

Despite repeated consumer and dealer requests to eliminate it, NBD insists on keeping the feature, calling it "a distinguishing advantage of NBD."

It might be noted that the feature was invented by NBD's owner.

Part 2: Market Research
3. RESEARCH PEOPLE, NOT NUMBERS

The goal of market research is to predict human behavior: what new products or product features will customers respond to?

In Western countries, marketers use sophisticated and complex formulas and techniques to make their projections about customers.

For the Japanese, predicting human behavior cannot be accomplished through scientific formulas or questionnaires. The best way to predict human behavior, they believe, is through direct contact.

Marketers—or, even better, managers—must speak directly with consumers. They must observe consumers using the products. They can then use their intuition and knowledge about the marketplace to predict how customers will react to new products or product features.

When researchers from Japanese diaper companies interview mothers, for example, they do so in the home while observing the mother changing her baby.

Honda's *sangen* approach (see page 87) is another case of Japanese intuitive, hands-on market research.

Getting Close to the Customer

Because Western marketing depends so much on highly sophisticated techniques, only marketing professionals are involved. The Japanese method of observation and intuition involves employees from all over the company.

Japanese companies, for example, will ask their designers, engineers, salespeople, and managers to talk to customers, listen actively, and think creatively about what customers might want in the future.

In the West, independent agencies and specialists collect and analyze market research data. Managers, much less engineers and designers, never get near a customer and may not even know what one looks like. How easy is it, for example, for a tall customer and a small customer in a questionnaire to average out to medium height?

Other Types of Information

While Japanese marketers downplay formal market research, that does not mean they act without being informed.

Japanese marketers pay close attention to "hard" market data, such as shipments or in-store turnover figures, which can be broken down by variables, such as brand, product form, or outlet.

They also pay great attention to environmental data, such as general information about the lifestyles of consumers. Japanese marketers are content to look at any information that helps them know their potential customers better.

HONDA'S *SANGEN* APPROACH TO RESEARCH

Observing the customer in the context of buying or using the product is what Honda calls the *sangen* or "three actuals" approach to market research: actual product, actual person, actual situation.

For example, Honda designers and engineers in California researched improvements to their cars by observing people in Disneyland's parking lot. The way drivers and passengers entered and exited cars led the designers to create wider front doors and seats closer to the door so that women with skirts could get into the driver's seat more easily. The way users opened the trunk helped Honda find the required angle for the hatchback door in the up position. And realizing that American drivers swung their elbows wider than Japanese drivers led to a hollowed-out door design.

Part 3: Intuitive Marketing Strategies

4. TRIAL-AND-ERROR MARKETING: WHY IT WORKS

Before a Western company launches a new product, it engages in a long, drawn-out product positioning process. Here's how product positioning works:

The company will first select a specific customer target segment. It will then test—extensively—product concepts against the preferences of customers in that target segment. The company will use the results of these tests to fine-tune the product's features, design, and style. It will develop an advertising campaign aimed specifically for the target customer group.

Finally, it will launch the product.

Intuitive Incrementalism

The Japanese have a different approach, one called intuitive incrementalism. Japanese companies don't do much a priori (before-the-fact) testing and analysis. Instead, after talking with customers and dealers, they will follow their intuition and launch a product, but on a small scale. Then they will get feedback from the market, ponder it, take another small action, get more feedback, take more action, and so forth.

Japanese thus enter markets incrementally—little by little.

Toyota, for example, didn't enter the U.S. market with a long line of different models. Instead, it came to the market in the late 1950s with a car called the Toyopet. Just one model.

How did it choose that model? Intuition. Toyota believed that big cars were more likely to be successful in the United States than small cars. The biggest car Toyota made was the Toyopet.

Trial and Error

The problem with using your intuition is that it may not be right. The Japanese know this and that's why they act on a small scale.

Intuitive incrementalism is a trial-and-error process. You try something based on your intuition. If it doesn't work, you regroup and try again.

The Toyopet was a flop. It just was not sturdy enough for U.S. highways. The success of the Volkswagen Beetle, meanwhile, gave Toyota the idea that there would be a market for a smaller car. So Toyota withdrew the Toyopet and successfully introduced the little Corona.

Then, one by one, it introduced the Corolla, the Celica, and the Cressida, and never looked back.

Close to the Customer

Although the Japanese act intuitively, they do not take shots in the dark. As explained earlier, they do some market research based to a great extent on conversations with potential customers and other players in the market.

Thus, Honda started selling small motorbikes after American buyers asked for them. And Canon moved into specialty camera stores after many personal visits from Canon managers.

Because they take small steps and enter markets incrementally, the Japanese can adjust their strategies to the preferences of customers, just as Toyota adjusted its strategy in entering the U.S. market.

Why Intuitive Incrementalism?

Why did the Japanese choose this trial-and-error approach to marketing?

First, the intuitive incrementalism approach is consistent with Japanese faith in intuition and direct experience. The best way to know if a product works is to put it on the market and to wait for feedback from customers, not to do fancy scientific analyses.

This is especially true for foreign markets. Despite their successes, the Japanese don't feel that they can ever fully know, and thus predict, foreign consumer behavior. The only way they can be sure about what will happen in a foreign country is to give it a try (on a small scale) and see. Western businesses, in contrast, are not afraid to move decisively into foreign markets.

Another fundamental reason for the Japanese intuitive approach is that when they first started marketing new products, their strategies were obvious. Starting from scratch after World War II, the Japanese didn't create new markets but entered markets already created. Competitors and customers were already in place.

The obvious marketing strategy was to imitate and learn from Western competitors and license their technology. A strategy based on imitating competitors does not need lengthy strategic planning or product positioning.

PITFALLS OF INTUITION AND INCREMENTALISM

Intuition and go-slow incrementalism don't always beat out a priori strategic thinking. Here's why:

1. You commit simple mistakes because the first step is so quick. Honda's first research team arrived in the United States at the end of motorcycle season.
2. You don't always screen out obvious losing strategies. A little research would have shown the Shiseido cosmetics company that U.S. drugstores only bought what big-city department stores bought. Instead, Shiseido lost time trying to sell directly to small-town drugstores.
3. You don't anticipate problems because you think everything can be fixed later. Mitsubishi ignored warnings about a public backlash against foreign ownership of Rockefeller Center. The purchase became a public relations and financial disaster.

---

5. THE POWER OF IMITATION AND CHURNING

The Japanese are competitor-driven. They focus their marketing strategies on following and imitating what the competition is doing, then offering a competing version of the product. They quickly add more and more features to make this new version of the product more attractive.

In response, of course, competitors add their own new features. This high-speed, tit-for-tat circle of imitated and modified products is called churning.

For example, the success of the Honda Accord in the late 1970s led quickly to the Toyota Camry, the Nissan Stanza, and the Mazda 626. Another example is the Sony videocamera that was soon followed by competing products from Matsushita, Sharp, and other firms.

How Churning Helps Everyone

Since all of the Japanese companies imitate, and imitate so quickly, no company can be a leader for very long. How do Japanese companies survive, and even thrive, in this cutthroat, churning environment?

The answer is key to the worldwide success of Japanese companies: churning is synergistic. Synergies are advantages, created through cooperation, that add up to more than the sum of the parts. Think of the equation $2 + 2 = 5$. Thus, churning doesn't cause Japanese imitators to destroy each other. On the contrary, it gives all of them additional advantages over an incumbent, who often stands alone.

UNIQUE AND FAILING

Churning not only helps imitators but can actually hurt companies introducing unique products. Uniqueness is no longer a competitive advantage.

For example, Sharp introduced a videocamera with a small TV screen in the viewer. This revolutionary feature hasn't been copied by other videocamera makers, hurting its sales. Similarly, Japanese imitation is the best thing that could happen to the newly designed Ford Taurus, whose sales have also been below expectations.

For example, a company by itself can have a hard time convincing parts suppliers to invest in machine tools for their new designs. When all the companies introduce the same new design, parts suppliers aren't afraid to make the investment. Parts and components are available and tested out earlier, thus helping the companies put quality products on the market quicker.

Demand-Side Synergies

Supply-side synergies, exemplified above, are joined by even more valuable demand-side synergies. When a group of Japanese imitators introduces new features or products into a market, for example, those features often become the new market standard—at the expense of the lone incumbent.

The reason: Consumers are always afraid of making mistakes. If many companies are offering the same products or the same features, they are reassured that the features are desirable or worthwhile. Imitation and churning help customers accept new features or products.

TARGET THE LEADER

In the 1950s, companies like Toyota and Sony entered foreign markets at the low end to gain a foothold in the new market. That strategy is being taken over by companies from other Asian countries. The Japanese strategy, meanwhile, has changed to a target-the-leader approach.

Japanese competitors now take aim at a leading brand, benchmark and reverse engineer the product, then develop a similar or better product at a better price. Thus, Toyota was able to build a luxury car that within two years was rated higher than a Mercedes.

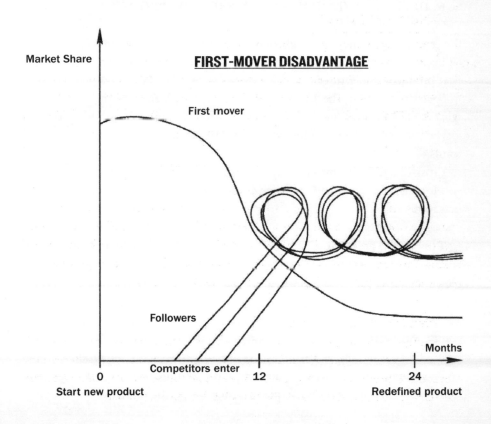

FIRST-MOVER DISADVANTAGE

For example, the Volkswagen Rabbit's new design, featuring a sloping hood and high back, was quickly copied by Honda, Toyota, Nissan, and Mazda. As a result, the new design became the norm and was readily accepted by customers.

In contrast, the classic styling of the Chrysler K-car was seen as old-fashioned.

The First Mover Loses

Churning synergies eliminate any first-mover advantage—the advantage of the pioneer company that creates or discovers a new market.

Look at the illustration on page 91. The first mover has all of the market share at the beginning. Then three competitors enter and within twelve months take over half of the market. As the first-mover market share continues to plunge, the three churning imitators continue their battle. This is how the Japanese entered and dominated new markets.

Part 4: Getting It Done

6. DEVELOPING "NEW AND IMPROVED" PRODUCTS

Continuously developing new and improved products is the cornerstone of the Japanese incrementalist approach to new markets. Beginning with better clones, the Japanese batter customers of targeted competitors with a barrage of new products and features.

Speed is essential. The Japanese have cut development time by combining what in the West are sequential activities—market research, product design, prototype production—into simultaneous activities conducted by cross-functional teams.

Cross-functional teams not only help Japanese companies speed up product development, but also help these companies choose the right features or products to develop.

The QFD Technique

The popular Quality Function Deployment (QFD) technique is a good example of the cross-functional approach to Japanese product development. QFD is essentially a two-step technique. The first step is to find out what customers like about targeted products. After selecting a competitive brand as a benchmark, the company collects information from potential and current users of the product—asking them, for example, what they like and don't like about the product.

Then engineers use reverse engineering and expert judgment to link what customers liked about the product's performance to specific design characteristics.

They can thus identify design specifications that must be included in the product they are developing.

The importance of cross-functional teams is apparent here. Engineers and designers must understand directly how their technological skills translate into customer benefits. Team members must also keep in mind production issues such as the cost of manufacturing a new design. Using the QFD matrix as their guide, design, production, and marketing functions work together to create a new, competitive product.

Hits and Misses

Not all new Japanese products hit a bull's-eye, of course. But the poor quality of new Western products gives the Japanese a chance to catch up.

The customer target segment is in the upper-right-hand box below. A Western

TARGETING vs. CHURNING

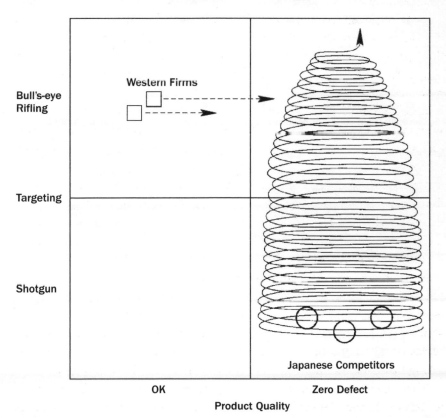

firm's product fits target customer preferences but misses because of poor quality. Japanese competitors offer high-quality products, but they don't meet customer preferences.

The illustration shows Japanese competitors making adjustments continuously to respond to customer preferences, thus churning toward the target market before the Western firm resolves its quality problems.

STARTING FROM SCRATCH

As Japanese successes have pushed companies to the forefront of many industries, they are finding fewer or no models to benchmark and improve upon. They are having to become more innovative, capable of creating products from scratch.

As expected, even when starting from scratch, the Japanese don't put any faith in the painstaking, in-depth market research common with Western innovators. Confident in their intuition and hands-on customer research, companies such as Sony develop products first, then create the markets for those products. Their attitude is that it is better to shoot many arrows and hope that one hits rather than aim carefully with one—and miss.

Teams, Not Loners

Also as expected, the Japanese do not depend on lone inventors for innovative ideas. They prefer to give a cross-functional team a general mission that, through open-ended brainstorming, gradually evolves into a specific product.

Nissan, for example, assigned a new product team to develop a "European car." Several team members drove a car from Brussels to Milan to get a "feel" for what it meant to be a European driver. Different seat designs were tested in the UK, using only European drivers.

The team translated their experience and experiments into recommendations for tighter handling and steering than usually offered by Nissan, and for changes in seat designs to fit the size and weight of European drivers. The result: Nissan's "Primera" won the European Car of the Year award in 1990.

Part 5: The Marketing Mix
7. THE FOUR DECISIONS OF MARKETING

Marketing decisions can be categorized as a mix of the four Ps:

- Product, including product line and new products.
- Price, including price position in the market.

• Promotion, from advertising to point-of-sale promotions.
• Place, or the choice of a distribution channel.

In the West, different companies will place their emphasis on different Ps. In the United States, for example, Unilever promotes its products heavily but is less successful in distribution. Kimberly-Clark is known more for product quality and less for its promotion and advertising efforts.

Unlike their Western counterparts, Japanese companies are more likely to agree on which elements in the mix are most important. Product, as covered on the previous page, comes first and foremost. Whether it is a new product or a me-too version, all Japanese companies take pride in their product. Nothing else counts if the quality of the product is questionable. The other three elements are then brought into the mix to add value to the product.

First, offering quality products at low prices is, as shown below, an important part of creating a superior value package. Promotions and advertising, as discussed in the box below, play a different role for the Japanese than for Western marketers. Promotions in the West are used to compete head-to-head with competitors. The Japanese avoid explicit attribute comparisons, preferring to use promotions to build up brand image through soft, feel-good campaigns.

Finally, Japanese firms view distribution channels as vital in keeping the company close to its customers, not just as a means of distributing their product. The quality of a company's distribution channels thus plays an important role in the ultimate value of a product.

ADVERTISING: THE POWER OF IMAGE AND FEELING

Unlike advertising in the West, Japanese advertising pays little attention to the specific features or attributes of a product. The reason: Japanese firms quickly copy successful features of a competitor's product. Therefore, functional attributes don't differentiate one product from another.

In response, Japanese advertisers try to differentiate their products through "softer" aspects of value. They highlight the feeling or spirit that a brand creates rather than specific features. The symbolic value created by this type of advertising cannot be easily copied by competitors.

The Japanese have imported this style of advertising to the West with mixed results. While Toyota's "Oh, What a Feeling!" campaign has been very successful, Nissan's recent Infiniti ads veered too far from the product and confused Western consumers.

8. PRICE: POSITIONING PRODUCTS FROM THE START

Japanese and Western companies use price in different ways.

Western marketers distinguish between list price and temporary price cuts. The list, or recommended, price is the price that positions the product in the market. To compare products, consumers look at list prices. When it comes to buying the product, however, Western consumers can often find special deals and price cuts through coupons, in-store promotions, and rebates, for example.

The Japanese believe in setting competitive prices but then letting those prices stand. Product quality and service should sell the product, not temporary price cuts.

Some Westerners may scoff at this statement, pointing to past charges that the Japanese "dumped" products into new markets at artificially low prices to build market share. For the Japanese, however, entering new markets at low prices is only logical. Part of the value of a product is its brand name. Products entering new markets have no brand value and, therefore, should not cost as much as brands already in place.

Target Pricing

Even when the Japanese develop a brand name, they are still reluctant to raise prices significantly. One explanation is that the Japanese prefer to focus on long-term building of sales and market share over short-term profits. The Japanese also believe in the experience curve: as sales go up, companies acquire experience that reduces unit costs, thus increasing profits without raising prices.

But the major reason for consistently low Japanese pricing is neither of these things. Japanese companies keep prices low because they include the issue of price in their manufacturing decisions.

Western companies set prices to provide margins over costs. For the Japanese, it's the other way around. They set production and other costs to meet predetermined target prices. They then use value engineering, in which product designs and production methodologies are chosen based on the cost targets, to manufacture products at the required cost levels. Japanese companies thus choose a targeted price position from the start. They see no reason to go lower—even temporarily—afterward.

9. DISTRIBUTION: STAY CLOSE TO THE CUSTOMER

In the West, distribution is a matter of getting the product to the customer. Products flow from different manufacturers to central clearing points (wholesalers) who collect, rearrange, and disperse the merchandise to retailers.

For the Japanese, this system breaks off the connection between manufacturers and customers. Japanese firms believe that staying close to the middleman is an important way of staying close to the customer (a central theme, as we have seen, of Japanese marketing). Thus, they put a lot of effort into building long-term and exclusive relationships with their channel members.

This emphasis on relationships is why the Japanese don't have the central clearing points common in the West. Instead of handling many or all of the competing brands, wholesalers and retailers in Japan are usually dedicated to one or a few manufacturers. Manufacturers control and support these distributors in a paternalistic type of relationship—offering help, expecting loyalty in return.

Foreign Distribution

Even in foreign markets, manufacturers retain much of their power over their channel members. One reason this dominance is accepted by foreign distributors is because Japanese companies often offer a leading market share in the industry.

Just as important, Japanese companies offer foreign distributors the same support they offer their Japanese distributors, including technical, financial, and training help. The Japanese reinforce this support with frequent personal visits—a key to maintaining motivated, high-performing middlemen.

For example, managers often find that distribution conflicts can be easily resolved in person. And middlemen who have been visited and listened to by management are more likely to pass on customer and competitive information to headquarters.

Saving 7-Eleven

The 7-Eleven retail chain offers a vivid example of the difference between Japanese and Western companies' relationships with distributors.

In the U.S., 7-Eleven stores operated strictly by a manual that standardized products, store layout, and other aspects of the business. There was little personal contact between management and retailers.

In contrast, 7-Eleven's Japanese licensee, Ito-Yokado, actively encouraged and supported innovations by individual store managers, sending roving field supervisors to the stores to help in any way they could. As 7-Eleven stagnated in the U.S., it continued to grow in Japan. Eventually, Ito-Yokado bought out its American parent.

Creating Channels

How do the Japanese create distribution channels in foreign markets? As with all aspects of marketing, they count on hands-on research and trial and error. And, as always, this method can lead to successes or initial failures.

For example, when their market shares were still low, Nissan and Toyota correctly chose to develop relationships with existing dealers for American and European cars.

The Shiseido cosmetics company, on the other hand, decided to enter the U.S. market by dealing directly with drugstore chains—a mistake since buyers for drugstore chains usually follow the lead of the big metropolitan stores. Only after Shiseido redirected its marketing efforts to the big department stores did it begin to crack the market.

Sooner or later, Japanese companies find the right distribution channels and build the relationships that turn these channels into value-creating assets for the company.

Part 6: Final Thoughts
10. LESSONS FOR THE WEST

Here are five major marketing lessons to be drawn from the Japanese intuitive methods described in this summary:

1. Nurture grass-roots relationships with consumers and middlemen so that you can make intuitive judgment calls when necessary. Blind intuition without an understanding of the market is dangerous, leading to mistakes in predicting customer behavior.
2. Balance sophisticated market research techniques with intuition about markets and customers. Numbers are necessary, but intuitive judgment based on hands-on research is also important.
3. Take one step at a time. Today's markets are unpredictable. Enter new markets incrementally and be prepared to make adjustments. This approach gives you vital speed and flexibility.
4. High functional quality is just the starting point. A product's status, image, and customer service will differentiate it from other products in the eyes of customers.
5. Forget the idea that a company can "own" a market. Imitation is too easy; any competitor can shift customer preferences.

A Note of Caution

Japanese companies test the waters quickly, then make adjustments. Westerners won't take a step until they've completely defined a long-term goal.

In the past, the Japanese method worked well since it was clear what immediate first steps, such as benchmarking and imitation, needed to be taken. But now that Japanese companies have become leaders, the first steps are not always obvious.

Japanese managers must create new, visionary objectives for their companies to guide the marketing strategies of the future.

THE ONE TO ONE FUTURE
by Don Peppers and Martha Rogers

O n a recent British Airways trip to London, I was delighted to discover that the in-flight movie would be shown on a screen installed into the back of the seat in front of me. What I didn't immediately realize is that instead of watching a specific film the airline had chosen, I would be able to pick from a menu of eight very different movies (action, love stories, comedies, new releases, a hit from the 1970s, a foreign film, etc.). Of course, if I didn't want to watch a movie, I could always listen to the scores of audio choices, from music to comedy to news.

My customized flight experience was predicted by one-to-one gurus Don Peppers and Martha Rogers in their 1993 book, *The One to One Future*. Mass marketing was dying, to be replaced, the authors insisted, by individualized marketing—what they termed 1:1 marketing. For example, they predicted that airplane seat backs will be equipped with phones and interactive video screens connected by satellite to programming providers and catalog merchandisers—an essentially accurate vision of my personalized experience (as for the shopping, most airlines place the Sky Mall catalog in every seat).

The fundamental enabler of 1:1 marketing is technology, the authors write—and this was before the popularization of the Internet and all its one-to-one ramifications: interactive blogs, customers participating in the creation of their products and services.

Peppers and Rogers also foresaw the popularity of customer relationship management. One-to-one marketing required the organization to transform itself into a customer management organization instead of a brand management organization.

Of course, mass marketing is far from dead. Car and beer commercials still scream at you from the television. In fact, as proposed in *Mass Affluence,* a book by Paul Nunes and Brian Johnson, mass marketing is being applied to products that would never have been mass marketed before, such as teeth whitening products.

But while 1:1 marketing did not fully replace mass marketing, the authors' vision of individualized or customized marketing as an integral part of a company's marketing strategy was right on target.

Don Peppers and Martha Rogers, Ph.D., founding partners of Peppers & Rogers Group, are leading thinkers in customer relationship management strategies, specifically the customized marketing approach they coined as 1:1 marketing. Peppers and Rogers introduced 1:1 marketing in their first book, 1993's *The One to One Future,* which is summarized here. Other bestselling books by the authors include *Enterprise One to One* (1997), *The One to One Fieldbook* (1999), *The One to One Manager* (1999), *One to One B2B* (2001), and most recently, *Return on Customer* (2005). *Business 2.0* magazine recently recognized Peppers and Rogers as among the most important business gurus of the past century, while Accenture's Institute for Strategic Change ranked both among the Global "Top 100 Business Intellectuals."

THE ONE TO ONE FUTURE
A New Era of Marketing
by Don Peppers and Martha Rogers, Ph.D.

CONTENTS

THE SUMMARY IN BRIEF

Mass marketing is making the same product for everyone, putting it in every store, then shouting its features and benefits to everyone. And shouting is the correct word. Your first goal in mass marketing is to be heard above the cacophony of thousands of competing messages. That's far from what your goal should be—to generate sales and loyal customers.

What's the opposite of this noisy mass-media system of marketing? It's to communicate directly with customers, individually, rather than blaring at them in groups. It's to use media that permit this (and the slow and cumbersome postal system isn't the only way). That's the "1:1 future" described in this book.

But are we ready for this? More specifically, have the media been created that can identify these potential customers, then permit you, the marketer, to both talk and listen to them? "The technological support structure is half in place," say the authors, "and the other half is coming sooner than you think."

By the end of the decade, magazines will offer personalized advertising and editorial content. Half the homes in the United States will have fax machines. Airplane seat backs will be equipped with phones and interactive video screens connected by satellite to programming providers and catalog merchandisers. Microwave ovens and VCRs will respond to your spoken commands. As many as five hundred television channels will be available.

The real advance—one of the greatest in communications since Alexander Graham Bell gave that command to Mr. Watson—will be in the use of optical fiber lines capable of carrying thousands of times as much information as a TV cable into your home and office. What is not in place is a realization in business that mass marketing is on its way out, and that only losers will fail to adapt now to the opportunities of this 1:1 future. This summary will open the eyes of business to these opportunities.

THE COMPLETE SUMMARY
1. INTRODUCTION

A technological advance—the emergence of mass media—made possible the development of mass marketing. Today, the advances of the Information Revolution—computers and a wealth of new communications methods—are changing mass marketing into something new and entirely different—1:1 marketing. Mass marketing means selling a single product to as many customers as possible. It's car ads in *Time*, headache remedies on TV. The aim is to make the product unique in a way that appeals to as many people as possible, then publicize that uniqueness with mass-media methods that persuade the audience to buy.

A Different Approach

As a 1:1 marketer, you won't be trying to sell a single product to as many customers as possible. Instead, you'll try to sell a single customer as many products as possible, over a long period of time and across different product lines. To do this, you will concentrate on building unique relationships with individual customers on a one-to-one basis. Many of the tools to do this are available today. More and more of them will be offered.

Your Challenge

The challenge to you, as a marketer, is to understand the capability of these tools, and to know when and how to use them. In the past, your job has been to learn what customers want. Now, using these new tools, your job will be working with dialogue and feedback, learning what this customer wants. Of course, the quality of your product and service will still rank high as factors in your success. But in the 1:1 future, you will be measuring individual satisfaction with your product and service. It will come directly from each customer, talking one-on-one to you.

How It Works

Let's see how this works in its most simple form. You own a small florist shop. Just before Mother's Day, you advertise a special in the newspaper. You're not too hopeful. You may get more than your usual share of that holiday business—if your competitors don't advertise a special, too. You recognize that the ad and the markdown of your offer will cut profits. Too, you're attracting onetime customers. They will go to your competitors when offered similar inducements the next time.

That's the old, mass-marketing method. Here's the new one.

Last year, one of your customers had you send flowers to his mother on Mother's Day. Three weeks before that date this year, you sent him a card. It reminded him of the holiday, told him he had sent his mother spider lilies and freesias at a certain price last year, and said a phone call to you would put a beautiful bouquet on his mother's doorstep this year. What do you need to sell flowers that way? Only a personal computer and some common sense.

Mass marketing, for flowers or mass products such as cars, is far cheaper per person reached. No argument. But 1:1 marketing is much less expensive per sale completed when you make the effort for a proven, paying customer.

2. AIM FOR SHARE OF CUSTOMER, NOT SHARE OF MARKET

To make 1:1 marketing profitable, you aim for share of customer, not share of market. In mass marketing, you're accustomed to selling as much product as you can to as many customers as you can. You're concentrating on share of market. Now your goal is to ensure that each customer who buys your product buys more product, buys only your brand, and is happy with it. That's working for share of customer.

Here's why that approach is important. If you have a 10 percent market share, for every dollar spent on products like yours, you get a dime. But that doesn't mean everyone buys your brand 10 percent of the time. More likely, 80 percent of them buy your product 12 percent of the time, or 20 percent buy your product 50 percent of the time.

If you're practicing 1:1 marketing, you'll identify and stop wasting your money on trying to sell to those 20 or 80 percent who won't buy your product. You'll concentrate on getting the rest to buy more of your product. How will you do it? By using interactive media and computers that track individual customer transactions and permit you to talk with each customer personally.

Change Your Thinking

If you are one of those whose careers have concentrated on the intricacies of mass marketing, you will find it difficult to move away from what you have developed into almost a science. Try this: Stop thinking of customers as on–off switches. Think of them as volume dials. Your job is to turn up each volume dial. That means thinking beyond today's purchase to those in the months and years ahead. It also means—and this is important—recognizing that each future transaction depends on that customer's satisfaction with the previous one.

A FAMILIAR RING

Does this "new" method of 1:1 marketing sound familiar? It should. It's been around for centuries. It's the corner grocer knowing Barbara Smith likes brown, not white, eggs. It's Joe the barber, without being told, not taking too much off the sides when cutting Jim Smith's hair.

It's an old method, but with new tools to reach millions more customers. The grocer and barber relied on their memories. Today, the computer will remember for you the individual purchases and interests of millions of customers. New communication techniques will let you chat with them.

Car dealer Carl Sewell, in the book *Customers for Life*, thinks this way. He estimates that a customer entering one of his dealerships' showrooms represents a potential lifetime value of over $300,000, counting new cars bought plus service on them. His thinking, like that of all 1:1 marketers, goes beyond that. They recognize there isn't an "average" customer. The average supermarket customer is worth $3,800 a year, but the bread buyer for a family of six must be recognized as worth far more than the lone bachelor.

Get Their Names

To work in this direction, get your customers' names and addresses. Waldenbooks does it by enlisting their customers in a frequency-marketing program the first time they buy a book. There's a small charge for the program, but they get their money back quickly in discounts. That discount provides the incentive for them to use the program card each time they buy a book. And the card links them and their book choices with any Waldenbooks sales efforts in the future.

A COMPARISON OF THE TWO MARKETING METHODS

Mass Marketing	1:1 Marketing
It requires product managers who sell one product at a time to as many customers as possible.	It requires customer managers who sell as many products as possible to one customer at a time.
Marketers try to differentiate their products.	Marketers seek to differentiate their customers.
Marketers try to acquire a constant stream of new customers.	They also seek new business from current customers.
Marketers concentrate on economies of scale.	Marketers focus on economies of scope.

3. LEARN FIVE THINGS ABOUT YOUR CUSTOMERS

Forget those expensive geodemographic studies that tell you what soap the residents of Block A in City B use. The conclusions are suspect, and, more important, they don't give you, a 1:1 marketer, the information you need.

To increase your share of customer, one customer at a time, you need answers to these questions:

1. Which customers are your most valuable ones, and why?
2. Which of your current customers aren't worth catering to at all?
3. Which customers will give you more business by referring others to you?
4. Which prospects would you most like to convert to customers?
5. What types of consumers do you consider real prospects?

Identify Your Best Customers

The reason for identifying your best customers is the Pareto Principle: 80 percent of your business comes from 20 percent of your customers. This differs a bit by business, but the principle remains unchanged. And so does the aim: to do all you can for these customers.

Airlines identify them with frequent flyer programs, then "loyalize" them by offering various conveniences and privileges such as upgrading to better seats. Catalog firms and credit card companies use a "decal analysis" system that divides their customers into ten groups by value to the company. A catalog company uses that information plus knowledge of what customers have bought to decide which catalogs and how many each year to send to each customer.

Get Rid of the Losers

It's equally important to identify, then get rid of, your worst customers. The horror stories of some doctors, lawyers, and accountants demonstrate that this is particularly true in many service industries where customers can be more trouble than they're worth.

That's the flip side of the Pareto Principle, that 20 percent of your customers require 80 percent of your time and effort. It's easy to identify them. The next step is to accept their patronage when offered, but not to allocate company time and energy to retain them.

Cherish the Proselytizers

Your very best customers are those who are so happy with your product or service that they refer others to you. Encourage them. Companies using member-get-a-member promotions reward those who assist them, often with gifts such as leather notebooks. Reward them for participation, such as when they offer names or serve as references, and not for results.

The *Official Airline Guide* staff members have such a promotion program and use the names tactfully but directly. They write to prospects, referring to the recommending subscribers by name, and mentioning that they said the prospects might like to receive the guide.

Customers Get Customers

MCI has a "Friends and Family Program." Any customer can identify up to twenty long-distance phone numbers that the customer can call at a 20 percent discount. The catch is that those twenty other numbers must also be held by MCI customers. Thus MCI's most satisfied customers are calling close friends and relatives, urging them to convert to MCI.

Dinner, Theater—and Cars

The luxury automobile line Lexus invites two or three hundred likely prospects to a dinner and a play or concert. The offer is clear: Accept our invitation, and we'll also display our new Lexus line. We will not pressure you to buy, but we want you to see our cars.

Their sales representatives don't pressure the guests. Instead, they invite a large number of Lexus owners they've identified as upscale, positive people who love their Lexuses. At dinner and later, these owners are mixed in with the prospects to provide all the sales appeal needed to win over many of the prospects.

IDEAS? FROM CUSTOMERS?

Sure. Why not?
Once you begin a share-of-customer strategy, you will help customers solve their problems. By working together, you will learn something from them that you can pass along to other customers. But don't stop there. Many companies have employee-suggestion programs. Why not the same for customers?

Try using an 800 number for this. You may not get a lot of response, but a few good suggestions will make it worth your effort.

Treat those who respond as friends. That means a note of thanks, or an unexpected present if the idea is used.

---

4. REORGANIZE YOUR FIRM FOR 1:1 MARKETING

Shifting to 1:1 marketing demands that you reorganize your marketing staff. If you are now organized to manage brands, with brand managers supported by advertising, sales promotion, and public relations services, this change will be monumental. You will be shifting to a customer-management organization in which every customer, by name, is the responsibility of one—and only one—individual in the firm. Each marketing manager will have a portfolio of customers and will be charged with building your company's share of customer for each of the customers in that portfolio.

The duties of your product managers will be changed, too. No longer will they be trying to sell their products to the most customers. Their job will be to support the customer managers by developing and providing the products those managers need to increase their customers' lifetime values.

There is still a role for advertising and brand names, but in this 1:1 organization, the emphasis has shifted to individual customer communications.

Precedents for Customer Management

This reorganization may sound radical, but there are precedents. IBM has "relationship managers," each in charge of a major customer such as USAir and Ciba-Geigy. The job of those managers is to know what share of the customer's computer business IBM has and to know about those customers to make sure that IBM gets as much of that customer's future computer business as possible.

Customer-based organizations are common in law firms, accounting firms, advertising agencies, and companies doing business with large accounts. American Express has long been respected among marketers for its ability to track and analyze individual transactional data. In 1992, it completely reorganized, assigning every AmEx card member to a "loyalty group." Each group is under the direction of a marketing manager. As an example, one loyalty group consists of frequent business travelers, identified by the company records. The manager of this group is responsible for keeping its members satisfied and loyal to AmEx by offering special card features such as paid car rental insurance or restaurant guides.

This organization is far different from the earlier one in which managers were in charge of the various types of AmEx cards and often worked in conflict with each other. For example, customers shifting from one AmEx card to another might receive a congratulatory letter from one card manager and a letter from another manager berating the customer for letting the other card lapse.

HOW TO CREATE PORTFOLIOS

An early stumbling block in reorganization often is creating the portfolios of customers. Chaotic efforts in this area will only increase the difficulties faced by marketing managers. To avoid this, put together customers who have something in common. Assigning customers with the same problems to a single portfolio will make the customer manager's job distinct and manageable.

Another way is to divide customers by their profit to the company. This makes it easier to single out for special treatment those with the highest predicted life-time value to the firm.

Finally, you can group customers by demographic profiles—single mothers, Hispanics, achievers, or teenage boys.

5. THE CUSTOMER MANAGERS TAKE CHARGE

In 1:1 marketing, the customer managers are the new kids on the block. More than that, they will take over the decision-making authority of many who consider themselves firmly ensconced in their positions.

The need for this change is obvious: Since the managers' goal is the satisfaction of their customers, they must be involved in product and service quality, and increasingly in new-product development. This means they will become line managers, assigning tasks to improve products, production, and service.

Because of that, the role of product and marketing service managers must change. Their job now is clear: to provide what customer managers need to achieve customer satisfaction.

To make this organizational change without bloodshed, top management must sell the concept of 1:1 marketing to the entire organization. It must stress the importance of the change to the future of the firm. Next, it must use the same lubricants it has in past departmental conflicts—negotiation, compromise, and team management.

Evaluating the Customer Manager

Use only one criterion to evaluate and reward customer managers: the increase or decrease in the total lifetime value of the customers in each manager's portfolio. This is exactly the same as awarding stock options to management. It's recognizing that, because of managers' work, an increase in the value of those portfolios (or the stock options) means an anticipation of greater profits.

The market itself sets a value on stock options. Valuing a customer portfolio is more difficult. There is no market for customer lifetime values. But they can and must be statistically projected and mathematically guessed. Any model that predicts this is only as good as the data and analysis that go into it. But with a reasonable amount of care, many models will serve the purpose.

Long-Term Results

There's a valuable benefit to your company from this method of reward. Under product management, the corporate concentration is on short-term actions for this-quarter results. While 1:1 marketing still pushes sales and rebates, the focus of customer managers is on the lifetime value of customers, and that means long-term results.

Looking Ahead

Visit a brokerage house for an example of customer management in action. Corporate headquarters has a specific job—to get helpful products and tools in the hands of individual customer managers. These include recommendations on stocks and bonds to buy, the view of their economists on what lies ahead, and printed material. Computerization has permeated the industry in every way from analyzing stocks to managing large portfolios to reporting transactions. Because of this, the brokers who lived comfortably on a few good clients a few years ago now can handle dozens. More important, they can give better service.

As this technology becomes cheaper and more accessible, even companies offering small-ticket products will find it profitable.

FINDING THAT LIFETIME VALUE OF A CUSTOMER

At a simple level, you can use a spreadsheet and a little common sense to calculate a single customer's lifetime value. That value is composed of a set of probabilities, multiplied by a number of future values and costs, and discounted back to the present to account for the time value of money.

Remember the florist shop at the start of this summary? The worth of a customer could be estimated this way: You could guess that there is a 60 percent chance of getting the customer's business that year by mailing him a card. If the customer orders that Mother's Day gift, there might be an 80 to 90 percent chance he will do the same in subsequent years. There also might be a 25 percent chance of getting other business. You can then begin the calculations based on nothing but your judgment. By tracking this buyer and other customers carefully, your ability to track lifetime values will improve.

It will take more than a PC spreadsheet to figure this in large companies with complex operations. But it is still a very manageable proposition with current information-processing technology. This is not marketing science fiction.

---

6. PREACHING IS OUT; DIALOGUE IS IN

The scales are tipped in your favor as a marketer. You can talk to customers and prospective customers in dozens of ways—commercials, ads, packaging messages, outdoor advertising. How can they talk to you? They can write, but it's a lot of trouble. They can reach you by phone, particularly if you have an 800 number. And that's about it.

But don't think for a minute that customers don't want to communicate with you. And, as a 1:1 marketer, you want to go beyond immediate selling to lock them in as longtime customers. You understand how mass marketers bargain with customers through the mass media: "Watch my commercial and I'll show you this TV program free." Your message will be different: "I'm bringing you something of value. In return, I want to hear from you. Tell me about yourself."

Create Opportunities

If you want to begin a dialogue with customers, make it easy for them to reach you. Many companies have voice-mail systems for their employees. Why not for customers? Allow them to call in and leave a question or comment. Tell them, "We cannot answer your call right now, but if you will leave a message at the tone, we will have an answer for you in twenty-four hours. You can retrieve your answer by calling back and accessing our voice-mail system. Your personal, temporary, voice mailbox number is pound (#) 2322. If you would prefer us to call you back, be sure to tell us your phone number and suggest a convenient time to call."

Two-Way Fax

The fax bulletin board is a new use of the fax. Having access to a list of what is available on the board, you call the bulletin number on your fax phone, press the right number for the bulletin-board item you want, then hang up. The item is immediately printed out on your fax.

MacWarehouse links this with information about the computer products it sells. The customers thumb through the MacWarehouse catalog and find equipment they want to learn more about. They call the company's fax number, press in the box number for the item, and in seconds receive a detailed spec sheet and description of the product.

Give a Fax

For some business-to-business relationships, the marketer could profit by providing a machine for the customer. This would also ensure a two-way relationship. One example would be a pharmaceutical company getting the latest research on drugs to physicians. Because sales reps would have to make fewer visits to physicians' offices, savings would quickly pay for the machine. In addition, the drug company would establish a closer relationship with its customers.

Opportunities with Computers

New openings for marketing are provided by the fast growth of the number of computer-literate customers equipped with a computer and modem and linked via phone lines to interactive computer services such as Prodigy and CompuServe.

Here is true 1:1 marketing. Customers can initiate the dialogue. They can consider offers, comparison shop, ask about products, see them on the computer screen, purchase them—and register their complaints, if they are dissatisfied—all without leaving their computers.

WANT TO BE PAID, JUST FOR LISTENING?

FreeFone, a Seattle telecommunications and marketing firm, pays its subscribers to listen to marketing messages. When signing up, they fill out a detailed questionnaire. When making a telephone call, they can press two special numbers, then the number they are calling. This routes the call through FreeFone's computer. They hear a five-second commercial "informational message," personalized and tied to the information given on the questionnaire. By pressing designated keys, they can get more information, or coupons, for example.

This system is linked to the call being made. For example, if you call Domino's Pizza, the message could invite you to "Press 0 to connect your call to Pizza Hut, and we'll take $2 off your order, guaranteed to be delivered to you in thirty minutes or less." For listening to these messages, subscribers get as much as $20 a month, depending upon the number of messages listened to. They can bypass the messages (and not get paid) by not pressing those two special numbers.

---

7. FURTHER AHEAD: DRASTIC LIFESTYLE CHANGES

The impact of the Information Revolution extends far beyond 1:1 marketing and the exchange of goods and services. Already it reaches—and it will go further—into the jobs we have, where we work, how we communicate, even with whom we socialize. Name an activity, some part of your life, and this Information Revolution will have an impact on it. Some you will like, some you will hate.

What are the ways?

Access to Information

Today we're far down the road toward having virtually immediate access to everything that has ever been recorded or printed and made public. Libraries are heading toward the ability to locate, search, sort, copy, and store in digital form anything that has been in print. More and more material is available on screen rather than in hard copy.

Back to Your Home

Two hundred years ago, the Industrial Revolution centralized the workforce. Workers left the land for the jobs in the city. The Information Revolution is already reversing that process, and eventually will send half or more of us back home, either to work or to draw unemployment.

In the past, our population has been divided between the "haves" and the "have-nots." The new division will be between the "theres" and "not-theres."

The "not-theres" will be those who can be linked to their customers or work-places by computers, faxes, and phones, and who can set up shop in the south of France, on Cape Cod, or in Vermont. The underprivileged will be the "theres," whose jobs require them to be somewhere in order to work. Theirs will be client-interface jobs, factory work, physical work. And there may never again be enough "there" jobs to support those who want them.

Middle Management

Futurists said years ago that information technology would destroy many middle-management jobs. Today they stress we're not in a temporary belt-tightening. This is a permanent, long-term shift in the allocation of business re-sources, made possible by technological change, and made necessary by the pressure of competition. Gone are the days when employees could bask in the security offered by major corporations. Today, those who work independently have found the place where they are appreciated, needed, and loved—and not easily fired. It's right in their homes.

A trend is growing toward moving low-skill work such as data-entry jobs anywhere on the globe. Cigna hired 120 young Irish workers to process medical claims. McGraw-Hill has trained 52 workers in the same country to maintain on computers the worldwide circulation files of their sixteen magazines.

Individuals Favored

The new technologies favor individuals over institutions. Everything monolithic—General Motors, NASA, public education, the Japanese juggernaut is on the endangered species list. Happily for Americans, the new technologies favor the diversity of American capitalism and competition over both Japanese conformity and Eurosocialism—but favor even more the free-market chaos of such countries as Hong Kong, Mexico, and Malaysia.

Replacing the big corporations in creating jobs are the small entrepreneurial businesses, twenty million in the United States now, and fast growing to the point where one in four households will include a business. Like the broad so-cial revolutions before it, this one will influence all of us. For some, it will mean suffering. For millions more, it will mean opportunity.

UP THE LOYALTY LADDER
by Murray Raphel and Neil Raphel

There are some business books that introduce revolutionary insights or methodologies never before seen or imagined. Such groundbreaking books, however, are the exception—there can only be so many Peter Druckers in this world. The contribution of many business books is not to break intellectual ground, but to give businesspeople the tools that help them understand, accept, and/or execute the mindset and actions that will lead to the success of their business. Often, these tools are simple but effective frameworks that help structure the thinking of executives. Michael Porter did not invent the value chain; by describing the process of converting raw material into a finished product as a value chain, Porter offered a framework, in the form of a metaphor, for understanding, planning, and implementing strategy that continues to be effective twenty years after his book, *Competitive Advantage,* was published.

Summarized in the pages that follow, *Up the Loyalty Ladder* also introduces a simple but effective metaphor framework, this one for managing customer relationships. The goal of a company, according to authors Neil Raphel and Murray Raphel (a father-son consultant team), is to bring in new customers and then move them up a loyalty ladder that turns them into dedicated advocates of the product or service. Because of their enthusiasm for the company and its products, customers on the top rung (the Raphels call them advocates) are not just buying your product or service; they are selling it. Through how-to tips, personal examples, and case studies, the Raphels show their readers what it takes to get the customers to move step by step up the rungs of the loyalty ladder.

Neil Raphel and Murray Raphel are co-founders of Raphel Marketing.

Neil Raphel has started several divisions of the company, including a book division (Raphel Publishing) and an annual marketing conference for the supermarket industry (Supermarket College). He graduated from Swarthmore College and the University of Texas Law School, and was president of a commodities trading firm in New York City. He is the co-author of several books, including *Tough Selling for Tough Times* and *The Loyalty Marketing Resource.*

Murray Raphel, chairman of the board of Raphel Marketing, is a leading speaker and consultant on direct marketing and advertising. The developer of Gordon's Alley (a multimillion-dollar shopping center in Atlantic City), he writes monthly columns for four magazines and an e-newsletter, *The Raphel Report*. He has authored or co-authored ten books on marketing, including his most recent book, *Selling Rules!*

UP THE LOYALTY LADDER
Turn Curious Prospects into Enthusiastic Advocates
by Murray Raphel and Neil Raphel

CONTENTS

THE SUMMARY IN BRIEF

Attracting customers and enticing them to return again and again is the basic challenge of any business. For without customers, you have no business.

But how do you get prospects—who languish on the lowest rung of what the authors call the customer "loyalty ladder"—to climb to the top rung and become enthusiastic advocates of your business?

This summary will show you.

You'll learn about sales, promotions, direct mail, referrals, community service, and other ways to attract prospects and make them walk through the door of your shop or office. Once in your business and ready to buy, they become shoppers—the next rung on the ladder.

You'll learn how not to scare away shoppers because of rude employees or unpleasant surroundings. You'll learn how to convince people to buy—and buy again—by treating them with respect, saying thank you in writing, and listening to their needs. Your shoppers, reaching for the next rung of the ladder, become customers.

You'll learn how to reward your good customers with special promotions, free services, and other extras. You'll learn the importance of always doing what you promised—and more.

Giving consistent good service and extra attention pushes your customers up the next rung on the loyalty ladder: they become loyal clients.

This summary covers the loyalty programs and other special treatment that you reserve for the very best of your customers. Rewarding these dedicated clients generously lifts them to the final rung of the ladder. They become advocates of your business, intensely loyal and eager to tell their friends and colleagues about you.

But first things first. Advocates were once just prospects that had to be found and brought into your business.

THE COMPLETE SUMMARY
Part I: Turn Prospects into Shoppers
1. FIND PROSPECTS AND PULL THEM IN

To attract prospects, you have to first locate them. Start by asking yourself, "Where do most of my current customers live?" More likely than not, that's where your prospects live.

Find out the total number of households that live in that area (your postmaster will know). Compare that number with the number of your customers to get an idea of the size of your prospect pool. If there are five thousand homes in the area, for example, and you have one thousand customers, you've just located four thousand prospects.

Pulling Them In

Now how do you get those prospects to come shop at your business?

First, reject any notions about having the largest selections and lowest prices in town. Those tactics may work for the Wal-Marts and Toys "R" Us's. They probably won't work for you.

Too much selection means high inventory costs and declining profits. Too-low prices lead to price wars, and nobody wins—except maybe the Wal-Marts and Toys "R" Us's.

Here are some other ways to turn a prospect into a shopper.

• *Create a major reason for a prospect to shop at your business for the first time.* Use sales and promotions, for example. Offer wanted items at cost or below. Write it off as advertising. That's what it is.

FOUR-MULA FOR SUCCESS

Here's a simple "four-mula for success" to help attract and keep customers. The authors predict this four-mula will grow your business by 10 percent per year. Its principle: make four contacts a day.

You can make these contacts either by phone, by mail, by reference, or in person, in any combination you wish (four by phone, two by mail and two by phone, and so forth). It doesn't matter how you do it, as long as you commit to four contacts day after day.

Prospecting

So whom should you contact? Start with friends and persons you know well. There are probably some who could use your product or service. But you never asked for their business.

To get more names for your four daily contacts, ask for referrals from, for example, acquaintances, suppliers, or customers. Financial analysts and insurance agents know that calling referrals is substantially more effective than cold-calling prospects.

Finally, you meet on average four new people every day: a fellow passenger on a plane, someone you're introduced to at lunch, a salesperson. Pass your business card around freely. If you ignore these contacts, you may be letting potential customers slip away.

Building Loyalty

Don't use the four-mula for prospecting only. It is an effective way of keeping in touch with current customers.

Contact top customers to tell them about a new line of products now available at your store—or just to say thank you for buying. Your customers will remember the attention.

- *Ask present customers for names of prospects.* The best source of new customers is existing customers. Insurance agents and financial planners know this well.
- *Test direct mail.* Most prospects live in a specific area. Mail to everyone in this area, making them an offer they can't refuse—such as a free gift. Direct mail is one of the most underutilized tools of small business. It allows you to contact a large but targeted group of people, from prospects you're trying to attract to loyal customers with whom you want to stay in touch.
- *Get involved.* Most successful small business owners are involved in their communities. Through Little League, schools, civic clubs, business organizations, and other local organizations, you'll meet and impress prospective customers.
- *Emphasize training and learning.* Meet weekly with your staff to review what's new. And ask for ideas. Employees are a great source for innovative ideas to draw customers in.
- *Read. Watch. Listen.* Learn from others through trade journals, trade association meetings, or cassettes on your business area, or just by talking to a successful businessperson in your industry.
- *Do busman's holidays.* When you travel, shop at similar businesses. What are they doing that you can copy?

TOLL-BOOTH NETWORKING

Prospects can be found in the most unexpected places, as one enterprising stockbroker showed. He would maneuver in front of luxury cars at toll booths, then pay for his car and the car behind him. He would then ask the attendant to pass his business card to that car's owner. As the luxury car's owner pulled up, the attendant would refuse his money and give him the card instead. On the back, a handwritten note said, "If you think this is unusual, you should see how I trade stocks and bonds."

---

2. HOOK PROSPECTS WITH SNAPPY ADS

Newspaper and radio ads are a great way to attract customers. TV advertising is another option, but it's more expensive.

■ **Newspapers.** In newspaper ads, you have to catch the attention of readers as they flip through the pages. For this reason, the headline is one of the most important parts of the ad.

To catch attention, an ad headline must do one of two things: promise a benefit or invoke curiosity. Prospects don't care about your products. They care about the benefits that your products bring them. For example, the suits you sell may be a blend of Dacron and wool. So what? In your headline, say the suits can be "worn year-round."

As for curiosity, it's often done poorly because writers try to be too clever. Don't use outrageous headlines that have nothing to do with the ad. It may attract readers, but not for long.

After the headline, there is the copy. Here the rule is simple: Get to the point. Expand on the headline immediately. That's what got readers reading in the first place.

Write in the present tense and use short sentences and short paragraphs. You want to be snappy and interesting.

One final note: Somewhere use the word *free*—such as "Buy one, get one free." You'll be sure to attract readers—and customers.

■ **Radio**. Radio is a niche industry. Most stations specialize in a specific type of music or format.

This helps you, because radio stations draw listeners with similar interests. So if you want to find the prospects that share the same characteristics as current customers, just ask those customers what radio stations they listen to. That's the station you want to advertise on.

And if possible, buy time close to the news. That's when most people are listening.

In radio advertisements, there are two things you should do early and often: identify your product and promise the listener a benefit. Here are some other points:

- Keep the number of products you mention low so listeners remember something.
- Avoid amateurish jingles.
- Use humor. It sells.

■ **Television.** Thanks to the proliferation of cable channels, TV is becoming more competitive and more affordable. As with radio and newspapers, your TV advertisements should grab the attention of viewers quickly.

Show your product and how it works. (Infiniti learned, for example, that nature shots don't sell cars.)

Finally, don't be too clever. Fancy camera angles are confusing. And TV humor usually bombs.

Use Promotions

Imaginative promotions can attract thousands of shoppers to your place of business.

A Piggly Wiggly grocery store in South Carolina began a yearly "Grits Festival," including grits-eating races, bands, and the annual selection of Miss Grits.

Sound silly? Maybe, but fifty thousand visitors attend each year—in a town of twenty-five hundred people.

Of course, you don't have to host eating contests or beauty pageants. Celebrity signings or four-hour sales will do the trick.

Throw in a free gift or run a sweepstakes and even more people will come.

Part 2: Turn Shoppers into Customers

3. CONVERT BROWSERS INTO LOYAL BUYERS

Shoppers are prospects whom you have convinced to visit your place of business. But they still haven't made the buying decision.

Why do people buy? There are two basic reasons: good feelings, and/or solutions to problems.

You go to a restaurant to enjoy a good meal. You buy life insurance to guarantee income to your spouse and children in case something happens.

If you have the products or services that bring good feelings to customers, or solve problems, then you will make a sale.

Unless you scare the shopper away.

Make Shoppers Comfortable

Shoppers decide whether they are comfortable in the first eight seconds they're in your place of business. Disorganized or dirty physical surroundings and rude or unhelpful employees are sure ways to stop shoppers from becoming customers.

HOW TO LOSE A CUSTOMER

On a recent trip to a supermarket, one of the authors needed help finding honey. The first employee he asked told him, "Hey, I'm just part-time. I don't know where anything is." The woman behind the deli counter said, "All I know is what is behind my counter." The man in the meat department pointed to the blood on his apron and said, "I'm not in the honey department." No, he wasn't. The author left the basket half-filled with groceries and walked out. He had been a shopper; he never became a customer.

A shopper recently went to a car dealership to buy a car. The salesman, drinking a soda out of a can, walked up in a sweatshirt and said, "Hey—can I help you?"

"No thanks," said the shopper, who hurried to another dealership.

Build Customer Loyalty

Another shopper went to a deli counter in a large grocery store. Although no other customers were waiting, the clerk wouldn't serve her until she took a number. She took a ticket—but never returned to the store.

A shopper may buy something, but that doesn't necessarily make him or her a customer. Will that shopper come back?

Here are some ways to ensure that the onetime shopper becomes a loyal customer:

- *Capture their names.* You have to know who your shoppers are before you can treat them like customers. At the point of sale, get names, addresses, telephone numbers, and what they bought. Find out what they like and anything else that sets them apart as individuals.
- *Send thank-you letters.* This is one of the reasons for capturing their names. Thank-you letters impress shoppers and will push them to become valued customers. In the months prior to writing their book, the authors purchased between them a $5,000 air conditioner, a $600 TV set, a $28,000 car, a $100 pair of shoes, and a $300,000 life insurance policy. The shoe salesman was the only one to write a thank-you letter.
- *Give them a "bounce back" at the time of purchase.* Offer a discount on the next purchase, for example. Don't worry about losing money. You'll come out ahead in the long run.
- *Ask them what they want.* When Furr's Markets of Albuquerque remodeled one of its stores, it sent a questionnaire to eight thousand residents asking what they wanted in the new store. They took people's suggestions, such as a deli near the entrance and a bigger seafood section, and doubled their volume. A suggestion box to which you respond diligently is another way to ask customers what they want.
- *Offer an up-front guarantee.* When shoppers walk in, they should see a posted guarantee on all merchandise in the store.

HANNA ANDERSSON: A SUCCESS STORY

Gun Denhart preferred the soft, all-cotton children's clothing found in her native Sweden to the polyester clothing that dominated in the U.S. Naming her company after her grandmother, Hanna Andersson, Denhart decided to sell the Swedish-style children's clothing to American parents.

Denhart targeted prospects through a small ad in *Parents* magazine. Within ten years, she had built up a $50 million business, mostly from catalog shoppers. How was she able to attract and keep so many customers so quickly? First, she gives them what they want: sturdy but soft clothes that stay so brightly colored they can be handed down again and again. Equally as important, she treats customers well. New customers get a $10 gift certificate. Employees are trained to be happy and helpful on the phones. And if a customer isn't happy, a replacement is sent immediately, even before the original purchase is sent back. Now that's a guarantee.

---

4. WHY DO CUSTOMERS LEAVE YOU?

Ever wondered why a certain customer who used to buy what you have to sell doesn't buy anymore? There have been plenty of studies on why customers leave. And they all tell the same story:

- Fourteen percent of customers leave because of complaints not solved.
- Nine percent leave because of the competition.
- Nine percent leave because they moved someplace else.
- Sixty-eight percent leave for no special reason.

Let's rephrase that last part. Seven out of ten customers who used to buy from you left for no special reason. Do you believe that? Don't. There was indeed a reason, or a series of reasons, those customers left. For example:

- They left because you never told them you cared or that they were important to you.
- They left because you never said, "Thank you," and "Please come back and shop with us again."
- They left because every time they entered your store or business, employees were too busy to take care of them.
- They left because they had a question about a bill and were told, "The computer handles that."

Customers don't leave for "no special reason." They leave because you give them a reason. They leave because they are dissatisfied. More often than not they said nothing, they never complained. But they never returned.

THE GROUND RULES

Too many businesses treat with disrespect customers who buy things on sale. Customers are always customers and should always be treated correctly—if you want to keep them coming back.

A customer recently went to an airline counter with an upgrade certificate for a free trip to Hawaii. The agent looked at the coupon and said, despairingly, "Oh, you've got one of these." "Yes," admitted the customer, "and 'one of these' means that I am a very good customer of your airline." The agent sighed. "Well, I guess I'm going to have to fill out the paperwork." Annoyed, the customer retorted, "I don't think you understand the ground rules. Let me tell you what they are. You are overhead. I am profit."

---

5. LISTEN TO YOUR CUSTOMERS

The best way to keep your customers is to listen to them.

Make sure your salespeople take the time to listen rather than trying to "talk" customers into buying.

General Electric recently did a customer survey to find out why sales weren't increasing. The most quoted answer: "Your salesmen talk too much."

Surveys and Focus Groups

Another way to listen to customers is through customer service surveys such as the questionnaires left in hotel rooms.

Or try focus groups. Get together ten to fifteen people that represent a cross-section of your customers by age, ethnic background, income, and so on. Emphasize that you're more interested in what they don't like about your business than what they do like. It's very important to try to find out what you are doing wrong. The reason: most customers don't complain—they just leave.

Databases

Technology is now available that lets you prepare complete databases on every customer and customer purchase. Use these databases to learn about your customers, follow up on transactions, and find out where problems occurred.

A study of the databases will show you which customers no longer shop at your business. Contact these customers, and find out why they left.

If you listen to your customers, you can give them what they want—and you show that you care.

THE BOOMERANG PRINCIPLE

Feargal Quinn, Ireland's leading supermarket owner, believes businesses should practice the "boomerang principle." Instead of worrying about bringing new customers in, businesses should make sure current customers return.

"At present," Quinn says, "your approach may be like playing golf, where the idea is usually to get the ball to travel as far away from you as possible. When you throw boomerangs, your objective is different, your strategy is different, and the way you judge your results is different."

A simple example: many stores slyly put candy in checkout lanes where children can spy them—and badger their parents as they wait in line. Quinn took the candies away. His supermarkets sold less candy, but had happier customers.

Also, customers get generous bonus points with each purchase to be used against merchandise or gifts. In the short term, Quinn may be giving up profit. But he knows the customer will be back.

Part 3: Turn Customers into Clients
6. MAKE YOUR BEST CUSTOMERS FEEL IMPORTANT

Make your best customers feel important and appreciated. As loyal customers to your business, they deserve it.

And treating them in a special way will make them reach for the next rung on the loyalty ladder. From good customers, they'll become dedicated clients returning again and again to your business.

Rewards

Here are ten ways to show your appreciation:

1. *Advance notice of everything.* Let these folks know first about special offers, sales, and so forth. These are your first-class customers. Mail first-class.

   And specifically tell them they're the first to know—or they won't realize they're being treated specially.
2. *Special promotions for them alone.* Forget the holidays. For loyal customers, sales just happen for no reason at all. Unscheduled. Again, be sure to tell them that this is something just for them.

LITTLE EXTRAS

L ittle unexpected gifts make customers feel appreciated and prompt them to come back to you with their business.

For example, if you sell VCRs, include free videos with each purchase. Or put gourmet foods in just-purchased refrigerators.

One furniture store always offered a little extra with the furniture it delivered. Dining room sets came with vases of roses. Lounge chairs arrived with magazine racks. Bedroom sets came with two pillows. All at no charge.

---

3. *Free services for which you normally charge a small service fee.* Don't charge them for gift wrapping, overnight shipping, or any fee service.

4. *Gift certificates from noncompeting stores.* Everybody wins. Customers appreciate the gift, other stores appreciate the business, and you are building loyalty.

But make the gift certificates worthwhile. Giving them "$50 off your next $500 purchase" is no gift.

5. *Free gifts at unannounced times of the year.* For example, send your best customers an unexpected gift certificate for some wanted item at your store—for no reason except that they're good customers.

One store offered one hundred of its best customers canvas shopping bags with the name of the store prominently displayed on them. In return, it had one hundred walking billboards all over town. And in many cases, when the customers came in for the bags, they bought something to put into them.

6. *What they want is what they get.* Overnight alterations? Same-day delivery? A special service? No problem. Customers climbing the loyalty ladder are always right.

7. *You're available when they want you.* Did someone forget to pick up a pair of altered pants for a meeting that night? Reopen the store—and convert a customer into a client instantly.

8. *The "extra" service that sets you apart.* Example: one hotel offers to transfer guests' hotel bags onto their planes and is rewarded with a dedicated batch of clients.

9. *They know who I am.* The customers know you're communicating with them by using computers, but it still builds loyalty to hear a business refer to them by name.

10. *Loyalty programs.* Establish special clubs with specific benefits such as price breaks. The more loyal the customer, the better the benefits offered.

HOW CASINOS TREAT THEIR HIGH ROLLERS

Once every six weeks, a limousine picks up executive Stan Golomb at his house and drives him to Chicago's O'Hare Airport. He then takes a plane to Atlantic City and stays in a plush casino hotel room for a few days. Golomb's room, airfare, meals, and limousine are all picked up by the casino where he gambles—rewards for being a loyal customer.

Casinos offer all businesses lessons in how to treat their good customers.

First, casinos know their customers. They know the names, addresses, habits, and likes and dislikes of the big spenders.

Second, casinos are ready to cater to their top customers. They've figured out the math and know that despite the costs of limousines, airfares, and hotel rooms, they will still come out ahead.

Casinos pamper their high rollers. What about you? What are you doing special for the most loyal of your customers? Many businesses can't even identify their best customers, much less offer them special deals. Other businesses offer special deals such as sales and coupons for the next purchase. But they offer these benefits to *everyone.* They aren't singling out the high rollers.

Don't Go Too Far

One note of caution: Do the math. Know how much to give, and when to stop.

There must be a relationship between cost and return, says Robert Renneisen, president of Atlantic City's Claridge Casino Hotel, "whether you're talking about a rebate at your car dealer or a sale on peas in the grocery store or a free roll of quarters at the casino."

7. DO WHAT YOU PROMISED . . . AND MORE

One of the first reasons customers become clients is that you consistently do what you promised.

If you promise, for example, repairs finished by a certain time, make the deadline. If you promise the lowest prices in town, deliver them. If you promise an accurate estimate, stick to it.

If you keep your promises, customers will keep coming back, becoming clients and even advocates.

It sounds simple. But every customer has stories of broken promises by businesses. Those fantastic rates advertised by hotels, for example, turn out to be "per person/double occupancy." True, it's in the fine print. But customers still feel they are paying double what they were promised.

Customer Satisfaction

Consistently providing the promised service or product will bring you clients. But you should go beyond customers' expectations. Aim higher than customer service; aim for customer satisfaction.

For example, a Lands' End catalog customer calls and orders a shirt. The shirt is sent promptly. That is good customer service.

A Lands' End customer calls and wants to order a present for her brother. But she doesn't know her brother's size. The operator suggests that maybe the brother ordered from them before. She looks up the brother on the computer and finds records of previous purchases, including sizes. That's customer satisfaction.

"NO, I CAN'T!"

A consultant recently stayed at a hotel where all the employees wore "YES, I CAN!" BUTTONS.

Hurrying for a plane, the consultant asked the receptionist if the hotel could mail some slides.

No problem, said the receptionist. Just take them to the bell captain.

The bell captain disagreed. "We don't do that; that's not our job."

The consultant suggested the bell captain take off his "YES, I CAN!" button and replace it with one that said, "NO, I CAN'T!"

---

8. PROMISE WHAT YOU ALREADY DO

An advertising account manager was touring the plant of one of his largest clients, a brewery.

He noticed some men dressed in rubber suits using live steam to clean bottles. Won't help for advertising, he was told. All breweries use steam to ensure bottles are hygienically cleaned.

Nevertheless, the account manager created a successful national campaign proclaiming "We Clean Our Bottles with Live Steam." The account manager knew that it didn't matter that all breweries did the same thing—because the customers didn't know.

Don't assume that customers appreciate the special efforts you are taking on their behalf. Let them know. Your customers will be impressed, and return again and again.

Incidentally, other breweries soon placed ads saying they also steam-cleaned their bottles. Customers probably considered them unimaginative copycats.

FROM THE RAPHEL FILES: TWO STORIES OF CUSTOMER SATISFACTION

L et's look at two cases of creating customer satisfaction.

Happy in Honolulu

One of the authors, a regular traveler to Honolulu, was unhappy with the service at his hotel.

He called the Kahala Hilton, another hotel in which he frequently stayed, said he was dissatisfied with his current accommodations, and asked if there was a room available. The operator said rooms were available and added: "I see that you usually stay in room 318. [The author had never noticed.] That one is unavailable, but we can give you the room just above it." She quoted the rate and the author taxied over.

At the hotel, the clerk informed him that a mistake had been made. The room had a balcony and was therefore more expensive. "But we quoted you the lower rate, and that's all you will pay," she said.

The author went to his room and found a tray of assorted island fruits with a message from the manager: "Sorry your vacation didn't begin well. From now on you'll have a great time."

Every day, he found a new tray of fresh fruit in his room.

The author left the hotel a dedicated client of the Kahala Hilton.

Cold Dishes, Warm Service

One of the authors went to a restaurant with friends. Two of the meals were not hot enough, and the authors pointed this out to the waitress. The waitress apologized and immediately reheated the dishes. That was good service.

At the end of the meal, the waitress said, "I'm sorry for your inconvenience, and we want you to have complimentary coffee and dessert." That was customer satisfaction.

Of course, the author became a loyal patron of the restaurant.

Part 4: Turn Clients into Advocates
9. REWARD LOYALTY WITH SPECIAL TREATMENT

On the final rung of the loyalty ladder stand the advocates.

These are not just good customers or longtime clients. These are customers so impressed with you that they sell your company and products to friends and acquaintances.

If you followed the suggestions in this summary, from thank-you notes to new shoppers to free gifts for loyal clients, you've been preparing customers to become advocates.

You can have your clients reach for that final advocate rung by rewarding their loyalty. Create generous loyalty programs for them alone.

Loyalty Programs

Loyalty programs reward customer loyalty with special treatment. This special treatment can include receiving free merchandise or services, special offers not available to other customers, and special privileges.

Rewarding loyal customers is nothing new. Stamp or bonus point programs, in which with every purchase customers receive points that can be redeemed for gifts, have been around retail for years.

Loyalty programs took a giant leap forward with American Airlines' AAdvantage Program, one of the first times such programs were applied in the service industry. Other airlines and hotels quickly followed with "frequency" programs of their own.

THE PRIVILEGE OF LOYALTY

Give your best customers privileges other customers don't have. For example:

• The usual checkout time for hotel guests is noon, but for advocates, it's 6 P.M. And put fresh fruit in their rooms with a "thanks-for-coming" note.

• Send advocates special offers with no minimum purchase needed to enjoy savings.

• Give advocates gift certificates on their birthdays.

• Don't make advocates wait. Give them exclusive phone numbers and special members-only waiting lines.

To better provide the privileges that your best customers want, know what they want. Have advocates fill out in-depth personal surveys.

And at least once a year write to ask them what they would like to see from you.

Usually, the programs allow customers to accumulate points toward future purchases. They also give customers special privileges (for example, late checkouts from hotels or special lounges in airports).

■ **Clubs.** In most cases, the loyalty programs are structured around clubs. Closed clubs are loyalty clubs for which customers pay to participate. For example, anyone can shop at Wal-Mart, but customers have to pay an annual fee to get into Sam's Wholesale Club.

THE HOTEL AND THE BAKER

Here's what two very different companies offer loyal clients.

Sheraton Hotels

From a customer survey, Sheraton discovered that the usual perks of hotel clubs (free rooms, upgrades, late checkouts) all came in second to customers' preference: air miles.

Sheraton built a new program around air miles.

Customers who stay a minimum of two days per year earn two air miles for every dollar spent on reservations. Customers who stay four days per year earn three air miles for every dollar.

At this level, membership is free. For $25, clients receive three miles for every dollar spent on reservations plus special privileges such as upgrades, express check-in and checkout, and gift premiums.

Dr. Oetker

Dr. Oetker, a baking products company in Germany, also based its program on a customer survey. The survey showed that most customers were older. Many potential new customers (younger women) didn't know how to bake.

The solution: A Dr. Oetker Baking Club aimed at eighteen- to thirty-eight-year-old women with children.

For $25, membership brings:

• Recipes on a regular basis.
• Product samples.
• Discounts on travel with Movenpick and Holiday Inn.
• Children's recipe contests.
• A hotline to their "test kitchen" for baking problems.

The Dr. Oetker Baking Club has a membership of one hundred thousand young bakers. And these customers take their baking seriously: the test kitchen hotline receives almost seven hundred calls a month.

Open clubs are either open to everyone or open upon invitation. Frequent flyer programs, for example, are usually open to everyone. Special gold card clubs for frequent hotel guests are often based on invitation only.

No matter how they are structured, all loyalty programs have the same goal: to give those customers that keep coming back special treatment. This ensures that they'll keep returning.

And if asked for a recommendation, customers will immediately think of your company.

SCORING POINTS
by Clive Humby and Terry Hunt
with Tim Phillips

While discussions about marketing often focus on efforts to bring in new customers, the best companies know the immense value of marketing to current customers. The adage that it is more expensive to acquire customers than to keep them is by now a cliché. Few companies, however, are as adept as Tesco in marketing to their customers.

Most business book readers will probably not recognize the name of the large UK grocery store chain: Tesco has no stores in the Americas and yet pops up time and again in business books on both sides of the Atlantic. The reason is that even U.S.-centric business book authors (of which there are far too many) have to acknowledge the exceptional success of Tesco.

Tesco has the world's most successful retail customer loyalty program. With 400,000 customers, it's the world's most successful Internet supermarket. (Read any books that say Internet grocery stores just can't work? Well, they're wrong.) With 3.4 million customers, it's one of Europe's fastest-growing financial services companies. With 221,000 employees, it's the UK's largest private employer. And Tesco keeps expanding—more than 65,000 of its staff work outside the UK.

The summary of *Scoring Points: How Tesco Is Winning Customer Loyalty* by Clive Humby and Terry Hunt with Tim Phillips will tell you how Tesco's success stemmed from its exceptional customer loyalty scheme: the Tesco Clubcard.

Tesco launched a fourteen-store pilot program of the card that immediately began generating detailed statistics about who spent what, and when and how those customers responded to personalized offers; it was clear to Tesco's executives that they had an opportunity to differentiate themselves from their bigger competitors. Within three short months, the program had been expanded to all of Tesco's six hundred stores.

Ironically, the first result of the card was too much data about customers—or at least too much for Tesco to be able to fully process. As explained in the summary, "Instead of building the largest data store it could, Tesco set out to build the smallest store of data that would give useful information." Tesco's goal was not to accumulate data; it wanted to get to know its customers in a way that would help it better serve those customers. The success of the Clubcard is proof of how well it has achieved this goal.

Clive Humby is chairman and founder of the leading marketing analysts company dunnhumby and a visiting professor at Northwestern University in Chicago. Terry Hunt is chairman of EHS Brann, one of the largest direct marketing agencies in the world. Humby and Hunt were the major outside influences and implementers in the development of the Tesco Clubcard. Tim Phillips is a well-known business journalist who appears on BBC TV and *Radio and Sky News.* He is currently managing editor of *Performance Plus magazine.* He published *Knockoff: The Deadly Trade in Counterfeit Goods* in 2005.

SCORING POINTS
How Tesco Is Winning Customer Loyalty
by Clive Humby and Terry Hunt with Tim Phillips

CONTENTS

THE SUMMARY IN BRIEF
Launched in 1995, Tesco Clubcard is the world's most successful retail loyalty program. Since then, Tesco has transformed its relationship with its customers. Today, Tesco is the United Kingdom's most successful retailer and the world's most successful Internet supermarket. It is also a leader in the financial services market and perhaps the best retailer in the world at managing customer relations. In this summary, you will learn how Tesco went from being just one of

three grocery chains in Great Britain, fighting for its share of customers and their wallets, to the undisputed leader. You will see the action behind the scenes as Tesco begins to learn exactly why customers shop at Tesco and what they want from the retailer. By creating the world's leading customer relationship management program, Tesco has learned a lot about what it takes to retain those customers and induce them to spend more. Through its innovative Clubcard, Tesco has learned that rewarding good customers is great for business. What Tesco has learned from its program will inspire others just now launching loyalty programs or trying to leverage the information theirs provides into sales.

THE COMPLETE SUMMARY

1. QUESTIONS OF LOYALTY

Loyalty, in day-to-day life, implies monogamy: one choice above all others. Retail loyalty isn't like that. There isn't a customer alive who will consider using one shop for every need. When retailers look at winning and keeping loyal customers, the best they can hope for is a little extra goodwill, a slight margin of preference, and an incremental shift in buying behavior. Together, however, these benefits can add up to a massive contribution to a business's financial success.

Types of Loyalty

There are four types of loyalty on which retailers have come to rely. The first is "purge" loyalty in which the retailer slashes prices to make itself the preferred place to shop. The second is "pure" loyalty, which is dependent on a two-way dialogue between the retailer and customer. Next, "pull" loyalty depends on attracting customers by giving a related special offer with a purchase, such as a buy-one-get-one-free deal. It's an inducement to create sales by encouraging customers to buy new items. Finally, "push" loyalty means creating a program to encourage customers to use a way of shopping they haven't used before, such as offering a combined credit card and loyalty card or making prices cheaper on a Web site. Push loyalty is what loyalty programs are all about.

Creating Value

Loyalty programs produce positive results in six ways:

- Customers make purchases more often, having made a conscious choice to commit to your brand in exchange for a reward when they sign up.
- Loyalty programs give you the ability to mass-customize marketing communications. Using customer transaction data, you can individually target marketing.

- Loyalty program information is very valuable if it is analyzed. The data is exact and becomes a high-value asset itself.
- Loyalty programs let you track trends, giving you early warning of significant changes in how customers are shopping, what they are choosing, and what they aren't doing.
- Loyalty programs minimize waste by targeting offers to those who are most likely to want them.
- Loyalty programs promote trust and open the way to an expanded relationship when it's time to add services and products to the marketing mix.

Making Loyalty Pay

Loyalty programs aren't cheap—they require a substantial investment in cash. For a large retailer, start-up costs can run $30 million in the first year, and annual costs will run between $5 million and $10 million.

Loyalty programs also require a huge investment in time and IT resources. For example, Tesco employs nearly one hundred people whose main job is to manage its Clubcard process.

And before you start, consider the cost of stopping. If you don't get it right and you have to end the program, customers may perceive your actions as breaking the bargain. Once customers embrace a program, they are likely to be very reluctant to have it taken away. Customers quite reasonably consider that the benefits they received are theirs by right, and react poorly to any perceived reduction in the value they receive from your company.

A related problem is split loyalty. What happens if all your competitors also start loyalty programs? Will customers carry a second and third card, all from the competition? The result may be that customers don't have a preference, but all the competitors are saddled with the cost of running the programs.

This may be less of a problem than it first appears. After all, it is unlikely that any customer will never shop at another store. All a loyalty program should expect to achieve is a slightly larger share of what customers would spend without the program. Persuading a customer to use the pharmacy or to buy three bottles of soda rather than one is a small change in behavior, but can considerably boost sales and profitability.

Loyalty Program Basics

Before you decide on a loyalty program, consider the different ways you can structure one. First, you must decide whether the plan will be opt-in or automatic. Generally, you are better off with an opt-in program rather than signing up everyone whose name and address you already know. (This may violate privacy laws in some jurisdictions.)

Next, decide whether the program will be anonymous or personalized. For example, a coffee shop that uses a discount card entitling the holder to the eleventh cup free may not need the customer's name and address—its success will be measured by whether there is an increase in sales. A grocery store, on the other hand, may want to gather as much information as possible to better target shoppers.

Will your program be flat-rate or top-down? Flat-rate programs reward all customers, while top-down programs give greater rewards to those who spend the most. A top-down example is British Airways, which rewards the most frequent flyers with more and greater benefits, like faster check-ins and better upgrades. Just be sure to think through your approach first—you risk upsetting customers if next year they don't reach the same reward level.

Finally, decide whether your program will feature rewards on demand or on cumulative value. The risk with the second approach is that you can carry, as some airlines do, a large financial liability for accumulated points. But if you use an on-demand system that gives customers a periodic reward, such as a discount at checkout, you don't accumulate long-term liability.

CLUBCARD ON TRIAL

In November 1993, the British press began following the introduction of Clubcard at Tesco. The press reported that soon after a test launch, over 50 percent of customers in test locations elected to join the program. Soon, rumors spread that a Clubcard national launch was imminent. Until then, the grocery chain was struggling to keep up with the industry leaders and needed something to give it a boost.

Tesco tried a rewards program in the 1960s, when it introduced Green Shield Stamps. Though successful for a decade, the gimmick ran its course and became an expensive distraction. Customers began valuing low prices and didn't want to lick stamps for rewards. But the grocer had trouble letting go of the program. Finally the program was replaced by price cuts and larger stores and the public was delighted. Management vowed to continue innovating.

Tesco launched the pilot Clubcard program and was surprised at the results. Within three months, Tesco analyzed the test results and launched a national program. It already had the technology to track every item purchased at all stores and at what price and time. All they needed to capture were the name and address of who bought the goods. Clubcard did that.

You will also have to decide which rewards customers most value. If you use a points system that allows customers to accumulate miles, points, or another unit measure toward rewards, remember that the units they save will have a perceived currency value. If you make changes to the reward plan that devalue the "currency," you will face angry customers.

Another approach is to offer a discount at the register to those in your rewards program. Simply put, you will have two price lists—one for members and another higher price for everyone else. Yet another approach is to offer information as the reward, such as a newsletter tailored to the customer's interests. Finally, you can give rewards, such as special shopping days or free snacks at the airport.

2. BECAUSE WE CAN

Tesco's experiment with its loyalty program, Clubcard, has been extremely successful. After a pilot program began generating detailed statistics about who spent what, and about when and how those customers responded to personalized offers, it became clear that the program was an opportunity to overtake the competition. The plan went ahead when executives announced, "We ought to do this because we can."

So urgent was the desire to take advantage of what had been learned in the pilot program that the small group working on the program was asked to expand from a fourteen-store pilot to all six hundred stores within three months. The race for first-mover advantage was on.

To make the twelve-week deadline, the team worked over Christmas and in secret. Rumor had it that Tesco's two major competitors, Safeway and Sainsbury's, were also considering loyalty programs. Plans included having over ten million cards ready for anticipated demand and setting up the system so that every customer who signed up had the card immediately.

Tesco worked hard to impress on staff how important the program was going to be. With staff enthusiasm, management calculated that far more customers would sign up. Everyone from managers to checkout clerks was expected to tell customers about Clubcard.

The last challenge was to get press attention. Three days before the national rollout, the press heard about the national launch for the first time. "Tesco says 'Thank You' to customers," read the press release. A media frenzy followed with radio and television coverage all across Great Britain.

Within days, over 70 percent of all Tesco sales were being recorded and matched to Clubcard holders—3.5 million transactions a day. Two weeks later, seven million cards had been delivered to stores, yet supplies were nearly exhausted.

Tesco had calculated that it needed to see a sales increase of 1.6 percent to cover the costs of the launch and the membership cards. The initial sales spike was near 4 percent and then settled well above 2 percent, making the launch a stunning success.

What Made the Launch a Success?

Clubcard is a case study in how to roll out a large marketing initiative quickly, efficiently, and with maximum impact. Here are the reasons why:

- Momentum: By accepting management's challenge to move ahead quickly, the team gained first-mover advantage.
- Simplicity: The message was right: "Save on your shopping today." It was simple and direct and a perfect match to the company slogan "Every Little Helps."
- Control: The team in charge was given the freedom to create the program based on the trial data.
- Involvement: Everyone, including the front-line staff, was involved.
- Preparation: Everything was in place, including phone help lines and the IT infrastructure.
- Ambition: Clubcard had to prove itself big to convince shareholders and management that it would work over the long term. It set ambitious yet reachable goals based on early testing.
- Commitment: The Tesco board was enthusiastic and committed to making the program work.

THE CLUBCARD EFFECT

Tesco Clubcard team members hoped for a few months to establish the program before their biggest competitor, Sainsbury's, retaliated with its own offering. It didn't happen for eighteen months. Meanwhile, customers spent 28 percent more at Tesco and cut spending at Sainsbury's by 16 percent.

The eighteen months following the introduction of Clubcard won Tesco time and turned customer data into knowledge it could use to take on the competition. The program let Tesco build customer loyalty by demonstrating that it appreciated their business.

---

3. DATA, LOVELY DATA

Clubcard could have been little more than a targeted discount, as many retail loyalty programs were. But they didn't survive. The true value of Clubcard is in the data it generates. Tesco recognized that and used it to change the way it does business.

However, making the data Clubcard provided usable was a challenge. At first, there was too much data and too little time—the challenge of analyzing every purchase from every cardholder was wholly beyond the technology available. IT's technology simply wasn't there yet. But today, Tesco has the capacity to take the information from every shopping basket processed through its checkouts and use it to drive marketing and management decisions.

The first thing the team did was to create a matrix of data samples to achieve a statistically valid picture of customer behavior. It took 10 percent of the data once a week, processed it, and applied the findings to the other 90 percent. After a few years, the company created a "Customer Insight Unit" filled with geographers, who are statisticians, who have spent a lot of time applying statistics to understand how customers behave. They could crunch through the sample data, see patterns, and then make recommendations.

Measuring Customer Loyalty

Creating a successful loyalty program requires you to match good marketing skills and commercial pragmatism with a hard-headed attitude toward data. This is especially clear in the way loyalty is measured. The basic measurement is known as RFV—recency, frequency, and value. Any shopper regularly using a loyalty card can be measured by monitoring how he or she behaves according to a mix of those criteria.

Recency is a simple measure—recording when the customer last shopped. A true sign of customers deserting a retailer is a decrease in a group of customers' recency behavior. But recency alone is a poor measure of loyalty. It must be combined with a measurement of the type of shopping the customer does.

Frequency is a simple measure of how often you shop—and is a rough guide to how robust the relationship is between the customer and the brand. But it, too, is an incomplete measure.

Value is an indication of the profitability of your customer base. A decline means a smaller basket size, which means more purchases are being made elsewhere. It is more than a measure of the value of a shopping trip—it is a measure of how much "value" the customer perceived the retailer is providing.

The advantage of RFV is that it can be quantified accurately and the information it provides can lead to action. For example, RFV analysis can highlight a group of vulnerable customers that needs more attention.

What Tesco Learned About Data

Instead of building the largest data store it could, Tesco set out to build the smallest store of data that would give useful information. It simply wanted a usable resource to better understand what customers did and to predict what they might do in the future.

Tesco started not from "What would we like to do?" but from "What can we realistically do and still make a profit?" Clubcard became a massive consumer behavior laboratory. Retailers have always experimented with price and range to see what works; now Tesco could measure exactly what worked in any store. When it did something wrong, it knew it in days. When it did something right, it could implement it nationwide in weeks.

Perhaps most useful was segmenting shoppers so that Tesco could target refund offers and coupons to those who really wanted them. In fact, after Clubcard, redemption for coupon mailings went from 3 percent to over 70 percent.

4. FOUR CHRISTMASES A YEAR

One of the most popular features of Clubcard is the quarterly check that customers get as a rebate/reward for buying at Tesco. Four times a year, loyal customers get refund vouchers. Each mailing gives Tesco a sales bump similar to what retailers see at Easter and Christmas. The first mailing to five million Tesco customers was an expensive leap of faith that paid off handsomely.

Each mailing includes the earned rewards voucher and additional discounts on individual products targeted at specific groups of consumers. These product coupons achieve redemption rates as high as 70 percent—not bad when you consider that direct mail marketing responses rarely climb over single-figure percentages.

The decision to give customers their rewards through direct mail worked well. Tesco looked at its established retail calendar and integrated Clubcard mailings into it. This way, store managers could gear up with special stock and customers wouldn't take the benefits for granted. Instead, they would eagerly anticipate their quarterly mailing.

As time went on, the mailings became more complex. For example, the fifth mailing had one hundred different letters targeting different customer segments and preferences. By 1999, there were 145,000 variations. Today, the mailings are truly individual with each mailing customized to the specific customer. And each packet contains coupons for four items the customer already buys and two for related products the customer hasn't bought yet, but which other customers with similar buying profiles have bought.

BANANA MAN

W̲ho in their right mind would buy a half-ton of bananas at their local grocery store? That's what Phil Calcot did in January 1997. He was a Tesco Club-card customer who responded to a special offer the grocer made on the fruit. The store offered extra points to be added to the reward voucher customers receive four times a year. Buy a three-pound bunch, and you would get an extra twenty-five points on your account. That made the bananas better than free—he earned a profit on each bunch. He bought 942 pounds of bananas and had fun giving them away for free in the neighborhood. When he got his bonus check at the end of the quarter, he had a $50 profit.

5. THE QUARTERLY ME

The largest circulating magazine in the United Kingdom isn't a standard like *Cosmopolitan* or *Reader's Digest*. Instead, it is *Clubcard Magazine*—with a print run of 8.5 million, four times a year. It's part of a trend. In 2003, eight out of the ten highest-circulation magazines in the United Kingdom were titles published by brands as part of their marketing and customer relationship management programs.

Tesco's emergence as a major media owner happened in much the same way as it became the leader in loyalty programs—it wasn't the first, but it was the most single-minded. It used its new customer knowledge to launch a highly successful magazine. Advertisers are happy to pay five or six times what they would pay to advertise in a regular national magazine.

The magazine is sent free with the quarterly mailing, and is again cus-tomized to the segment the customer belongs to. Because it targets the front cover, some of the articles, and the ads to specific groups, it has become known as the "Quarterly Me" magazine.

Advertisers see the value of the expensive space Tesco sells because the grocer can give them real data on the effectiveness of the ad buy. Tesco tracks the product sales before the magazine mailing and after so it can demonstrate the short- and long-term effects. Sales increases by brand run anywhere from 1 to 27 percent.

The first full magazine mailing came in May 1996. Customers didn't know it, but there were five different versions—for students, families, young adults, older adults, and those over sixty—depending on the information provided when the customer signed up for Clubcard. The only issue that failed was the student-focused one—mainly because students move too often for the mailing to make sense. To give an idea of how the magazines differed, one Christmas issue aimed at over-sixty readers offered a chance to win a trip to the theater and tips on winter gardening, while the issue aimed at young adults offered a chance at a trip to Thailand and a guide to curing hangovers.

6. YOU ARE WHAT YOU EAT

Tesco encountered some problems along the way. A few years into the program, management was ready to address five main business problems. These were:

- *Price sensitivity.* How could Clubcard help Tesco set competitive price levels that generated significant sales without starting a price war?
- *Ranging for customers.* How could Clubcard help Tesco determine the range of goods to make available at stores to satisfy what customers wanted to buy?
- *Range creation.* Could Clubcard data help Tesco lead rather than respond to emerging customer tastes?
- *Promotions.* How could Clubcard data help Tesco see if promotions were working or whether customers were cherry-picking the best deals?
- *Competitive attack.* How could Tesco use Clubcard data to take aim at the competition?

The common denominator of these challenges was the need for better-quality knowledge of customers. The analysts knew they had to create robust new groupings of customers, new ways to predict behavior, and a shared language that could easily describe customers.

The Loyalty Cube

Imagine that all a company's customers can be placed at various points in a three-dimensional cube. The first axis of the cube has to be the customer's profitability today. For example, a retiree who cooks from scratch may be very loyal but not as profitable as a less loyal customer who drops by twice a week for a prepared meal and a bottle of wine. The second axis measures future value and contains two elements: how likely a customer is to remain a customer and headroom—how much potential there is for the customer to become more valuable in the future. Finally, there is the last axis: championing. Customers can serve as ambassadors for the brand.

Tesco concluded that the differences among customers existed in each shopper's basket: the choices, the brands, the preferences, and the trade-offs each made in managing his or her grocery budget. The basket could tell a lot about two dimensions of the loyalty cube. First, it could quantify contribution simply by looking at the profit margins of the goods each chose. Second, by calculating the calories in the cart, it could measure headroom. Just how much of a customer's food needs did Tesco provide?

Tesco set about examining the details of each cart on the presumption that "you are what you eat" and that it was possible to reconstruct the life of a customer by examining the shopping data. The first hurdle was that one cart was not enough since the purchase might indicate a birthday party or a rare dinner party. Tesco used a 10 percent sample of data to model customers from their shopping behavior.

Baskets Become Buckets

Tesco analysts pondered the task of analyzing baskets and came up with a solution—they would analyze a "Bucket." The Bucket was the combination of products that appeared from the makeup of a customer's regular shopping baskets. Each Bucket was defined by a "marker": a high-volume product that had a particular attribute. It might typify indulgence or thrift, or indicate a tendency to buy in bulk. They then searched for other items bought more often than would be expected in combination with one of the markers. The end result was eighty different Buckets.

Each customer's Bucket score was used as a measure of how he or she liked to shop. Using cluster analysis (a statistical method), Tesco grouped customers with similar profiles over a number of variables. Putting the data into three dimensions, Tesco analysts could place the score in three Buckets as a point inside a cube. If those three Buckets suggested a type of customer, then they could see similar shopping patterns.

The next step was to get insight into why customer behavior fit into a particular Bucket. By looking at the clusters, they could answer the why. In all, there were twenty-seven different clusters identified. These became known as the Tesco Lifestyles.

7. LIFESTYLES BECOME HABITS

Lifestyles was not a perfect program. One weakness was that a few of the product Buckets did not seem to help decide which customers were in which clusters. If a product Bucket is going to define you, it should be a significant part of what you shop for, and not all eighty Buckets were equally important. In effect, eighty Buckets and twenty-seven Lifestyles may have broken customers down too much.

The next challenge was to create new customer groupings that were large enough to be cost-effective to use, but with a richness of common interest to paint a meaningful picture. Tesco came up with a plan that it dubbed the "Rolling Ball."

Project Rolling Ball set about assigning attributes to the food in shopping carts, such as "adventurous." First, the team defined a few products themselves. Olive oil and the ingredients for Malaysian curries were "adventurous." The team then looked at who bought these ingredients or foods, and what else they bought, after excluding the items just about everyone buys (bananas and milk, for example). Eventually, every Tesco item received a grade in one of twenty attributes. A food that only the adventurous bought received a high adventurous rating. Eventually, four hundred products might earn an adventurous rating, but the last fifty products found by the analysts might have a higher rating in another attribute, such as "fresh." The statistical ball had rolled into another new attribute category, if you will, and it was thus time to start focusing on finding products for this new attribute.

Grading the foods allowed Tesco to cluster customers into Lifestyle segments. But Tesco went one step further when it discovered that when customers shopped was also important. Adding this data to the mix created an extra segmentation to understand customers—a segmentation that used not only what people bought, but when people shopped. This segmentation was called Shopping Habits.

Avoiding the Big Brother Label

Any time you collect data on people, some will raise privacy concerns. To avoid the allegation that you are becoming some sort of Big Brother spy into private lives, you may have to do some proactive public relations work. Tesco understood this from the beginning.

One approach Tesco took was to publicize the good that went with learning what people were buying. For example, Tesco was able to demonstrate that it was using the information it collected to do good. Tesco used demographic data to:

- Track sales of allergy-free products and then persuaded the manufacturer to expand the product line;
- Track which nonorganic products organic shoppers bought and added to the product line based on actual need;
- Add over seven thousand local products by learning where shoppers preferred locally produced alternatives.

8. LAUNCHING A BANK

The next step for Tesco was to launch Clubcard Plus. The idea came from listening to customers who wanted to pay with their Clubcards, too. Tesco's development team came up with a unique idea—a card that let customers prepay and paid interest on the balance in the account. Clubcard Plus became an interest-bearing savings account. Basically, customers were able to debit money from their other accounts into Clubcard Plus, based on their average shopping bill. The reward was additional loyalty points for using the account to buy groceries and a modest overdraft provision letting customers borrow a month's worth of purchases at low interest. The plan ended up being the first step in the Tesco Personal Finance program.

To run the new "bank," Tesco partnered with an established bank. Tesco offered the program to its most creditworthy one million customers even though its credit risk was minimal (it didn't want to risk alienating customers by rejecting their applications). The program was a success, with over sixty thousand people signing up in the first few months. Those customers then began spending more per trip. Publicity about the program's interest payments (which were higher than most banks') led to new customers opening accounts.

Unfortunately, the program didn't sustain its early success owing to the increasing popularity of bank debit cards that could be used everywhere. Some Tesco customers still use the card, but the company has since expanded into more traditional banking products. It now offers a Visa credit card and loans. The credit card lets shoppers earn extra Clubcard points for all their purchases.

9. THE BABY EXPERTS

When Tesco looked at the information it was collecting through Clubcard, it discovered that families with babies who bought baby products at Tesco were more valuable than those with babies who didn't. It then set out to convert the nonbuyers. It discovered that those nonbuyers were spending their baby-product budgets at a leading drugstore, even though they were paying about 20 percent more. To make matters worse, the drugstore began offering its own loyalty program, and because its prices were much higher, it could offer a bigger discount.

To convert the nonbuyers, Tesco tried something different—it appealed to the emotional needs of new parents rather than to their rational side. The result was the Tesco Baby Club. Baby Club was opt-in and a soft sell. It positioned Tesco as an expert on baby care. Advice and special offers were targeted to each mother's pregnancy and the age of her child up until twenty-four months. The result was excellent. In the first two years, 37 percent of all British parents-to-be joined and the retailer increased its share of the baby market by 24 percent.

10. FROM MOUSE TO HOUSE

Customers want convenience as well as good prices. To meet that need, Tesco has begun using the Internet as a channel, letting customers order online through Tesco.com. By 2003, Tesco online had 1.3 million monthly visitors to the site that offers twenty thousand grocery items and wines, as well as travel and financial services. Customers can also buy books and CDs, as well as electronics, all delivered by eight hundred Tesco.com branded delivery vans.

Tesco is now the largest Internet grocery retailer in the world. Tesco experimented with reviving home delivery starting in 1996. The major problem Tesco ran into was that customers were put off by the amount of time it took to prepare the first order.

To solve the problems, Tesco signed on with Microsoft and became the first full-service Internet grocery store. Selecting the order was made as easy as possible. Tesco also chose not to build special warehouses for its online division. Instead, Tesco provides a personal touch—using "personal shoppers" who shop the local Tesco. These shoppers use a special instruction sheet produced by a custom-designed software system that allows them to fulfill six orders at a time, taking the shortest route through the store. The goods are then delivered to customers at their convenience.

Tesco has learned that it takes two shopping sessions before customers become committed online grocery buyers. But the efforts are clearly worth it. Today, Tesco.com has 380,000 active customers. Of those, only about one-third are replacing regular trips to brick-and-mortar Tesco stores. Another third were regular customers, but now they are spending more per year at Tesco. The rest are entirely new customers.

A BIGGER DEAL

Gradually, it became apparent that getting a coupon for a modest amount off your grocery bill four times a year was not enough. Customers wanted something more exciting, so more excitement they got. In 1999, Tesco announced that Clubcard points could be spent on seasonal Clubcard Deals—on anything from hotels to movies. The program launched with publicity boasting "a million cheap tickets" with partners from KLM, Virgin, Eurostar, and Disney. High-spending customers could quadruple the value of their points by using them on Clubcard Deals.

With the success of its online grocery business, Tesco is looking into expanding its offerings online. It wants to sell more books, music, and electronics. Clubcard remains an important part of this marketing strategy because Tesco knows its customers very well. Using Clubcard data, Tesco has been able to look at the similarities and differences between virtual shoppers and those who come into the stores.

What's Next for Tesco?

Tesco has begun expanding its stores into Ireland, Continental Europe, and Asia. For example, in South Korea, Tesco has teamed up with Samsung and is offering electronics as well as groceries. In the United States, Tesco is teaming up with Kroger—the fifth largest retailer in the world. The two companies are working to expand Kroger's loyalty program by applying the lessons learned from Clubcard to the American market.

Tesco continues to face challenges. First, it is focusing attention on a segment of its shoppers who haven't benefited greatly from promotions and special offers—those loyal customers who still make meals from scratch. Tesco wants to please these customers with deals relevant to their needs.

Tesco is also experimenting with checkout coupons. Clubcard members receive coupons they can immediately use for items in their carts. The coupons serve as an instant reminder of the value of Clubcard.

HOW TO DRIVE YOUR COMPETITION CRAZY

by Guy Kawasaki

In the crowded world of marketing authors, Guy Kawasaki stands out for his enthusiastic and energetic manifestos, whether he's talking about pushing change through resistance (*Rules for Revolutionaries*), launching a new company (*The Art of the Start*), or, in the case of the book whose summary follows, developing the strategy to beat the competition. Of course, he does not use the phrase *beat the competition,* which would be too sedate in the world of Kawasaki. You have to "drive your competition crazy!" This is even more fun, according to Kawasaki, if your competition happens to be a giant, entrenched corporation and you happen to be a small upstart. As he notes in the book, you want to take on a mighty opposite.

Kawasaki has some experience with taking on mighty opposites. He was a member of the Apple team in the early 1980s that decided it was going to take on and beat IBM. (On his Web site, Kawasaki writes about landing a job at Apple right out of business school: "When I saw what a Macintosh could do, the clouds parted and the angels started singing.")

While his enthusiasm is infectious, his books are popular because they are also filled with specific how-to steps—and scores of examples to back him up. Honda, General Electric, Harley-Davidson, and Levi Strauss are just some of the better-known companies referenced in *How to Drive Your Competition Crazy.* The summary you are about to read also features a variety of David-and-Goliath face-offs including Kiwi International against American Airlines; Wilson Harrel and his cleaning product Formula 409 against Procter & Gamble; and Bob Curry and his Ace Hardware store against Home Depot. Kawasaki's readers are also treated to stories about small but clever businesses, such as the nursing home that turned itself into a small town, complete with post office, bank, library, beauty parlor, soda shop, and even a mayor and town council.

Guy Kawasaki was born in Hawaii, received his MBA from the University of California, Los Angeles, and was one of the original Apple Computer employees responsible for marketing the new Macintosh in 1984. He is currently the CEO of Garage Technology Ventures, a Silicon Valley venture capital firm. He is the author of eight books, many of them bestsellers, including *The Macintosh Way*, *Selling the Dream*, *Rules for Revolutionaries*, and, most recently, *The Art of the Start*.

HOW TO DRIVE YOUR COMPETITION CRAZY
Create Disruption for Fun and Profit
by Guy Kawasaki

CONTENTS

THE SUMMARY IN BRIEF

In 1984, Guy Kawasaki was part of a high-level team on a mission to destroy a competitor. The tactics the team used included anything that would disrupt the existing marketplace and create advantages for his company's products.

Kawasaki's job at this upstart company, Apple Computer, was software evangelist. He had to convince developers to create software for the

Macintosh—something absolutely necessary if Apple were to survive, let alone help bring about the downfall of the hated competitor IBM.

Kawasaki and friends happily worked ninety hours a week, fueled by zeal. They were on a crusade to change the world and prevent domination by IBM's "blue-suited meanies."

To disrupt the market, they created a user-friendly interface, something the world had not only never seen but never thought possible. Next, they fostered innovative software like desktop publishing programs. Third, they incited customers to "evangelize"—sell—for them.

Though Apple didn't topple IBM, Kawasaki and his crew succeeded at driving Big Blue crazy and winning a big chunk of the computer market. They also had a great time.

Kawasaki learned lessons from all this that can be applied to your business: To create advantages that diminish the power of industry leaders (or just everyday competitors) takes clear, shrewd thinking; guts; hard work; and a willingness to buck convention. It means knowing yourself and your competitors, and understanding your customers so well that you can give them what they want and need—even before they think of it.

By the time you've read this summary, you'll have the tools and insights you need to disrupt your market and increase your revenue and profitability substantially. And work will be a lot more fun.

THE COMPLETE SUMMARY
Part I: Lay the Groundwork
1. FIRST THINGS FIRST: KNOW THYSELF

Before you start annoying your competition, spend a few hours getting to know yourself.

Basic Questions

Begin by asking, *What business are we really in?*

Most people define a business too narrowly. Wang, for instance, defined itself as making word-processing equipment. If it had defined the business as enhancing productivity, Wang might still be strong.

Honda, for example, knows it's not a car, motorcycle, generator, or lawn mower company. It's in the engine business, with a core competence in converting fuel to power.

Where do you see your firm in five, ten, twenty, and fifty years?

Most companies are short-sighted. Honda, in contrast, introduced a motor scooter to the American market in 1959. Twenty-seven years later, it introduced the Acura. This process took foresight and patience.

If prospects don't buy from you, from whom do they buy?

Wang probably thought its competition was other word-processing companies like NBI. Wang's real competition was computers and word-processing software, not firms making dedicated word processors.

Define Products and Services

These questions will help you understand your business and point to markets you could develop.

- What benefits does your product or service really provide?
- What are the most important reasons customers buy from you?
- How is your product positioned in the marketplace?
- Are customers using products in ways you never intended?

Honda again offers a good example. Motorcycles, it knows, offer more than just transportation. For many, they symbolize freedom and fun. Thus, Honda markets motorcycles to professionals and students.

PICK A "MIGHTY OPPOSITE"

Thomas Watson, Jr., of IBM said:

Make no little enemies—people with whom you differ for some petty, insignificant reason. Instead, I would urge you to cultivate "mighty opposites"—people with whom you disagree on big issues, with whom you will fight to the end over fundamental convictions. And that fight, I can assure you, will be good for you and your opponent.

Guy Kawasaki and others at Apple chose IBM as their mighty opposite because they saw IBM as centralized, autocratic, and at times user-unfriendly. Apple, in their eyes, was decentralized, democratic, and user-friendly.

A good enemy forces you to improve your company. In Apple's case, it even helped the company succeed.

Choose a mighty opposite of your own to battle with. A good choice: an older, richer company that leads the industry. But whatever firm you choose, make sure it's a worthy opponent. Says guerrilla marketer Jay Levinson, "If you're lucky, your competitors are good, smart, and working hard—they're not pushovers."

REALITY CHECK

Make sure you're gaining the right insights using this method:

1. List the top five reasons customers buy from you.
2. Using sales records, find out who your best customers are.
3. Take the top ten customers to lunch—one at a time—and ask them why they buy from you.
4. Compare your list and your customers' responses.
   The results will surprise you.

---

2. NEXT STEP: KNOW THY CUSTOMER

To know your customers, you have to get out and meet them. This is what you need to know:

- *Who is using your product?* The Thermos team creating a new grill (see story below) discovered that the "man of the house" was no longer chief barbecuer. Women grilled, too, and had different desires. For instance, they did not like messing with charcoal or propane tanks. (Note: Users may not always be the buyers. For example, parents buy toys for kids, which is why toy packaging so often screams, "Educational!")
- *How are products in your category used by customers?* Thermos discovered that many people used grills on small patios or balconies. That prompted it to come up with a compact, attractive design.
- *Are regulations or societal pressures changing your marketplace?* Thermos discovered that lighter fluid was banned in some parts of the U.S., making charcoal harder to light. Its solution: a high-intensity electric grill.

How to Get to Know Them

There are a number of ways you can get to know your customers:

The ad hoc team. This is how Thermos did it. It worked toward a short-term goal—creating a new grill—by sending a product development team into the field.

The corporate commitment. Harley-Davidson is committed to knowing its customers. Every employee, for instance, goes to motorcycle rallies to ride with customers.

The open channel. General Electric practices this method with its GE Answer Center, which provides answers or solves problems having to do with any GE product.

The scientific approach. This includes audits, consulting studies, and focus groups.

Though these methods can be valuable, don't fall in love with technology. A company with massive computing power for research but no real love for customers won't last.

ANTICIPATE THEIR NEEDS

Customers can tell you what they want from current products. But they are poor at knowing what they need beyond today's frame of reference. Could computer users, for instance, have asked for the Apple interface when all they knew was DOS?

It's your job to go beyond customers' articulated wants and serve their unarticulated needs. That means knowing them so well you can satisfy desires they don't even know they have.

---

3. KNOW THY ENEMY

Sam Walton of Wal-Mart used to roam the aisles of Kmart and Price Club, tape recorder in hand, taking notes on pricing and merchandising. Walton knew how to adapt an idea—and which ideas were worth stealing. Just as important, he knew what his competitors were up to.

Take a lesson from Sam and start watching competitors (including upstarts and niche players) closely.

Know these big-picture things about each competitor: its mission, goals, and objectives; whether it sees itself as market- or product-driven; whether it considers you its competition; and its strengths and weaknesses.

Find out the nitty-gritty stuff, too: What distribution channels does it use? How does it position products? How does it manufacture them? What are its pricing, discounting, and payment terms? How does it handle customer service? How does it get feedback from customers?

Ways to Get to Know Them

To gain competitive intelligence:

- *Be like Sam.* Go to the competitor's store. Get its catalog and price list. Gather promotional material.
- *Become a customer.* Buy the competitor's product or service to see how it handles after-sale support, service, and follow-up selling.
- *Invest in the competitor.* Buy a share of stock to receive reports.
- *Talk to the competition's customers.* Learn as much as you can ethically.

- Read everything you can about the industry and your competition.
- Attend trade shows and meetings. You may pick up knowledge of the competitor's strategic direction.
- Browse government records. Competitors often have to disclose much in public offerings, bids, tax assessments, patent and trademark registrations, and more. Look it up.

GRILL YOUR CUSTOMERS

In 1993, Thermos introduced the Thermal Electric Grill. It combined the high-temperature capabilities of gas and charcoal grills with the convenience of electric grills. This grill disrupted the marketplace and added significantly to Thermos's revenues.

Thermos did an extraordinary research job before bringing the grill to market. It convened focus groups and videotaped customers using grills. From these, it learned that people were tired of messy conventional grills, that people wanted more attractive barbecues, and that fire-safety laws often prohibited conventional grills.

Thermos, too, knew its real business. It applied expertise in insulation and heat transfer to the project, which ensured that the grill could achieve the necessary high temperatures. If Thermos had forgotten what business it was in, and if it hadn't gotten to know its customers, it might have created just another big, ugly, black barbecue.

Part 2: Do the Right Things
4. FOCUS ON CUSTOMERS

The best way to drive your competition crazy is to make your customers happy. To do that, you have to focus squarely on them. If you concentrate on beating the competition instead, you'll get into a tit-for-tat battle that may have little to do with pleasing customers.

Ask the Right Questions

Guy Kawasaki discovered a restaurant in Portland, Oregon, whose owner asked the right questions about what customers need. Called Old Wives' Tales, the restaurant features a huge playroom for kids that contains three boats, a train, a tunnel, and more. The playground, and the orange slices served when you sit down, keep kids occupied and happy.

Why would owner Holly Hart use space that could fit at least twenty revenue-producing seats for a playground? Because she noticed that parents have a difficult time having a relaxing dinner out when young children are along. They tended to gulp and run at full-service restaurants, but they weren't always satisfied at the places that already had playgrounds for kids: fast-food joints.

Hart asked, "How can I redefine the dining experience to make it more pleasant for families?" Business has boomed ever since.

Provide Imaginative Solutions

Eventide Lutheran Home in Moorhead, Minnesota, asked the right questions about what people want in a nursing home. Knowing that most nursing homes breed loneliness, isolation, and boredom, Eventide gave its home a small-town feel. It has a post office with antique mail boxes, bank, library, beauty parlor, barbershop, and even a soda shop. Residents elect a mayor, and a town council brings its concerns to management.

Eventide encourages community organizations like the Rotary to hold meetings in "town," and the soda shop hosts birthday parties for residents and grandchildren alike.

Any doubt that residents prefer Eventide to other homes? Focus on the customer, and imaginative solutions emerge.

Provide a Complete Product

When people buy something, they want to take it out of the package and use it right away. You can satisfy customers by making sure that you provide everything they need to get started.

Paint firm Standard Brands, for example, sells a customer-pleasing kit that includes a roller tray, roller handles with extension, drop cloth, roller covers, and a paintbrush.

BREAK DOWN BARRIERS

When you focus on your own convenience, you often make customers leap over barriers to do business with you. Take a cue from these barrier-removing companies:

• Blue Cross and Blue Shield of Massachusetts has information and service centers in two of the state's large malls. "We made a decision to meet our members . . . where they are," said the organization's chief operating officer.

• Mervyn's, a California retailer, shows it knows how to handle crowds. When things get busy, it rolls portable sales terminals to wherever they're needed.

5. CONCENTRATE ON A DECISIVE POINT

In 1796, Napoleon, with thirty-five thousand men, faced an army of Austrians and an army of Sardinians with sixty thousand men between them.

Napoleon attacked neither army directly, but a point where the two joined. He secured this weak point, then turned on the Sardinians. They surrendered. Three days later, so did the Austrians.

Dividing and conquering works in business, too. It helps you use your resources most efficiently, it minimizes retaliation, and small victories breed confidence.

Find a Niche

If you know your advantages and the capabilities of your competition, you can detect exploitable, market-busting niches. Use this method:

1. Determine the most important features of your product or service, as well as those of your competition. Include soft features such as service and warranty.

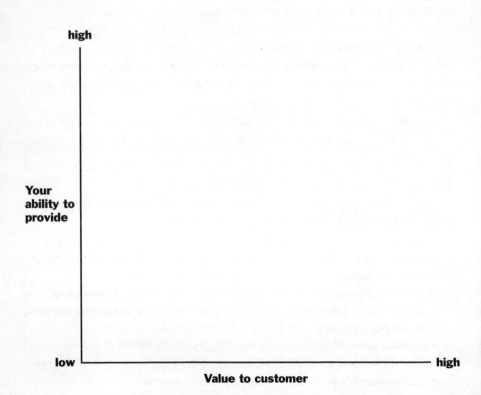

2. Draw a graph like the one on page 156 and position the features on it based on your ability to provide them and their value to buyers.

3. Look for features near the top and to the right where your competition is absent. There's your niche.

Provide Alternatives—or Value

Another way to find a decisive point of attack is to provide an alternative to the leader. For example, Pepsi provides a carefully crafted alternative to Coke: If you're stodgy, drink Coke. If you're hip, drink Pepsi.

Finally, you can create a decisive point the old-fashioned way: Increase the value of your product or service. Don't lower the price (price wars are nasty); increase the warranty length, improve support, guarantee delivery, or provide inexpensive upgrades.

6. TURN CUSTOMERS INTO EVANGELISTS

Back in 1984, everyone expected Apple's eventual demise. While even the experts thought that the Mac was a nifty computer, they figured it was doomed because it couldn't run the standard MS-DOS operating system.

The naysayers could not foresee that Apple would muster a band of "raging, inexorable, thunderlizard evangelists" who would provide emotional and technical support and spread the word to millions. Such early adopters—evangelists all—made the Mac a success.

Create a Cause

Evangelists need a cause. They want something they can believe in and want others to believe in it, too. "It" can be a product like the Macintosh, a company like Saturn, or a set of beliefs like environmentalism.

Do you have great products or services that could become a cause? Match your product with these cause characteristics. A cause:

- *Embodies a vision.* A cause is a radically different way to change the world—or at least make a dent in it. More than a good idea, it's a calling.
- *Seizes the high ground.* Its intent is to make the world better by, for example, improving productivity, cleaning up the environment, or empowering disenfranchised groups.
- *Redefines experience.* Its effects are irreversible, such as how the Mac forever redefined the concept of user-friendliness in a computer.
- *Catalyzes strong feelings.* You love or hate the product or idea.

VIRTUAL DEALERS

Garden Way, which makes Troy-Bilt rototillers, makes good use of the cultish behavior of Troy-Bilt owners by sending prospects to nearby volunteers for demonstrations. The firm recruits Troy-Bilt owners into its "Good Neighbors" program by giving them a discount or a free attachment at the time of purchase.

Beyond a dealership network, then, Garden Way has a "virtual" network of Troy-Bilt evangelists. It must drive competitors nuts.

Find the Right People

You have to aim your great product at the right people. When Apple first started marketing the Mac, it aimed at senior executives it believed could order in large numbers.

Those in the executive suite, however, were too far removed from the use of computers. Explaining computers to them was like explaining clouds to fish. Also, they were committed to existing standards.

Apple thus went after grassroots users: secretaries, temps, artists, students, interns, and so on. These people ultimately made the Mac successful.

To find those who will commit to using your product or service, start with existing users. It's easier to raise them to higher levels of commitment. And don't be afraid to ask for help. People like to help companies that create great things, and they want to go with winners.

Let them help you however they can. Some will want to demonstrate your product, some will want to write about it, others will work to persuade friends to switch. Let a thousand flowers bloom.

Finally, get the product into the hands of the user. Be free in dispensing samples or offering "test drives." When W. L. Gore introduced Glide dental floss, it sent samples to every dentist's office in the U.S.

Don't Forget Employees

Your employees should all be evangelists. After all, their salaries depend on the firm's success.

All employees of airline Kiwi International are trained to see themselves as salespeople. They even visit local travel agents—for no pay—to evangelize Kiwi.

IGNORANCE CAN BE BLISS

One company adept at driving competitors crazy is Hewlett-Packard. Unlike many of its competitors in the high tech field, HP doesn't fall in love with the technology it creates. It tries to look through the eyes of the customer.

With the market for microwave products slowing, HP replaced the Microwave Division with the Video Communications Division.

It found a market for potential products, division chief Jim Olson told Guy Kawasaki, in a matter of months. It's now making test equipment for TV studios, a video server, and a plain-paper video printer.

How did the division find a ready market so quickly? By acknowledging its ignorance and using it to advantage.

"We took our current R&D and marketing engineers and . . . sent them to attend trade shows and meet customers," said Olson. "We told people we didn't know anything about the industry, but that we thought we had a lot to offer. We listened better than if we went and talked to other microwave engineers."

Olson also refused to hire a bunch of video experts. "One of the ways to drive your competition crazy is to succeed at seeing the forest from the trees, and we could do that because we had never been in this forest before."

Ignorance, for HP, was "incredibly empowering. . . . There's no way anyone could do what we did without taking a fresh viewpoint of how to talk to customers, how to listen to them, and how to take what they tell you and go back and execute."

A measure of success: a rep for a top competitor said HP has "made my life miserable."

Part 3: Do Things Right
7. WORK TO ESTABLISH BRAND LOYALTY

Staying focused on customers is doing the right thing. Getting people to buy again and again is one aspect of another important business task, doing things right.

Systematize the Process

One way to establish loyalty is to systematize the process. Dick's Supermarkets, a chain in Wisconsin and Illinois, has made that a science.

First, Dick's employees regularly comb newspapers, new utility-account information, chamber-of-commerce announcements, and other sources. They look for the names of new residents, newly married couples, and families with newborns.

Each family on Dick's list gets a barrage of enticements. For example, newly arrived families get a welcome letter from the nearest Dick's. In it are coupons good for two free items each week for three weeks.

A few weeks later, another letter comes with more coupons. A year later, yet more. "If we can bring people in six times, we feel we can convert them into regular customers," says Dick's president.

Start Early

The earlier you snag 'em, the better. Best Western hotels has a Young Travelers Club for kids eight to twelve. They get an "adventure journal" to record their travels, a pack with educational cards, a travel magazine, decals, and more.

For every dollar that club members or their parents spend, they get points that can be used toward items in a catalog. Coming soon: club rooms that might have anything from books to electronic games. "The motivator is to grow the next generation of Best Western customers," says manager Tom Dougherty.

Target Cubbyholes

A niche is based on product characteristics. A cubbyhole is based on specific customers in a market.

Polaroid targets a spacious cubbyhole, real estate brokers, through a program called the Polaroid Real Estate Photography Workshop. Attendees receive instruction on using photography to best serve customers (for example, shooting pictures that house hunters can take home). For $10, brokers receive instruction, a camera and film, a booklet, and discounts and special deals.

WHAT'S "COOPETITION"?

The Atchison, Topeka, & Santa Fe Railway stunned the freight-moving industry by forming an alliance with trucker J. B. Hunt.

Here's how the alliance works: Hunt picks up a load from a shipper and takes it to the railroad. The train hauls it to the yard nearest the destination, where another Hunt truck picks it up and delivers it.

Customers get fast, door-to-door service for a low price—and only one bill. Hunt saves fuel and wear and tear on trucks. The railroad gets business it wouldn't have had. And the alliance cuts down on traffic and pollution. Coopetition, anyone?

Besides providing a skill brokers can use immediately, Polaroid makes them feel wanted and offers experience with Polaroid products. It's a great way to create loyal customers.

Build Cocoons

Don't lose loyalty you've worked hard to gain. Smart companies use "frequency marketing" techniques to keep customers on board.

The New York Times, for example, has a program for residential subscribers. Members receive discounts from restaurants and other businesses. That creates incentives to keep subscribing.

CANNIBALIZE YOURSELF BEFORE OTHERS EAT YOUR LUNCH

Sly companies sometimes create brands that appear to be their own competition. An article by Suzanne Oliver in *Forbes* explained how one company did it.

"They'll Eat You Up"

A trade show attendee pointed to a slick new line of yellow power tools by an outfit named Dewalt and said to Nolan Archibald, chairman of Black & Decker, "These guys are going to eat you up." Archibald merely smiled; B&D makes Dewalt tools.

Joseph Galli, the B&D employee who thought up the idea, wanted to position the tools above industry leader Makita, so he priced them higher than the Makita line. He also decided to control distribution. Dewalt tools can't be had in mass-market stores; they are sold only in hardware stores and at construction sites. The line is expected to account for $300 million in sales.

Self-Nibbling Not for All

Self-cannibalizing can be an effective weapon to drive your competition crazy and broaden your market share. It's not for everyone, though. First, your employees may have trouble adopting the different mindset another line might require.

Second, self-cannibalization is a luxury for those with the capital, production capacity, and personnel to go after incremental sales. In a sense, you have to earn the right to eat your own lunch by doing right by the customer in the first place.

But if you have the capability, do it to yourself before someone does it to you.

8. MAKE MOUNTAINS OUT OF MOLEHILLS

Sometimes it doesn't take much to drive competitors crazy. Richard Sears, of retailer Sears, Roebuck, was a master market disrupter.

In a pitched battle with competitor Montgomery Ward, Sears made a brilliant move. He trimmed the height and width of his catalog so it was smaller than Ward's.

When customers stacked their catalogs on a table, the Sears catalog would thus have to sit on top. That improved the chances that it would be looked at first next time a customer needed a new corset or saw.

You too can make these minor features of your products—molehills—loom large in the minds of customers. But to do that, you have to get inside their minds.

Eliminate Headaches

Begin by thinking of the problems that aggravate customers, then solve them. Sometimes, that's easy to do.

Servtech, a Minneapolis car-repair shop, eased an age-old aggravation—how do you get around while your car is in the shop?

No, Servtech doesn't taxi you to and from work. Instead, it picks your car up in the evening, does minor servicing that night, and has the car back in your driveway by 6:30 A.M.

Save Money

Another way to make mountains out of molehills is to save customers money. Innovative companies provide toll-free telephone numbers, offer free shipping, and more.

Hard thinking reveals even more creative ways to save customers money. Phone company Ameritech, for example, offers a new call-waiting plan. If you subscribe to it, you hear two kinds of beeps. One is for a local incoming call, while another signals a long-distance call.

Wouldn't you rather take the long-distance call immediately than dial the party back?

Exercise Questions

Answering these questions will help you figure out how to turn molehills into mountains:

- What would cause customers to use your product or service more frequently?
- What would cause customers to use more of your product at each occasion?

- What would encourage distributors to stock more of your product?
- What is the most fun customers have ever had with your product?
- How can you institutionalize having fun with your product?

9. PACKAGING: A DISRUPTER'S WEAPON

As the following examples show, packaging can be used to terrorize your competitors—and gain new revenues.

- Chubs Stackable baby wipes, made by l&f Products, come in one of four bright colors. The plastic boxes are interlockable, so babies can play with them as though they were giant Lego toys. Parents can also use the containers to hold items.

DAVID FENDS OFF GOLIATH

In 1992, Bob Curry's world nearly collapsed. That's when he learned that the huge hardware "category-killer" Home Depot was opening up a quarter mile away from his small Ace Hardware store. It didn't take long for Bob to learn important lessons:

Don't panic. Curry had heard that revenue at stores like his typically fell 20 to 25 percent once Goliath moved in. "We didn't want our people to be nervous wrecks, and we didn't want them to see that we were nervous wrecks!" said Curry.

Competition is good. "Home Depot really got us off our rear ends."

Maintain morale. Curry pays well, shares profits, and trains employees extensively.

Be realistic. Faced with price competition, "Customers won't be loyal for very long. They think the same way you and I do about our money."

Do what's right for the customer. "We try to get to know as many customers as we can in a personal way." Curry also opened on Sundays (business boomed) and strove to be competitive with Home Depot's prices. "We took four or five hundred items and gave them away."

Develop niches. Curry started selling propane, which now accounts for $100,000 in sales. And rather than just sell paint, he opened a paint department.

Know thy enemy. "When Home Depot first opened, we were there at least once a week."

Can David coexist with Goliath? Home Depot now sends service problems to Curry's store. "We work to build some kind of a bond between Home Depot and us rather than try to fight."

Curry's sales are up 35 percent.

• Amurol Confections Company makes a jar of candy tarts called Bug City. The lid is perforated, so when the candy is gone kids can use the jar by keeping bugs in it.

• An English firm, Reed Plastic Containers, makes a plastic container for paint that it markets to paint manufacturers. It's square with rounded corners to make stacking easier; it's clear so you can see what color paint is in it; and it includes a brush-wiping area and built-in lip for pouring.

Why use packaging as a competitive weapon? You want to use every opportunity to gain an advantage for your product when a customer is making up her mind: "If I buy Chubs, Junior can play with the box. If I buy another brand, he can't."

Part 4: Push the Envelope
10. SEIZE THE DAY

If you've done your work, the mere sight of your company's logo causes rivals to quiver. Now it's time to turn the screws.

Grasp Opportunities

Every so often, you have a chance to serve your competition's customers. That's what happened when American Airlines went on strike during Thanksgiving in 1993. American's tiny competitor, Kiwi International, went on the attack. It sent fifteen hundred faxes to travel agents alerting them of the availability of seats on Kiwi. It also put up signs that said, WELCOME AMERICAN AIRLINES PASSENGERS.

These choices were easy. Said Kiwi's marketing director, "We asked ourselves, 'What can we do to take advantage of the situation and encourage people to choose Kiwi?'"

First Interstate Bank of California was another organization that moved quickly to seize the day. Soon after Security Pacific Bank merged with Bank of America, Security began to close some offices. First Interstate scooped them up. It dispatched people, by truck, to branches that were closing. They urged customers to switch over by offering free checking for a year, free checks, and other things. For its efforts, First Interstate gained $1 billion in deposits.

Piggy Back

In a 1986 promotion, British Airways gave away 5,200 free seats for travel on June 10.

Virgin Atlantic wasn't about to let British Airways have all the fun, so it ran full-page ads that said in large type: "It has always been Virgin's policy to encourage you to fly to London for as little as possible. So on June 10 we encourage you to fly British Airways." In smaller type below, the ad read, "As for the rest of the year, we look forward to seeing you aboard Virgin Atlantic. For the best service possible. At the lowest possible fare."

Each time the media mentioned the giveaway, it also mentioned Virgin's response.

Create a Day

Levi Strauss commissioned a study on casual clothes in the workplace. The study found that 81 percent of respondents believed casual clothes improved morale, and 47 percent thought it improved productivity. Further, 46 percent said that they'd consider the option to wear casual clothing a good reason to go to work for a company.

Because widespread adoption of "casual clothes" days at companies would benefit it enormously, Levi Strauss went on a public relations blitz. This resulted in more than three thousand news stories.

Levi's went further: It put in a toll-free hotline that offered advice on how companies could adopt casual dress standards. It also created a casual-clothes-day kit—complete with case studies—for human resources managers.

PLAY WITH THEIR MINDS

O ne way to drive competitors crazy is to lead them astray.

One of the greatest stories of an entrepreneur playing with the competition concerns Wilson Harrel and his cleaning product, Formula 409. When Harrel had gained a 5 percent market share, Procter & Gamble began test-marketing a competing product called Cinch. Harrel found out that P&G planned to test the product in Denver, Colorado. In a daring move, Harrel discouraged reorders and curtailed advertising of Formula 409 in Denver. Cinch thus performed well, and P&G rolled it out nationally.

At that point, Harrel bundled a sixteen-ounce bottle of Formula 409 with a half-gallon size, and he sold the two for a huge discount. Anyone buying the bundle wouldn't need cleaning liquid for at least six months. This took Formula 409 customers out of the market, leaving many fewer customers for Cinch. In less than a year, P&G removed Cinch from the market.

11. TO SUCCEED, ACT LIKE AN OUTSIDER

Your competition may be playing by rules you needn't play by. Don't let assumptions or conventions hold you back. As author John Czepial said, "Fight fair, but avoid fair fights."

- *Ignore conventional wisdom.* Bank One teamed up with the American Association of Retired People to help seniors get credit cards. Normally, a bank issues a card based on credit history or current income. What if, like many elderly people, you have neither? Bank One bases its decision to issue a card on net worth. And the delinquency rate on this card is lower than average.
- *Ignore conventional practice.* Electronic Scriptorium in Virginia automates libraries, creates CD-ROMs, provides data entry, and more. Founder Ed Leonard had trouble finding a stable workforce until he uncovered a disciplined, educated, and productive group of people who could do top-quality work: monks.
- *Ignore conventional perspectives.* Finally, California requires contractors to warrant labor for a year. Rather than view the law as a nuisance, one roofing company considers it an opportunity: It calls each customer eleven months after installation to make sure everything is okay. The calls result in some warranty work—and a lot of new business and referrals.

CROSSING THE CHASM
by Geoffrey A. Moore

In this popular and seminal book, Geoffrey Moore argues that high-tech products require their own marketing strategies—the strategies for marketing milk, cars, or any other nontechnology product or service simply do not work.

The reason is because of the adoption life cycle of high tech goods. Specifically, new high technology products will be quickly bought by what Moore calls "early adopters": aficionados of high technology who are eager to try new products. In the past, marketers assumed that the pool of customers would grow steadily from a small number of high tech enthusiasts to a large number of mainstream buyers. In truth, however, many products languish in sales as they struggle to get accepted by the mainstream. There is a giant gulf   a chasm—between early adopters and mainstream buyers. The goal of marketing, Moore writes, is to somehow get your product to cross that chasm.

A speaker, bestselling author, and consultant, Geoffrey Moore is the founder of The Chasm Group and a co-founder and managing director at TCG Advisors. In addition to *Crossing the Chasm* and its follow-up, *Inside the Tornado*, Moore is the author of *The Gorilla Game* (with co-authors Tom Kippola and Paul Johnson), *Living on the Fault Line,* and most recently *Dealing with Darwin.*

Before founding The Chasm Group in 1992, Geoffrey Moore was a partner and principal at Regis McKenna Inc., and a sales and marketing executive at several software companies.

Moore earned an undergraduate degree in American literature from Stanford University and a doctorate in English literature from the University of Washington.

CROSSING THE CHASM

Marketing and Selling Disruptive Products
to Mainstream Customers

by Geoffrey A. Moore

CONTENTS

1. If Bill Gates Can Be a Billionaire
2. High Tech Marketing
3. Defining the Chasm
4. The D-Day Analogy
5. Getting Beyond the Chasm

THE SUMMARY IN BRIEF

To make money with disruptive technologies in this era, they need to be brought to market and adopted quickly. There is always someone right behind, catching up and trying to overtake you. The problem is that the initial marketing strategies and tactics necessary to break into the market of techies and early-adopting visionaries don't work once a company begins marketing to the mass market, where the real money is going to be made. The reason the mass market purchases a product and, in fact, the actual concept of the product they will purchase are different from those of the early adopters. It is crossing the chasm between the two markets that allows companies to extend and expand their technologies and make money. In this revised edition of his 1991 classic, Geoffrey Moore has updated his concepts and examples to better reflect the changes that have occurred in the technology world since the first edition.

THE COMPLETE SUMMARY

1. IF BILL GATES CAN BE A BILLIONAIRE

Though it is not an easy task to accomplish, the last two decades have been full of people who succeeded in the high tech industry, making it seem like a legitimate get-rich-quick opportunity. Bill Gates did it. Why can't you? Why can't every entrepreneur be a monumental success, especially when his or her products are superior to others in the field? Is Oracle better than Sybase? Microsoft Word better than WordPerfect? Pentium better than the Power PC? What makes one product take off while another flounders?

When products fail—whether superior to the competition or not—the company scapegoat is typically the VP of marketing. Meanwhile, the whole company fails, and the uncertainty of success makes capital more difficult to acquire. If the U.S. strategy for global competitiveness rests on outmarketing the rest of the world now that we can no longer outmanufacture them, why do so many in the high tech field get it wrong?

It turns out the current model for high tech marketing ignores an enormous gap between two separate markets: the *early market* dominated by a few *visionary* customers and the *mainstream market* dominated by a large block of *pragmatists*. Fortunes are made by those who cross the chasm between these two markets, and lost by those who fail in the attempt.

2. HIGH TECH MARKETING

Imagine that it is 1998 and General Motors is starting to commercially release an electric car. Ford and Chrysler will surely follow and these cars will work just like any other, except they will be quieter and better for the environment. When are you going to buy one?

Your answer tells a lot about how you relate to the *technology adoption life cycle*, a model for understanding the acceptance of new products.

"I want to be the first one on my block with an electric car."—innovator or early adopter

"When I have seen electric cars prove themselves and when there are enough service stations on the road."—early majority

"Not until most people have made the switch and it becomes really inconvenient to drive a gasoline car."—late majority

"Not until hell freezes over."—laggard

High Tech Marketing Model

Attitudes toward technology adoption become significant to marketing whenever people are introduced to *discontinuous innovations* that require them to change their current mode of behavior, such as a high-definition TV that is incompatible with today's broadcasting standards and requires the owner to seek out special sources of programming. *Continuous innovations*, such as a TV that promises sharper and brighter pictures, don't require any change in behavior.

Each group is distinguished by its characteristic response to discontinuous innovation and its psychographic profile. These profiles can be used to develop a high tech marketing model. The way to develop a high tech market is to work the curve left to right, using each "captured" group as a reference base for marketing to the next group. By maintaining momentum, a company creates a bandwagon effect, making it natural for the next group to want to buy, and keeping the company ahead of the next emerging technology.

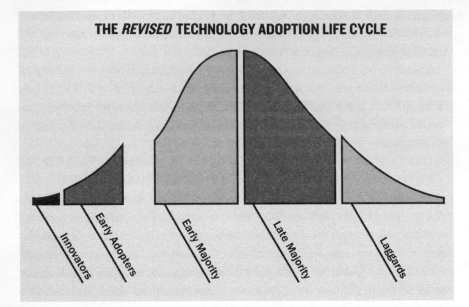

THE *REVISED* TECHNOLOGY ADOPTION LIFE CYCLE

Innovators · Early Adopters · Early Majority · Late Majority · Laggards

Cracks in the Adoption Cycle

Unfortunately, the experience of most in Silicon Valley is that the technology adoption life cycle doesn't work very well as a high tech marketing model.

The components in the model are unchanged, but between any two psychographic groups there is now a gap symbolizing the dissociation between the two groups. This is the difficulty any group will have in accepting a new product if it is presented in the same way as it was to the group to its immediate left. Each of these gaps represents an opportunity for marketing to lose momentum and fail to gain the profit-margin leadership in the middle of the bell curve.

■ **The First Crack.** The crack between innovators and early adopters occurs when an innovation cannot be readily translated into a major new benefit— one example being Esperanto. The enthusiast loves it for its architecture, but no one else can figure out how to start using it.

■ **The Other Crack.** The crack between the early majority and the late majority separates those who are willing and able to become technologically competent to use the new technology from those who are not. Examples are programmable VCRs and high-end office copier systems with protocols that are too hard for infrequent users to remember.

■ **The Chasm.** This deep and dividing chasm separates the early adopters from the early majority. This is the most formidable and unforgiving transition in the technology adoption life cycle. Often the customer list and order size look the same, but the basis of the sale is radically different. The early adopter is buying a change agent to get a jump on the competition. The early majority are buying a productivity improvement for existing operations. When promoters of high tech products try to make the transition from a market base made up of visionary early adopters to penetrate the pragmatist early majority, they are operating without a reference base and without a support base within a market that is highly reference oriented and highly support oriented.

High Tech Marketing Enlightenment

In the context of this book, the word *marketing* means taking actions to create, grow, maintain, or defend real markets, not to create illusions. For high tech organizations that real market is defined as

- a set of actual or potential customers
- for a given set of products or services
- who have a common set of needs or wants, and
- who reference each other when making a buying decision.

People tend to understand every part of this definition except the last idea. Part of what defines a high tech market is the tendency of its members to reference each other when making buying decisions—and that is key to successful high tech marketing.

Two Different Markets

If two people buy the same product for the same reason but have no way to reference each other, they are not part of the same market. If a company sells an oscilloscope for monitoring heartbeats to a doctor in Boston and the identical product for the same purpose to a doctor in Zaire, and these two doctors have no reasonable basis for communicating with each other, then the company is dealing in two different markets.

Similarly, if a company sells an oscilloscope to a doctor in Boston and then goes next door and sells the same product to an engineer working on a sonar device, the company is also dealing in two different markets. In both cases, the reason for the separate markets is that the customers could not have referenced each other.

Innovators, or technology enthusiasts, are the first to realize the potential in a new high tech product. They spend hours trying to get products to work; they forgive bad documentation and poor performance all in the name of moving technology forward. They buy HDTVs, DVD players, and digital cameras when they

(continued)

cost well over $1,000. As buyers they want the truth without any tricks, they want access to the most technically knowledgeable person to answer problems, and they want to be the first to get the new stuff. In large companies, technology enthusiasts can't make large purchasing decisions, but they can kindle the fire of interest with bigger bosses and provide feedback to improve the technology.

Visionaries can match an emerging technology to a strategic opportunity. They often work with large budgets and are highly driven by a "dream." The core of the dream is a business goal, not a technology goal. They're not looking for incremental *improvement,* but a *breakthrough.* Visionaries are also effective at alerting the business community to pertinent technology advances and are willing to serve as highly visible references. Because they are buying a dream, they are hard to please. They want to be very close to the development train so they can get off if they discover it is not going where they thought.

Pragmatists are the early majority and they represent the bulk of the market volume for any technology product, but instead of a dream, their goal is incremental, measurable, predictable improvement. Though hard to win over, pragmatists are loyal customers, often enforcing a company standard that requires the purchase of only the new product. Pragmatists care about product quality, the infrastructure of supporting products, and the reliability of service. References and relationships are very important to them, creating a kind of catch-22. Pragmatists won't buy from a company until it is established, but the company can't be established until pragmatists buy from it.

Conservatives, or the late majority, make up approximately one-third of the total potential customers, but high tech marketers don't exploit them well. Conservatives often fear high tech and are against discontinuous innovations. They tend to invest at the end of the technology adoption life cycle, preferring preassembled packages at a discounted price. The conservative marketplace provides a great opportunity to take low-cost, trailing-edge technology components and repackage them into single-function systems for specific business needs and extend the market for high tech components that are no longer state-of-the-art.

Skeptics, or laggards, only participate in the high tech marketplace to block purchases. They don't believe technology actually adds value, and they are always there to point out when new systems don't deliver on the promises that were made at the time of purchase. Their criticism can provide help in improving the product.

3. DEFINING THE CHASM

Each group on the technology adoption life cycle marketing model has its own preconceptions, biases, needs, and behaviors. In crossing from innovators to visionaries, companies can ride the momentum of the first to the second, and in moving through the pragmatists and conservatives, they can do the same thing. But the chasm between the visionaries and pragmatists is too wide for momentum.

Why Pragmatists Don't Like Visionaries

There are four basic reasons why pragmatists don't like visionaries:

1. *Lack of respect for the value of colleagues' experiences.* Visionaries are the first to see the potential of a new technology and its competitive advantage, so they see themselves as smarter than leaders at competitive companies. Pragmatists deeply value the experience of their colleagues in other companies.
2. *Taking a greater interest in technology than in their industry.* Visionaries define the future and are bored with the mundane details of their own industries. Pragmatists don't put a lot of stake in futuristic things.
3. *Failing to recognize the importance of existing product infrastructure.* Visionaries are building new systems from the ground up and setting new standards, so they don't expect standards and support groups to be in place already. Pragmatists expect all these things and shudder when they see visionaries ignoring the mainstream practices.
4. *Overall disruptiveness.* Pragmatists see visionaries as people who soak up the budget for their pet projects. If a project succeeds, they take all the credit while the pragmatist gets stuck trying to maintain a system so "state-of-the-art" that no one knows how to keep it working. If the project fails, visionaries are always a step ahead of the disaster, leaving the pragmatist to clean up.

4. THE D-DAY ANALOGY

To cross the chasm and enter the mainstream market is an act of aggression, because it is essentially a life-or-death situation. The solution is to target a very specific niche market, and focus on it with an overabundance of support. The technology will develop a solid base of references, collateral, and internal procedures and documentation by virtue of a restricted set of market variables. The D-Day Allied invasion of Normandy provides an excellent analogy.

- The long-term goal is to enter and take control of a mainstream market (Europe) that is currently dominated by an entrenched competitor (the Axis).
- The company assembles an invasion force comprising other products and companies (the Allies).
- The early goal is to transition from an early market base (England) to a strategic target market segment in the mainstream (the beaches at Normandy).

- The chasm (the English Channel) separates the company from its goal.
- The company crosses the chasm as fast as possible, focused exclusively on the point of attack (D-Day).
- The company forces the competitor out of its targeted niche markets (secure the beachhead).
- Then it moves out to take over additional market segments (districts of France).
- Finally, it achieves overall market domination (the liberation of Europe).

This strategy seems counterintuitive to the management of start-up enterprises, so it is rarely put into practice. But trying to cross the chasm without taking a niche market approach is like trying to light a fire without kindling. Most companies feel they do not have the time or money to develop and target a niche and so they become sales-driven instead of market-driven. But in order to succeed, companies need industry references, so they must completely satisfy the buying objectives of the customer by committing themselves to providing the whole product.

PALMPILOT'S SUCCESS BY SUBTRACTION

The PDA had been flailing in the chasm for years when the PalmPilot brought the category into the mainstream market. The beachhead target market for PDAs was the management team of high tech enterprises, who spend 100 percent of their time either in meetings or on the road. They need support for contacts and scheduling, but paper systems are hard to update and coordinate among individuals.

The first market entrants, the Sharp Wizard and the Casio Boss, were too limited in functionality. They had no calendars, phone books that could only be input manually, and no backup. Hewlett-Packard's LX line of palm-top computers provided too much, with a full keyboard, DOS, Lotus 1-2-3, and a word processor. Apple's Newton never got its form or pen recognition program right.

Palm created a product that was small and had an interface that was intuitive to all Mac or Windows PC users, a convenient docking station to upload/download information, and a pen system that actually worked. It was exactly what the niche—technology industry managements and others—wanted. It solved their problem precisely.

The companies that failed had overdesigned for the target market to hedge their bets. By trying to reduce their market risk, they actually increased it.

Of course, there is life after the niche, and that is indeed when the huge profits are made. The niche should be strategically selected so that it creates an entry point into a larger segment. When the Macintosh crossed the chasm, it chose graphic arts departments in Fortune 500 companies—not a large target market but one responsible for a broken, mission-critical process. After dominating that small segment, Apple was able to move to adjacent departments in the company such as marketing and sales.

Target the Point of Attack

What niche segment should a company choose when facing such a high-risk, low-data decision? Crossing the chasm is already high-risk, and now executives have to make the most important marketing decision in the history of their enterprise with little or no useful hard information. The market will not have experienced the product, and the company will have no experience working with the market. The people who have experienced the product—the visionaries—are so different from the new target customers—the pragmatists—that it is unwise to extrapolate results.

MARKETING STRATEGY CHECKLIST

When deciding on a niche, ask the following questions, each of which incorporates a chasm-crossing factor:

• *Target customer*—Is there a single, sufficiently funded buyer readily accessible to the intended sales channel?

• *Compelling reason to buy*—Can the pragmatists live with the problem another year? If possible, they will.

• *Whole product*—Does the high tech company have a complete solution to the target customer's compelling reason to buy?

• *Competition*—Has this problem already been addressed by another company that crossed the chasm before, and occupied the target space?

• *Partners and allies*—Are there relationships with other companies that are needed to fulfill the whole product?

• *Distribution*—Is there a sales channel in place?

• *Pricing*—Is the price of the whole product consistent with the target customer's budget?

• *Positioning*—Is the company credible as a provider of products and services to the target niche?

• *Next target customer*—Do these customers and partners facilitate the company's entry into adjacent niches?

Informed intuition, rather than analytical reason, is the most trustworthy decision-making tool to use. By trusting the right brain, people can draw conclusions based on isolating a few high-quality images and archetypes of a broader and more complex reality. Memorable images of consumers become *characterizations* such as teenyboppers or men wearing gray flannel suits, and each characterization suggests specific marketing tactics and represents characteristic market behaviors.

To find a niche, companies need to focus on *target-customer characterization*. Most chasm crossers get into trouble when they focus on a target market or segment instead. Create a customer profile for each customer and application of the product. Somewhere between twenty and fifty customer profiles will begin to turn into eight to ten distinct alternatives. Prioritize those eight to ten desirable target market segment opportunities and now there is a more helpful set of material to work with.

Committing to the niche market can be challenging for technology enthusiast entrepreneurs because they do not have the pragmatist response and don't trust in these market dynamics. What is most important is to choose swiftly and get on with it. It is not necessary to pick the optimal beachhead to be successful. The target customer will pull for the product if it solves a genuine problem. Commission market research early in the process to make sure the target is working.

Assemble the Invasion Force

Marketing is a war to create a market where the new product is the only reasonable buying proposition. Target markets that have a compelling reason to buy the product. To do that, the target customer must be presented with a whole product.

The whole product model identifies four different perceptions of a product:

1. *Generic product*—the product that is shipped in the box and is covered by the purchasing contract.
2. *Expected product*—the product that the consumer thought he or she was buying when buying the generic product. It is the minimum configuration of products and services necessary to have any chance of achieving the buying objective.
3. *Augmented product*—the product fleshed out to provide the maximum chance of achieving the buying objective.
4. *Potential product*—the product's room for growth as more and more ancillary products come on the market.

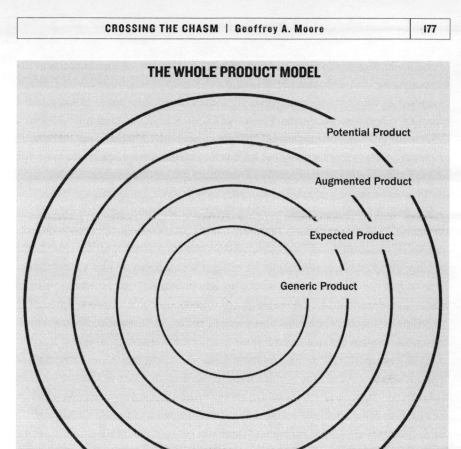

THE WHOLE PRODUCT MODEL

Potential Product

Augmented Product

Expected Product

Generic Product

At the introduction of any new type of product, the marketing battle takes place at the level of the generic product. As marketplaces develop and enter the mainstream market, products in the center become more and more alike, and the battle shifts increasingly to the outer circles.

To dominate a mainstream marketplace, produce the whole product. When compared to the technology adoption life cycle, the outer circles of the whole product increase in importance as one moves from left to right. Real techies aren't interested in whole products. Visionaries must take responsibility for creating the whole product to achieve their dream. Pragmatists want the whole product to be readily available from the outset. They like a product such as Microsoft that has books in every bookstore, seminars for training, office hotline support, and potential employees already trained. Even if offered a "great deal" on an alternative product, such as an office suite from Corel or Lotus, a pragmatist will ignore it because the whole product simply cannot match up. Pragmatists wait for a strong leader and then back that candidate forcefully in an effort to squeeze out the other alternatives.

The most important difference between the early market and the mainstream markets is that those in the former are willing to take responsibility for piecing together the whole product (in return for getting a jump on the competition), and those in the latter are not.

For now, a company needs to focus only on the minimum commitment to the whole product needed to cross the chasm—the whole product that ensures that the target customers can fulfill their compelling reason to buy. Traditionally, high tech has delivered 80 to 90 percent of a whole product to target customers, but rarely 100 percent. Anything less than 100 percent means that the customers either supply the remainder themselves or feel cheated. By solving the whole product equation for any given set of target customers, high tech has overcome its single greatest obstacle to market development.

Marketing partnerships and strategic alliances are a trendy way to increase marketing power, but they rarely work as well in practice as they do in the boardroom. Tactical alliances work better if their only purpose is to accelerate the formation of whole product infrastructure within a specific target market segment.

Define the Battle

After mapping out the whole product and recruiting the necessary partners and allies to deliver it, the only major obstacle left is competition. It is critical to define the competition, determine their current relationship to the target customer, and gauge how best to position the company to force them out of the target market segment. Any force can defeat any other force—if it can define the battle.

Pragmatists want to see strong competition, and if the company has just finished developing a new valid proposition with the visionaries, there is not likely to be much competition that the pragmatist will appreciate. In mainstream markets, competition is defined by comparative evaluations of products and vendors within a common category. These comparative evaluations bring a sense of rationality that is extremely reassuring to the pragmatist. Since competition is a fundamental condition for purchase, it is necessary to create it.

Competition will not come from competitive products so much as from alternative modes of operation. Locate the product within a buying category that already has some established credibility with the pragmatist buyers and then position the new product as the indisputably correct buying choice. Establish the market alternative—the company that the target customer has been buying from for years—and the product alternative—a company that has also harnessed a discontinuous innovation and is positioning itself similarly. Acknowledge the competition, which gives the new product credibility, but differentiate from them. Focus on the values and concerns of the pragmatists, not the visionaries. Create a value profile of target customers, identify what they would see as the most reasonable competitive set, develop comparative rankings, and then build a positioning strategy around those comparative rankings.

SILICON GRAPHICS

Silicon Graphics targeted the postproduction film-editing process in Hollywood. Traditional editing was done by cutting and splicing film, but if a desired image wasn't on the film, the only solution was an expensive reshoot.

Silicon Graphics developed a radically discontinuous innovation: If the image you want is not on the film, *put it there*. Digital editing trumped analog methods, and traditional vendors couldn't match it, making them perfect market alternatives. At the same time, asking artists to embrace computers and asking their producers to pay for them created a credibility crisis. But Sun and Hewlett-Packard both had Unix workstations that were leading edge and thus worthy product alternatives to Silicon Graphics. Both companies validated Silicon Graphics, but neither company had undertaken the exceptional commitments needed by the film industry.

Silicon Graphics showed their seriousness simply by showing the back of all three workstations. Both Sun and HP had the standard ports for connecting to traditional computer peripherals and networks. But the Silicon Graphics workstation also included half a dozen other ports that hooked it to devices specific to the film-editing industry. They had made a niche commitment the others had not.

Launch the Invasion

Distribution and pricing are the final pieces of the D-Day strategy. Choosing the channel that makes the pragmatist customer most comfortable is the primary goal. During that time, also develop pricing that motivates the channel. Use distribution-oriented pricing to attract customer-oriented distribution.

Distribution Channels

The most prominent kinds of distribution channels are:

Direct sales—This consists of a dedicated sales force in the direct employ of the vendor that focuses on calling on major accounts. (IBM)

Two-tier retail—Vendors ship to the first tier, which stages inventory and manages credit for the second tier. (Ingram)

One-tier retail—These are superstores that for the bulk of goods sold, fulfill both the wholesale and retail functions in a single entity. (CompUSA)

Internet retail—This is either one or two tier and is optimized for consumer offers that don't need significant configuration or support. (Dell)

Two-tier value-added reselling—These are typically "No-name," local value added resellers (VARs) that specialize in a particular technology and act in the customer-facing role for products that are too complex for retail. (Web sites)

National roll-ups—The market occasionally rolls up local VARs into a nation-wide chain. (ICON)

Original equipment manufacturers (OEMS)—These are two- to four-tier transactions where a direct sales force go to manufacturers that integrate the purchased product into their own systems, and then sell the systems. (American automakers)

Systems integrators—This is not really a channel, but a project-oriented institution for managing very large computer projects designed specifically for the customer.

The various channels are optimized for different purposes. Direct sales forces are best for creating demand, while retail superstores are best for fulfilling it. The immediate goal when crossing the chasm is to create mainstream demand, but developing a channel that can fulfill this demand will be important very soon. Systems integrators and VARs work well for providing the whole product and making a large profit, but they are not optimized for volume delivery. To cross the chasm, use direct sales as a demand-creation channel to penetrate the target market. Then use the distribution channel that best handles volume without losing the whole product.

Pricing is also difficult because there are so many perspectives competing for the controlling influence:

Customer-oriented pricing—This varies greatly with customers' different psychographics and can be based on the perceived value of owning cutting-edge technology, cost of an institutionalized trailing-edge technology, or comparisons with the competition. The key pricing strategy is premium margin above a norm set by comparison.

Vendor-oriented pricing—This comes from internal issues of cost of goods, cost of sales, and promised rate of return. These factors have no immediate meaning in the marketplace. It is the worst basis for pricing decisions in the chasm.

Distributor-oriented pricing—The price visionaries pay is probably too high, so don't let it be an issue for the pragmatist. Without pragmatists there is no demand. If the price is too low, there is no margin to motivate the channel.

The best solution is to set pricing at the market leader price point, reinforcing claims to market leadership, and build a disproportionately high reward for the channel into the price margin, a reward that can be reduced as the product becomes more established in the mainstream.

5. GETTING BEYOND THE CHASM

The chasm is not merely a marketing problem. Its effects extend to all areas of the enterprise. Finance, organizational development, and R&D must all be ready to aggressively attack the mainstream market, because the postchasm enterprise is bound by the commitments made by the prechasm enterprise. Usually these commitments were made on the fly for the early market and they take much effort and money to fix when they do not work in the mainstream market. The company effectively molts and becomes a different entity, and the entire organization must be prepared.

The purpose of the postchasm enterprise is to make money, unlike the prechasm entity, whose purpose is to create a new product. Early market entrepreneurs are not primarily focused on making money, so their actions do not conform to traditional management theory that assumes a profit motive. They make financial commitments with consequences they cannot or will not understand. They acquire prechasm investors by projecting hockey stick forecasts of revenue, instead of a more likely staircase projection of profit with plateaus.

So how do managers and investors change their behavior to neutralize the chasm? Investors can only expect to make a reasonably predictable ROI when a sustainable whole product is created and installed in the mainstream market—not before. They should not be fooled by projections indicating otherwise. Management must change from pioneers to settlers. Once the organization crosses the chasm, management may find that pioneers become a liability with their inclination to innovate, not administrate. Ideally, these people can be transferred to another project in the enterprise, but, if necessary, to another company.

Finally, when crossing the chasm, companies should add two new job titles: the target market segment manager, who stewards the visionary's product to learn about what will be needed for the whole product, and the whole product manager, who prepares the whole product by working out all the bugs and adding improvements that will make it applicable to the mainstream market.

UNLEASHING THE KILLER APP
by Larry Downes and Chunka Mui

Appearing at the height of the digital age, Larry Downes and Chunka Mui's primer on digital strategy, *Unleashing the Killer App,* was one of many books that sought to explain to companies how to exploit the new world of the Internet and e-mail. Downes and Mui coined the phrase *killer app* to describe the technology application that companies would discover and leverage to their advantage. One example of killer app was Dell's use of the Web to sell computers directly to the market.

The bulk of *Unleashing the Killer App* is focused on the fundamental steps in developing a digital strategy that have since become accepted wisdom, such as cannibalizing your markets, creating communities of value, giving away information, and concentrating on information assets. To the credit of the authors, the examples they cite (all included in the following summary) are not only the usual American suspects, but include firms such as the giant German conglomerate VEBA AB, British Petroleum, and Barclay's Bank.

Of course, the technology boom went bust, and after the outrageous IPOs (and outrageous Super Bowl commercials) only a few of the imaginative, crazy new technology companies are left standing.

Does that make *Unleashing the Killer App* obsolete? Not a chance. Companies of all sizes are discovering exactly what Downes and Mui argued: if you know how to leverage technology, the Web and the Internet offers a new world of opportunities. Bricks-and-mortar did not disappear to the extent some of the more ultra techno-enthusiasts predicted, but the fundamental steps in developing a digital strategy are still important lessons for today's companies to learn.

Larry Downes is a speaker, writer, consultant, and adjunct professor at Northwestern University. Chunka Mui is a partner with Diamond Technology Partners and executive editor of *Context.*

UNLEASHING THE KILLER APP
Develop Digital Strategies That Help You Dominate the Market

by Larry Downes and Chunka Mui

CONTENTS

THE SUMMARY IN BRIEF

A wave of killer apps is sweeping across the business world. For many individuals and firms that are prepared, it promises unbelievable opportunities. For others, expecting business as usual, it threatens failure.

Killer apps (applications) are inventions, goods or services, that change the world dramatically and often quickly. The cotton gin was one. Henry Ford's Model T was another.

Today's killer apps include the personal computer, electronic funds transfers, and the first word-processing program. Many more are on the horizon, created by technological and economic forces and promising both opportunities and perils. The driving force is the science of semiconductors, which has moved the world's economy from an industrial to an information base.

More specifically, it is our ability today to transform information into digital form so it can be manipulated by computers and transmitted by networks. The Internet is the result of this ability.

The authors offer in-depth case studies, discuss some of the key tools and techniques of digital strategy, and are most helpful in describing what a business must do to unleash the killer apps and profit from them.

First, "You must learn to see them coming." Next, be prepared to act. That may mean putting together laboratories, finding business partners, or creating new business models.

Most of all, you must have "the corporate will to take the big leaps." Without that, you may be doomed to failure.

Frightening? Of course. A killer app that threatens the very existence of your business may be in the development phase today.

What can you do? A good start is to get the basic understanding this summary offers you on turning that killer app into an opportunity.

It can be done. It must be done.

THE COMPLETE SUMMARY

1. THE LAWS OF DISRUPTIVE TECHNOLOGY

Digital technology has become the most disruptive force in modern history. Two basic principles explain why.

The first is Moore's Law, named after Intel founder Gordon Moore. More than thirty years ago, Moore observed that each succeeding generation of semiconductors was both more powerful and smaller than the last but the cost of producing them remained the same. This happened, he said, every eighteen months.

Thus, Moore's Law reads, "Every eighteen months processing power doubles while cost holds constant." This explains why your state-of-the-art computer equipment is obsolete a year and a half after you purchase it.

What Moore's Law doesn't explain is how the new technologies spread so quickly. To understand this, you need Metcalfe's Law.

Robert Metcalfe, who founded 3Com Corporation, noted that new technologies are valuable only if many people use them. A telephone, for instance, is useless by itself. Several telephones are handy but not particularly valuable. A million phones make up a network that is both valuable and powerful.

According to Metcalfe, the usefulness of a network equals the square of the number of users. Whatever you create becomes more valuable as more people use it. And the more valuable it becomes, the more users it attracts.

At a certain point, this creation of yours will achieve critical mass. How quickly it does so depends upon how inexpensive it is to use. Buyers weigh the usefulness of a good or service against what it costs them to try it.

The Internet is a good example. It achieved critical mass in 1993 because it was and is based on open, public standards. The Net gives away its secrets, allowing it to grow by leaps and bounds.

CHANGE THE PLAYING FIELD

You don't have to fall victim to killer apps if you know how to exploit them. That's what Dell Computers is doing.

Dell sells over $3 million worth of goods and services a day over the Internet. Selling through the Web reduces inventories because Dell doesn't have to wait for dealers to pass on the orders. And, since electronic commerce allows the company to take customer payments directly and immediately, Dell can convert the average order to cash in twenty-four hours.

By contrast, the average order takes rival Compaq thirty-five days to convert. And inventories are heavy at Compaq. That's because it continues to operate through dealers instead of killer apps.

Second-Order Effects

Initially, technological change affects technology. Once it reaches critical mass, however, other systems—our social, economic, and political arenas—are affected although more slowly than the speed of technological change.

Government, for example, was completely unprepared for the advent of electronic commerce on the Net. It is only now attempting to regulate it but the technology is changing faster than government can enact the laws.

Killer apps are the result of the Law of Disruption. They are the collisions of exponential technology adoption and incremental social changes. If you have ever had an uncomfortable sensation that technology is moving faster than you are, you have experienced the Law of Disruption.

The only antidote is to unleash killer apps yourself. To do so, you must develop a digital strategy.

2. BECOME A BUILDER OF DIGITAL STRATEGY

Throw out your old strategic plan. You no longer can expect to predict the future based on the present; technology is changing the business environment too quickly. You need a digital strategy in today's digital era.

Digital strategy differs from old-fashioned strategic planning in several significant respects. Traditionally, for example, an appointed team—often senior managers—met for a limited time to create a plan that would guide an organization for the next three to five years. These plans typically treated technology as a tool to achieve proposed changes.

In the world of digital strategy, technology *causes* change, creating both threats and opportunities for your firm. Digital strategy is dynamic, demanding constant rethinking by everyone in your organization. You don't have time for detailed analysis so you must learn to depend more on intuition and ideas.

POSTAL SERVICE SAYS, "OUCH"

The United States Postal Service had it made. For the two hundred years of its history, it had a legal monopoly on the delivery of first-class mail.

Then those on the Internet learned about e-mail. They didn't have to find stamps and address envelopes. And e-mail reached its destination in minutes, not days. To add insult, e-mail users were soon referring to first-class mail as "snail mail."

E-mail quickly reached the killer app status, and the Postal Service never saw the threat until it was too late to act. It was left with two hundred thousand vehicles, eight hundred thousand sorters and deliverers, and thirty-six thousand local post offices handling lighter and lighter bags of mail.

Meanwhile, the use of e-mail boomed and improved. Senders now are sending reports, greeting cards, photographs, and files in less time than it would take them simply to find an envelope of the proper size.

Postmaster General Marvin Runyon isn't the only executive staggering from the blow of a well-placed killer app. An interview of thirty leading CEOs and another four hundred senior executives surveyed found confusion in every industry. The executives agreed that technology was changing the basics of their businesses. Many felt competition was changing in ways made possible by technologies, ways they didn't fully understand. Only a few said they knew how to respond to all the changes—and they may have been "whistling in the dark."

For example, when Playboy Enterprises CEO Christie Hefner launched a photo archive on the Web, initially giving away digital photographs, she had "an instinctive feeling" that the time was right. The site was so successful that Playboy soon was able to sell enough advertising to pay the upfront costs to develop the site.

Build from the Ground Up

Developing a digital strategy is similar to building a structure. You start by reshaping the landscape, the environment in which you do business. You do this by outsourcing to your customers; cannibalizing your markets; developing goods and services that are unique every time; and creating communities of value.

Every structure contains a network of systems you must connect. Build these connections by turning each transaction into a joint venture; making change painless for customers; depending on electronic interfaces; and giving away as much information as you can.

Finally, define the interior: your organizational structure. Replace the old one with a new one that concentrates on information assets; scraps your value chain; creates a portfolio of potential killer apps; and learns from the children.

These twelve design principles, discussed on the following pages, comprise a building code. Use it to develop your own killer apps.

TAKING THE FIRST STEPS AT VEBA AG

VEBA AG is Germany's largest conglomerate, with total annual revenues of more than $42 billion. The company includes divisions in electricity, chemicals, oil, transportation, real estate, trading, and wholesaling.

CEO Ulrich Hartmann wanted to move VEBA from the Industrial Age to the Information Age. Each division had expertise and customer data that other divisions could use, but organizational and technical hurdles prevented information from flowing.

An assessment of how VEBA used digital technology revealed it lagged behind industry leaders in other countries. This became clear at workshops run by a digital strategy project team. Live demonstrations with the Web, CD-ROMs, and virtual reality software showed VEBA executives just how far behind they were.

The presentations surprised the VEBA officers and got them thinking about ways they could get more involved with their companies' information systems resources. Several announced they would take responsibility for introducing new technology. Others said they planned to experiment with technology that other markets and industries already were using. They began to discuss how they could partner with each other to achieve these goals.

They opened the door to ideas and, in doing so, took the first steps toward digital strategy.

---

3. OUTSOURCE TO YOUR CUSTOMERS

You may already be outsourcing certain functions, such as purchasing, accounting, and data processing, that your company used to provide in-house. Outsourcing often is more efficient—allowing you to concentrate on what you do best—and it may be cheaper, thanks to dropping transaction costs.

Digital technology takes outsourcing to the next level: your customers. You can have them perform your data collection and customer service functions by creating a Web site that allows them to enter and track orders, manage purchase orders, and construct and develop products.

FedEx's package-tracking system is a good example. The database allows customers to use their own computers to follow their packages' travels.

Recognizing the killer app potential of its system, FedEx added other features such as the digitized signature of the recipient and software that allows customers to schedule pickups and print out airbills on their own equipment.

Holiday Inn's Web site helps travelers locate the hotel nearest their destination, check availability, take a virtual tour, and complete their reservations. The system even recommends the next closest Holiday Inn if the first choice is full. The process is entirely customer-driven.

Let Customers Develop Products

Who better to help you develop products than the end users? Make it easy for customers to help you and make the rewards for doing so, such as customized products or faster turnaround times, worthwhile.

CASE STUDY: DIGITAL STRATEGY AT BP, GERMANY

C hris Brennan, regional manager for British Petroleum's gas stations in Germany, wanted to find a new revenue source. In Germany, stores have closing curfews. Gas stations and attached convenience stores are exempt. Brennan decided to capitalize on this competitive advantage.

He and his team identified the digital technology they needed, partnered with select merchants and credit card companies, and created the BP multimedia shopping kiosk.

Each kiosk presented a touch-sensitive screen on which customers could view short videos, choose merchandise, and get advice on everything from planning a party to the latest fashions. The next day they could pick up all their goods at the gas station.

German shoppers loved it. They were fed up with limited store hours, dirty facilities, and rude clerks. They began to use the kiosks for more of their everyday shopping, even when they purchased groceries.

Within a month of launching the pilot in Munich, Brennan and his team redesigned the software several times and increased the number of participating stations. At that point, they told BP headquarters what they'd done.

This is how strategy is done in the digital age. Applications, strategic partnering, and creative thinking are in. Lengthy analysis and top-down dictates are out.

Hüls AG, a leading specialty chemicals manufacturer in Germany, is getting consumer input through a virtual design lab. The lab design not only is simple to use, it's cheaper and more reliable than traditional communication channels such as phone calls, faxes, mailings, and meetings.

In Hüls's virtual lab, interaction is continuous and communications are direct. Make sure you can make the same claim about your Web site.

4. CANNIBALIZE YOUR MARKETS

You may be reluctant to launch new products or services that will compete against your existing offerings. But in today's accelerated digital era, you must become your own competitor. Although this means you may lose some of your existing market share, you can use killer apps to open whole new markets.

Marvel Entertainment Group released the first issue of a new comic book title on the Web well before it came out in print. It was so popular that sales of the print version weeks later actually broke records. Marvel since has created a weekly "cybercomic," available only online.

Securities broker Charles Schwab slashed its commission for, and gives away software tools to, its Internet customers. Why? Because cyberspace competitor E*Trade was offering its customers lower prices over the Net.

Schwab and other firms that eat into their markets realize that they may lose current market value if they don't move into cyberspace. Upstart competitors already are there. So are an increasing number of customers.

New Media, New Rules

Cannibalizing today's business is especially critical for information providers. Information on the Web flows freely and can be easily reproduced and distributed by anyone, anytime.

The key is to recognize that digital media are not extensions of old media. They require a new approach, new rules, and a new attitude.

The Wall Street Journal set up a Web site clearly different from its paper edition. The site links stories to more detailed archival information, hosts discussion forums between readers, and offers a database of the latest financial, stock, and company filings, data, and news releases.

More than six hundred thousand subscribers signed up for the free trial period. The trial's success attracted paying subscribers, creating a new generation of product for The WSJ.

5. DEVELOP GOODS AND SERVICES THAT
ARE UNIQUE EVERY TIME

Technology makes it cheap and easy for you to tailor products and services to each individual customer. Author Stan Davis calls this approach mass customization.

Pointcast's computer screen saver, for example, delivers whatever content the user chooses, from business news to sports to gossip.

Users of Intuit's Quicken Financial Network can enter their stock holdings on Intuit's Web site and get up-to-the-minute reports of their portfolio performance. The site also offers a retirement planner that calculates individual retirement incomes.

These products are popular because customers like personalized products, especially when they do the personalizing. The advantage to you is that they become vested in your system, providing you with more data than you're likely to get from a direct mail survey.

Even a public utility is capable of providing customized service. In fact, utilities must learn to customize because rapid deregulation means customers soon will get a chance to choose their suppliers.

Some utilities are using time-of-use or real-time pricing, offering remote control of appliances, and providing customized billing for corporate customers. Others are taking a "gateway" approach, selling telephone, home security, and entertainment services in addition to power.

Cable and telephone companies, meanwhile, also are vying for the opportunity to provide this gateway into customers' homes.

These companies and utilities are treating each customer as a separate market. News services and travel, retail, and entertainment firms are doing so as well. Soon everyone else, including your own company, must follow suit.

6. CREATE COMMUNITIES OF VALUE

The real power of digital technology is that it makes it so easy for people to communicate with each other and with you. Tap this power by creating communities of value for your customers.

ESPN's SportsZone service offers subscribers sports information, play-by-plays of games in progress, and discussion forums. It also manages fantasy leagues that allow players to draft teams and play against others based on the changing statistics of real-life athletes. The site's popularity is mushrooming.

You can provide more value by targeting issues about which individuals are passionate. Games and sports sites are particularly popular.

Mobil Oil built a Web site for racing enthusiasts who follow the company's involvement in Formula One racing. The site channels visitors to information about environmental issues important to Mobil, then invites them to e-mail their thoughts to their elected representatives. In this way, Mobil creates value for itself as well as for racing fans.

Manage Your Brands

Communities of value can make or break your brand. You can use these communities to promote your brand to many people at relatively little cost. However, unhappy customers can just as cheaply and easily create their own communities to air grievances about your brand. The "Untied Airlines" cyber-community is one example. It bills itself as "the Web site that offers frustrated former United Airlines passengers a chance to speak out." And they do.

Create an official forum that allows customers to express their feelings about your branded goods and services, and they won't need to create their own.

Take advantage of the information they give you in this forum. Develop life-long relationships by addressing customers' questions and complaints rather than ignoring them. Use their good experiences to promote your good name and goodwill.

Connect to Other Businesses

Most organizations begin building communities with buyers and suppliers. These types of business-to-business networks not only create value but also reduce cost.

One real estate developer, for example, created an intranet that makes repair data electronically available to approved contractors. Now the firm is looking at using the Internet to connect to tenants, suppliers, and other stakeholders.

7. TURN EACH TRANSACTION INTO A JOINT EVENT

In the future, firms will shrug off departments and turn to a network of partners to stay competitive. These partnerships will be short-lived, based upon single transactions rather than long-term contracts or alliances.

In fact, virtual firms have begun to do just that. Brewer Andrew Klein, for example, bypassed the investment bureaucracy and financed his microbrewery by selling stock in his company over the Internet. Klein then turned around and launched Wit Capital, an online investment service, to help other entrepreneurs do what he did.

To design any killer app, you must be able to identify potential partners quickly and get them to commit. You also must decide how intimate you want the partnership to be. Partnerships can range from basic awareness through interim relationships—such as licensing and joint ventures—to outright ownership.

Microsoft frequently partners. In 1996 it bought or invested in twenty companies to get early access to the technologies these firms were developing.

8. MAKE CHANGE PAINLESS FOR CUSTOMERS

The benefits your customers get from electronic commerce—customization, communities of value, participation in product development— will create problems for you.

You may have to transform your stores into showrooms or demo centers and improve your production and delivery systems to meet individual expectations. No matter how tough this process is for you, make it painless for your customers. They don't want to know about your problems.

Some electronic commerce start-ups are building businesses that do nothing but minimize disruption to customers. Cybercash, for example, was launched to make it cheaper and safer to send and accept payments over the Net. To ease customers' worries about giving their credit card numbers over the Web, Cybercash initially offered a simple third-party verification service.

Similarly, WebTV was developed to provide Internet access to consumers who are more comfortable with television sets than computers. This killer app adapts to the consumers' behavior rather than forcing them to do things the way computer makers think they should.

Make sure the killer apps you develop are easy for your customers to use. Security First, an Internet-only bank, initially presented a three-dimensional image of a bank on its site. Customers clicked on the information desk or a teller or security guard to learn different information about the bank.

The site evolved as people learned to use it. A revised site design responded to customers' preferences and previous activities. Last year the company sold the bank. Now it shows other banks how to serve in cyberspace.

9. DEPEND ON ELECTRONIC INTERFACES

Every direct contact with customers is an opportunity to improve your relationship with them and learn more about their needs. Yet most firms don't take advantage of this.

Digital technology can help. On the surface, it may seem less personal than direct human contact. But think back to your own most recent experiences as a consumer with the checker at the grocery store, a customer service representative, or a directory-assistance operator.

How good was the service? Did you get any service? Were you asked for information that would allow the company to serve you better in the future? Did you structure the transaction the way you wanted?

One commercial bank boasted that its policy guaranteed that every customer who called the bank would connect to a human rather than a machine. However, this didn't guarantee better service.

When account executives were busy, calls were rerouted to assistants who did little more than take a message. Worse, without a voice mail system, customers were unable to leave a message at all after closing hours.

Technology-based interfaces such as voice mail may seem cold and inflexible, but they're reliable. A number of systems, such as Wildfire, a voice-driven "electronic telephone assistant," can do some remarkable things such as screening, routing, and announcing your calls.

Some technology interfaces speak more than one language. Others adapt to users' skill levels and record interactions, providing a storehouse of information.

Equally valuable, these kinds of interfaces can reduce customer sacrifice: the difference between customers' ideals and what they settle for. Peapod, a Web-based home grocery delivery system, is doing this by providing direct data on customers' first and second choices to participating grocers.

Best of all, digital technology is almost never rude.

10. GIVE AWAY INFORMATION

In the early 1980s, IBM locked in its customers by selling them equipment that ran only IBM software. This closed-system strategy doesn't work anymore.

To succeed today you must share information, not hoard it. Develop killer apps that are as open as possible. The more people who use them, the more valuable they become.

That's how Netscape captured 80 percent of the browser market within months of its first product release in 1995. The company gave away copies of its software but sold advertising on its Web site and software tools for building other Web sites and intranets. It worked. In 1997 Netscape's revenues exceeded $500 million.

If your company sells information, consider giving it away and selling your expertise. If you don't, someone else will.

Cornell University, for example, currently offers a database of U.S. Supreme Court decisions that is easy to use, search, and print. Many government agencies offer their information directly to the public. These services are likely to put legal information provider LEXIS/NEXIS out of business because it sells information in a closed system.

The real value of what LEXIS/NEXIS provides is not raw data but the way the company enhances information with commentary, indexing, and organized notes services. Instead of charging for access as it currently does, the firm could sell its expertise on a subscription or transaction basis—answering specific tax questions, for example.

Information is public goods—it can be owned and used by everyone simultaneously. Give it away initially and you can create a ready market down the road.

11. CONCENTRATE ON INFORMATION ASSETS

As commerce moves from the marketplace to marketspace, your physical assets become liabilities. You don't need your trucks, factories, and licenses on the Net.

What you need are information assets. These include everything from expertise, trademarks, market intelligence, goodwill, and processes to corporate culture and identity.

Identify the information assets in your own organization. They may become the product or service you sell in the future.

Shift to Digital

The U.S. financial printing industry is turning the transformation from atoms to information bits to its advantage. The industry might have capsized when the Securities and Exchange Commission (SEC) announced that companies could file electronically with the commission beginning in 1996.

Instead, printers went after the electronic market. They capitalized on their expertise, their relationship to the securities industry, and their reputations for being able to do the work quickly and confidentially. These, not their equipment, were their assets.

The strategy worked. Financial printers were responsible for over 40 percent of the first electronic filings.

Even manufacturers and heavy industry must learn to reassess their assets. Information brokers already collect price and inventory information and use it to buy and sell commodities through a global network. In doing so, they undermine manufacturers' ability to set the prices themselves.

These companies can respond in a number of ways. They can focus more on specialty products, use technology to reduce inventory and handling costs, or do their own brokering.

One company that builds material pipelines is responding by building an information pipeline between itself and its customers and suppliers. Based on the open standards of the Internet, this pipeline will replace old communication channels such as phones, mail, and closed systems. The firm will be able to offer customers a virtual inventory of finished products, thereby reducing its physical inventory. For customers, this offers the promise of customization.

You must take stock of your own assets. Identify those that are at risk. One way to do this is to imagine how new competitors can use digital technology to compete against you without those assets.

Identify the functions you can outsource, then outsource them. Begin the shift to a more digital existence.

12. SCRAP YOUR CURRENT VALUE CHAIN

Every activity in your company that helps you produce and distribute your product adds value to that product. Collectively, these activities—from procurement to human resources, production to finance—form what author Michael Porter calls the value chain.

Killer apps have weakened traditional chains, wiping out the competitive advantage some firms have enjoyed. Don't try to squeeze any more value from your current chain of activities. Instead, scrap it altogether and create a new one by doing business digitally.

In the United Kingdom, Barclay's Bank has launched an electronic shopping mall, BarclaySquare. It costs relatively little to run the mall and yet produces a high profit margin. The company earns a percentage of all credit card transactions it clears for the cybermerchants.

By contrast, real-life shopping malls are expensive to operate, and revenues, typically rent, depend almost entirely upon location. That kind of competitive advantage quickly loses value against electronic malls that let consumers shop anywhere anytime.

The threat to your value chain probably will come from outside your industry. Unlike you and your competitors, new entrants aren't vested in the old value chains.

Amazon.com, a successful Internet-only bookseller, weakened the value chains of traditional bookshops by turning pricey stores, large inventories, and extensive staffing into disadvantages.

Bookshop chains, such as Barnes & Noble, only recently set up their own Web sites because they were afraid of cannibalizing their markets. While they hesitated, Amazon.com had an entire year without competition on the Web.

CASE STUDY: VIRTUAL FUEL COMPANY

Virtual Fuel Company (VFC) is the brainchild of a home heating oil company that hopes to increase its market share. The company is developing VFC in an effort to boost flagging retail sales of home heating oil to residents. Sales to residents generate 75 percent of its profits but the firm controls only 4 percent of the residential market where it operates.

VFC customers initially will order oil through the Web or by telephone. Future plans call for sensors on home oil tanks that will indicate automatically when it's time to refill so customers won't have to call the company at all. By outsourcing order processing to the customer, the company saves money it would have spent on a sales force.

The firm's supply and distribution network will be virtual. VFC will partner with leading transport companies to deliver the product, routing pickup and delivery schedules through the partners' systems. The infrastructure may be virtual, but savings to the customer and the company are real.

---

13. PUT TOGETHER A PORTFOLIO OF POTENTIAL KILLER APPS

If your company is like most others, it probably only underwrites research projects that guarantee a return on investment (ROI). However, this approach won't work if you want to invest in the kinds of innovation that lead to killer apps.

You can invest responsibly in experimental technologies by becoming a stakeholder in someone else's experiments. Doing this reduces your loss if the innovation doesn't pan out while giving you first crack at killer apps that do work.

Look at the OCI

Diversifying your investments allows you to manage your research dollars as a portfolio rather than a series of discrete projects.

The technique that will help you do this is called option-creating initiative or OCI. Instead of looking for a specific return, OCI weighs what you stand to gain against the price of an option in a technology, the price of taking full ownership of that technology, and the volatility of the investment.

OCI requires senior managers to get involved in technology investment decisions. They must take ownership of the portfolio and manage it. They must quickly abandon options that fail. Their companies' futures depend on it.

Seek Out Opportunities

Making effective decisions about technology works best in an environment that seeks out opportunities. The first step to nurturing such an environment is to develop a technology radar. This is the pipeline that feeds digital strategy.

Point your sensors in the right direction by focusing on digital technologies you can inspect and evaluate in the context of trial runs. You must be able to see the technology that's coming if you hope to exploit it.

Next, feed the pipeline. Tomorrow's applications are everywhere—in electronics stores, toy shops, and car lots and in newspapers and magazine articles. Check out what's happening in high tech companies. See what's on the Net.

Once you have identified a potentially useful technology, get others in the company to try it out. You can learn more from a simple demo than from the most detailed business plan.

14. LEARN FROM THE CHILDREN

If you're over the age of thirty, even if you are exceptionally cybersavvy, you are what Electronic Frontier Foundation's John Perry Barlow calls an "immigrant" of cyberspace.

Children are the natives. They grew up surrounded by digital technology. It was in their homes and in their schools. They have never experienced a world without the Internet.

If you want to succeed at digital strategy, talk with them. You can learn a lot.

MIT sociologist Sherry Turkle tells of a thirteen-year-old playing a sophisticated game that simulates the life of an ecosystem the player designs. Turkle worried that the game's complicated format would frustrate the boy.

"Don't let it bother you if you don't understand," he told her. "I just say to myself that I probably won't be able to understand the whole game any time soon. So I just play."

Hiring the children, or including them in the process of product development, is the easy part. What is more difficult is learning to see the world through their eyes. But that is the only way to develop a process that will help you discover, form, and unleash killer apps.

A New Way to Work

Young adults are different as well, particularly in their approach to work.

When a group of twenty executives from different European postal agencies toured game company Rocket Science, they were amazed at the company's culture. The oldest employee in the Silicon Valley company was under forty. People were running in and out of each other's offices and holding impromptu meetings to resolve problems as they came up.

Most impressive, however, was the attitude of Rocket Science's young workforce. "Everyone is smiling," said one postal executive. "They actually seem to be enjoying themselves. They're not working, they're having fun."

Killer apps flourish in work environments like this. Creating them isn't easy, but it's critical.

THE CASE OF LOTUS NOTES

Lotus Notes, a software product that allows organizations to share information over local and wide-area networks, was released in 1990 by Lotus Development Corporation.

The idea for Notes actually debuted in 1984 when PCs had barely penetrated the market. Lotus founder Mitch Kapor believed the idea had potential but knew the investment it required could put other Lotus projects at risk.

His solution was to form a new corporation solely to bring Notes from concept to product. Lotus funded the project, reviewed its progress, and could take it to market when ready, but Lotus did not own it. If Lotus stopped funding Notes, the new company could take it to market.

Lotus continued to invest and, five years later, launched the finished product. Had it been handled as an internal R&D project, Notes might have fallen by the wayside. Instead, it became the company's principal source of revenue.

THE ANATOMY OF BUZZ
by Emanuel Rosen

Word-of-mouth advertising is getting more and more attention from marketers. Companies have always recognized the power of the word-of-mouth recommendation—a third party extolling the virtues of a product or service is much more effective than an advertisement created by the product's seller. In recent years, however, marketers have more fully realized the extent to which they can impact and generate word-of-mouth recommendations. This realization has led to a new, and rather inelegant, term in the field: *viral marketing*.

Thankfully, author and consultant Emanuel Rosen uses the more evocative term *buzz* in his how-to guide on word-of-mouth marketing *The Anatomy of Buzz*. One of the first to try to explain how the process of buzz works, Rosen provides a comprehensive toolkit on how to create a buzz in the marketplace through word-of-mouth marketing. As the title suggests, Rosen first dissects buzz to reveal the invisible networks through which it travels. Rosen reveals network hubs—the influencers and opinion leaders who are at the center of networks. He also shows how marketers can work with network hubs to start the buzz, including actively "seeding" the product with key customers.

Originally an advertising copywriter from Israel, Rosen became VP of Marketing at Niles Software in Berkeley, California. He was responsible for launching and marketing the company's flagship product, EndNote—software for managing bibliographies. After selling his share in the company, Rosen spent two years researching the phenomenon of buzz and writing his book. He is now a sought-after consultant and speaker.

THE ANATOMY OF BUZZ
How to Create Word-of-Mouth Marketing
by Emanuel Rosen

CONTENTS

THE SUMMARY IN BRIEF

Today's consumers are skeptical, and they suffer from information overload. The result: they'll probably ignore the expensive television and print ads your marketing team creates. So how do people decide which car to buy, or which fashions fit the image they're looking for, or what new techno-appliance is a must for their homes?

The answer is word of mouth—the recommendations of friends and the buzz that develops in the marketplace. Buzz will make a new book soar to the top of the bestseller list, turn a "sleeper" movie into a box office superhit, or have parents lining up at toy stores to buy the new prize of the season. And buzz will help you sell your product or service—if you know how to create it. In this summary, you will learn exactly how to create buzz by understanding the following:

- *Buzz is an invisible network.* You will never really see how buzz moves from person to person, but you don't have to. You just need to understand that people need to communicate with one another, and figure out how to get them talking.
- *There are thousands of networks through which buzz flows.* These networks are loosely connected with one another. Buzz can start in one, but might not jump to another without a push. You will soon learn how to make the leaps.
- *In every network, there is a person who is the hub.* That person needs to be cultivated so he or she can spread the word about your product or service. You will soon

know how to identify and engage those influential people at the center of the network.

• *A great product is essential.* There's no reason to spread buzz if your product isn't compelling. It won't happen.

• *Networks must be seeded.* Before word of mouth can take off, each network must be seeded with suggestion. You will see exactly how and where to seed your product.

THE COMPLETE SUMMARY
1. THE BUZZ PHENOMENON

Most of today's marketing focuses on how to use advertising to influence individual consumer buying behavior. It ignores the fact that for many products, purchasing is part of a social process. People rely on "invisible networks" of friends, relatives, and co-workers for recommendations about everything from which movie to see to where they should vacation. This is buzz.

Buzz starts with a superior user experience; nothing will help your product if it doesn't deliver such an experience. If you want to generate buzz, you should underpromise and overdeliver. Then, instead of pushing the product on customers, let the product spread itself through the invisible networks.

WHAT IS BUZZ?

Imagine this scene. A teen stands outside a school leaning against a fence playing with a yo-yo. He's good. A younger child walks by and asks, "Where'd ya get it?" and "What kind is it?" The teen tells him it's called "The Brain" and "It's cool." This type of exchange is the basic building block of buzz. Buzz is the sum of all comments about a certain product that are exchanged among people at any given time.

Buzz can, of course, be negative. Angry car owners can e-mail their thoughts to all their friends, participate in chats with other car enthusiasts, create their own critical Web sites, or rate the car on a consumer site like Epinions.com. In the past, their complaints would have reached only a dozen or so. Now they can reach millions.

Why Buzz Is Powerful Today

Why has buzz taken on such a significant role in marketing? There are three reasons: noise, skepticism, and connectivity:

- *Customers can hardly hear you.* Consumers are suffering from information overload. In addition to facts and figures, they're exposed to an avalanche of ads every day. The result is that many consumers filter out the messages sent by mass media and listen to their friends instead.
- *Customers are skeptical.* The public believes very little of what they are told by companies. A recent survey illustrates the point: 37 percent of the public considers information that comes from a software company "very or somewhat believable." It's worse in other industries. Drug companies are believed by 28 percent of the public, car manufacturers by 18 percent, and insurance companies by 16 percent.
- *Consumers are connected.* They have new tools for sharing information. The Internet has added to this connectivity. Strangers can now share information in a variety of forums, most entirely outside your control. And this is just the beginning of a major power shift. Generation Y—those born between 1979 and 1994—shop by word of mouth. Using the Internet is second nature to them. As this generation gains buying power, expect buzz to become even more important.

HOTMAIL TAKES OFF WITH BUZZ

When Hotmail launched its Web-based free e-mail service, it experienced the fastest adoption rate of any new product ever—from zero to twelve million subscribers in just eighteen months! The Internet allowed buzz about the company and its services to take off. The premise was simple: give Internet users an e-mail service they could access from any computer with Internet access and offer it free of charge. Each person who signed up helped recruit new members because every e-mail sent through a Hotmail account included a message touting the free service.

Adopters and Networks

Traditionally, marketers have focused on placing consumers in categories based on the likelihood that they will adopt a new product or service. People are divided into five categories: innovators, early adopters, early majority, late majority, and laggards. But those who understand buzz will look beyond these classifications and adopt a network approach.

A network approach takes a microlevel look at the categories, for example, subdividing categories according to industry. Take two people—a retailer in the Midwest and a software programmer in Silicon Valley—who bought Palm organizers in 1999. The retailer could be considered an early adopter because he was buying the Palm organizer earlier than many people in his industry. The programmer, on the other hand, was behind the curve since the Palm organizer was already popular for people in high tech industries. As a result, the retailer is plugged into a network that has the most potential for future sales.

WHY WE TALK

Buzz is powerful because it is in our genes. We must communicate to stay alive. We talk because we are programmed to talk. Sharing information is essential. We also talk to connect, often about everyday things. We discuss products and services like what car we test-drove or what book we read. We talk to make sense of the world and the products available. Instead of doing independent research on products or services we need, we ask for recommendations.

How Important Is Buzz to Your Business?

Buzz doesn't affect all businesses the same way. The role it plays in your business depends on four factors:

- *The nature of your product.* Some products, like paper clips, won't generate buzz no matter what you do. There's nothing new about them. Products that do create buzz are exciting products, such as books and movies; innovative products, such as Web browsers and computer programs; personal experience products, such as hotels, airlines, and cars; complex products, such as medical devices; expensive products, such as computers and electronics; and observable products, such as clothes and cellular phones.
- *The people you're trying to reach.* Different audiences have different propensities for talking about products. Some of it is cultural, and some may be based on age. For example, young people tend to socialize more and be influenced by peers, while older people rely less on the advice of others.
- *Your customer connectivity.* The more connected your customers are to each other, the more you will depend on their buzz for future business—and the more open with them you must be. Producing high-quality products and services is crucial if you are supplying connected customers, because negative buzz will spread faster than positive buzz.
- *Your marketing strategy.* Your marketing strategy as well as those of your competitors might affect the degree to which you rely on buzz. For example, when Pepsi contracts to be the sole provider of soft drinks for a school district, the need for buzz decreases.

2. NETWORK HUBS HOLD THE KEY

Some people love to talk about a favorite product or service so much that they become "network hubs" in the world of buzz. Researchers typically refer to them as "opinion leaders," "power users," or "influencers." Of course, you won't find their names and addresses in any directory. Identifying them is much harder than renting a mailing list. But the rewards for paying attention to these people can be huge.

The first step in trying to find the individuals who act as hubs is to understand that such people come in all shapes, colors, and forms. In general, though, they can be classified into four categories.

First, network hubs can be categorized based on the number of people they reach. *Regular hubs* are regular folks who have developed an interest in a certain product category. *Mega hubs* are the press, celebrities, analysts, and politicians who provide powerful one-way links with people who listen to their message via mass media. For example, Oprah Winfrey propels books onto bestseller lists every time she recommends one for her book club.

Network hubs can also be distinguished based on the source of their influence. Some people are influential because they have demonstrated significant knowledge of a certain area, or at least have convinced others that they are experts. These *expert hubs* can make or break a product introduction. *Social hubs* are the members who are central to the group because they are sociable or charismatic and trusted by the peer group.

Reaching Regular Hubs

It is probably best to leave reaching the mega hubs to publicity experts, but you can reach the regular hubs if you know where and how to look for them. The acronym ACTIVE may help. Hub members are Ahead in adoption, Connected, Travelers, Information-hungry, Vocal, and Exposed to the media more than others.

3. THE RULES OF NETWORKS

There are ten principles at work in social networks that affect buzz:

1. *Networks are invisible.* We know our friends, and we may know our friends' friends, but that's where our direct view of networks stops. Networks are too complex to allow us to see much beyond the horizon.
2. *People link with others like them.* Scientists like to talk to other scientists, teenagers to other teens, and so on. The tendency for people to associate with those who are similar to them is called "homophily." Unfortunately, homophily is the main factor that limits the spread of buzz.

3. *Similar people form clusters.* People tend to form clusters when they share similar characteristics and interests in some dimension of their lives. These clusters can informally adopt products together. The good news for companies is that if your product becomes the standard within a cluster, it makes it difficult for a competitor to uproot your hold. Of course, this could work against you. Consider the case of Birkenstock sandals. In the early 1970s, the brand was adopted by alternative lifestyle clusters, so that wearing them was almost a political statement. It took the company years to convince others to buy them.

4. *Buzz spreads through common nodes.* We all belong to more than one cluster or clique, which is one way buzz spreads. To understand this idea, you must understand the "six degrees of separation" or "small world" concept, which is the belief that any two people are linked through a chain of no more than six other people. Any person can be reached through a limited number of steps. We are all linked to many clusters and networks.

5. *Information gets trapped in clusters.* Although there appear to be easy links between clusters, they are not always as connected as they seem. Consider this example. A software manufacturer has already sold hundreds of copies of a program that makes creating endnotes easy for academics at a large university, and is surprised to learn that a new customer is unfamiliar with the program. The reason is that she is a medical researcher, while the previous purchasers are all Ph.D.s engaged in basic research. The surgeon only interacts regularly with surgeons in her cluster, and not with other academics.

6. *Network hubs and connectors create shortcuts.* If you want to spread the word between clusters, you need to identify people who touch both clusters in some way. Many times, these people will be accountants, bankers, or lawyers who have strong and varied community ties.

7. *We talk to those around us.* Geography still matters, even with the advent of the Internet. Although we all have global ties, most of our ties remain with and to those within close physical proximity. Physical proximity is still an excellent predictor of those with whom we will share information.

8. *Weak ties are surprisingly strong.* Your closest friends are likely to be exposed to the same news you are, so they don't offer you the latest news. But those acquaintances in other close-by clusters receive different information, and are therefore a more likely source of news for you. Although you may view your tie to the cluster as weak, it is surprisingly strong when it comes to giving you new information. The lesson? Diversify your connections.

9. *The Net nurtures weak ties.* It's easier to maintain weak ties over the Internet. Consider how easy and unobtrusive it is to send a friendly e-mail. It's also easy to

create new ties over the Internet. For example, most people who use news-groups or online chats don't know each other well; they have weak ties. However, that doesn't mean that they don't exchange quite a bit of information. As a result, information travels much faster today.

10. *Networks go across markets.* People belong to more than one market, and are connected to people in more than one market. A business owner shopping for computers for his business and home, and who has a daughter in college who also uses computers, belongs to more than one market, and connects with yet another. As a practical matter, a dissatisfied customer in one market can easily spread that anger to another.

So What?

What does all this mean to you as a marketer? It means that if you market a product that lends itself to being talked about, your customers are very likely to be talking about it. Some are talking with their neighbors, co-workers, and friends, while others are talking with people in other countries. It's this combination of local and global networks that makes buzz so important now. If you understand these rules, you will soon understand how to stimulate the flow of buzz.

QUESTIONS TO ASK YOURSELF

If you want to create buzz, you have to know who your customers are and how you are reaching them. Start by answering these questions.

• From whom do your customers typically learn about your product?

• What do people say when they recommend your product?

• How fast does information about your product spread as compared with competitors' products?

• Who are the network hubs?

• Where does the information hit a roadblock?

• How many sources of information does a customer rely on and which ones are most important?

• What other kinds of information spread through the same networks?

---

4. HOW BUZZ SPREADS

Now that you understand the highway system of buzz, it's time to examine how buzz, the traffic, spreads through the system. A perfect illustration of the phenomenon is the buzz that made the novel *Cold Mountain* a bestseller.

The publishers printed twenty-six thousand copies of the book, and it started to sell well without much media attention. The sales were being pushed by word of mouth. A professor heard about the book in a newspaper review and asked his local bookstore to call him when it arrived. Both he and his wife liked it so much they bought three more copies to give to their parents and a friend. He also posted a review on Amazon.com, participated in a panel discussion on local-access television, and gave the book as an option for use in student projects due that semester. Six students read it, and five recommended it to others.

Meanwhile, another reader read a review in *Southern Living* magazine and bought the book. She estimated she told ten people about it and also posted a review on Amazon. A flight attendant who liked the book estimated she told at least fifty people. Soon sales clerks got excited about the book as positive comments came in.

The publishers also did their part in getting the book into important hubs. They contacted authors and told them about it. In addition, they printed more than four thousand advance copies of the book for reviewers, bookstore owners, and anyone else who might be expected to help build buzz. They also sent the author to talk to bookstore owners, clerks, and buyers several months before the publication date. All the effort paid off. The book sold an astonishing 1.6 million copies in hardback alone.

5. ACHIEVING SUCCESS IN THE NETWORKS

Before you can expect to generate buzz, you must have a superior product or service. No amount of advertising or PR will sell a mediocre product. The best buzz comes from attributes inherent to the product itself. These are *contagious products*, and they can be grouped into six categories:

1. *Products that evoke an emotional response.* A good example is the movie *The Blair Witch Project*. The buzz was driven by the fear the movie generated, especially in the first few weeks after its release, when people still believed that the footage was taken by the three students depicted in the film. For other products, the emotional response is the feeling of excitement and delight you get when a product exceeds your expectations.
2. *Products that advertise themselves.* Another contagious product is one that advertises itself. People notice the product and start asking for it. One example is the wheeled luggage bags first pulled by pilots through airports. Soon travelers wanted to know where they could get the same convenient carry-ons.
3. *Products that leave traces.* Some products propagate because they leave traces of themselves behind. For example, in the early days of desktop publishing, software often left a message on the artwork such as "I used Photoshop" or "I used my Mac."

4. *Products that become more useful as more people use them.* Some contagious products reward you if you talk about them. Telephones, fax machines, and e-mail work this way. In order for them to be useful, customers have to persuade others to get the product or service too. The spread of instant messaging software worked the same way. If you were the only one with the software, it wouldn't be very useful. In fact, it is only useful if you encourage all your friends to download and use it.

5. *Products that are compatible.* Your product must be compatible with the way potential users already do things. Take the Palm information organizer. People already kept schedules on their PCs and didn't want a complicated system for coordinating a portable organizer with their computers. The Palm device capitalized on this by being an extension of PCs rather than an entirely separate computing device. One step synchronizes your PC and Palm.

6. *Products that do the rest.* Cameras were invented in the 1820s, but it took Kodak to make them popular in 1888. One reason was the advantage touted in ads: "You press the button—we do the rest." Products that are easy to use spread quickly because customers are hungry for simplicity.

Accelerating Natural Contagion

Two things are needed to create buzz successfully. First, you need a contagious product. But that's not enough. Companies that get good buzz have learned to accelerate natural contagion. Every product starts with no one knowing about it except a few insiders. The buzz is zero. There is an enormous gap between the few people who know about it and the rest of the world. The product's creators have to reach out and spread the word in the rest of the network. The company must have at least one person who is obsessed with spreading the word.

Spreading the word requires hard work. You may have to organize a sales blitz to get moving. In some cases, that means ignoring traditional channels and trying new approaches. When the game Pictionary was introduced, the manufacturer hired actors to dress up as artists and take flip charts to parks and shopping centers. There they engaged potential customers in the game. The company leapfrogged over traditional distribution channels like toy stores right into the heart of consumer networks.

6. STIMULATING BUZZ: FIRST, WORK WITH NETWORK HUBS

One way to spread the word about a product or service is to convince those who are opinion leaders in their networks that they should tell others about it. The problem is that there is no simple way to identify these leaders. But there are tricks you can use to make the task easier. Always look for individuals who display the ACTIVE characteristics: more ahead in adoption, connected, travelers, information-hungry, vocal, and exposed to the media.

Sometimes opinion leaders come to you, asking for information. They hang around your booth at trade shows and e-mail you asking for updated information on new features. Others have to be sought out in likely places such as trade shows and conferences and as readers of trade magazines. Or perhaps a chat host on a topic related to your product is a likely candidate for spreading the word. You may also have to go directly into the field to locate grassroots network hub leaders. Also, keep an eye out for connectors between hubs: those people who can take word of your product from one group to another. Examples include visiting professors, exchange students, and temporary employees.

You can also identify hubs through surveys. For example, you could conduct a sociometric survey by asking all members of a given network for the name of the person from whom they would seek information about a particular service or product. The name that appears most often is the hub. You can also ask people in the network directly who the hub is. For example, the hub will be the "person you want to talk to if you want to get anything done."

WHY YOU NEED TO REACH HUBS EARLY

Approaching network hubs at an early stage can help your product reach critical mass earlier than it would otherwise. And once a product reaches critical mass, adoption gains enough momentum to become self-sustaining. It's crucial that you bring the product to their attention early. Address their concerns. Give them the facts. Tell them it's safe. Show them others who have already begun using the product or service. Once they adopt, they will give their seal of approval, making it okay for their followers to adopt and tell all their friends.

Once you have identified network hubs, you will need to keep track of them. Make everyone in the company aware of them. Your database should include names, phone numbers, e-mail addresses, and information about the scope and source of their influence. Timing in reaching out to those on your list is important. With a new product or service, it is critical to capture their minds and hearts before your competitors do.

Buzz needs ammunition. Give hubs something to talk about. For example, Jeep owners attend Jeep Jamborees. The activities they engage in there are likely to stimulate discussion within the network. Be sure to give them plenty of facts. Don't worry about boring hubs. Keep them up to date on improvements and milestones.

7. ACTIVELY SEED YOUR PRODUCTS

To accelerate the rate at which word about a product spreads, smart companies seed their products—at strategic points in many different clusters—with seed units.

A seed unit is an actual product or a representative sampling from the product you are trying to promote, which you place in the hands of seed customers. You can offer the seed unit at a discount, on a loan basis, for full price, or free; but the principle is the same: You give people in multiple clusters direct experience with your product. That way you plant the seed to stimulate discussion in multiple networks simultaneously.

FOUR RULES FOR A SUCCESSFUL SEEDING PROGRAM

1. *Look beyond the usual suspects.* Although seeding traditional channels is important, you must think broadly. Identify social circles, industry segments, or academic disciplines in which people don't talk about your product or services, and seed them.
2. *Put products in their hands.* Most of the time, the seed has to be the product itself. In some cases, like a book, a sample may be enough to stir interest, but generally people need the entire product to get excited. It has to be placed directly into their hands.
3. *Reduce the price barrier.* Make the product free for seed recipients if you can, or at least offer a significant discount.
4. *Listen for silence.* When you hear silence, the network is dead. Pay attention to dead networks and do further seeding to wake them up.

A good seeding campaign goes beyond mailing samples to a small group of press contacts and the industry elite. It must be sent to a large number of individuals in many networks. But seeding only works in categories that people will talk about, such as cars, books, computers, fashion, and other conversation products. The idea of selective seeding is to get people from different networks more involved with products so that they talk about them with others.

We value everything that is scarce, from baseball cards to places with restricted access. Remember this when trying to build buzz. But don't withhold too much information either. You need to build anticipation at the same time. One trick you can employ is the sneak preview. People who are invited leave feeling like they are in the know.

8. THE NEW VIRAL MARKETING

For years, companies have run campaigns in which they encouraged customers to spread the word to friends or relatives who might be interested in the product. With the advent of the Internet, the technique has been improved and renamed "viral marketing." You should consider using both the traditional tell-a-friend strategy and Internet viral marketing to increase buzz.

Give your customers the tools they need to make it easy to spread the word. One effective strategy is to give customers discount coupons to hand out. Another strategy popular with record clubs is to offer current customers a free gift for every friend they bring to the club. Other examples include MCI's "Friends and Family" promotion, which resulted in ten million residential customers switching to MCI from the competition.

SHOULD YOU GIVE INCENTIVES FOR REFERRALS?

To decide whether an incentive should be offered for a referral, keep these guidelines in mind:

• *Don't make the incentive the main motivation.* If you do, the message loses credibility. Keep incentives modest.

• *Ask customers what they think through interviews, focus groups, or surveys.* Or give them a choice of rewards.

• *Minimize loopholes and keep it simple.* You don't want customers taking advantage of the incentive without delivering a good referral. Don't encourage fraud.

If you want to use viral marketing on the Web, there are three principles you should keep in mind:

• Make your product part of the communications process. Viral marketing has the strongest effect if your product can be somehow incorporated into the communication between two people. That's why free electronic cards (Blue Mountain) and free e-mail (Hotmail) spread so quickly.

• Have your customers interact. Many companies that started selling on the Web acted as if they were conventional businesses. Then they discovered that getting people to spend time interacting with each other on the Web site worked much better. Examples include eBay, where sellers tell friends how much money they're making and buyers boast of what a bargain they got.

• *Prompt your customers to spread the word.* You may want to offer tools for your customers to spread the word. These may include prewritten e-mail messages that customers can forward to friends or online postcards that play a tune. Be careful not to appear too intrusive, though, or you will turn customers off.

9. DOES MADISON AVENUE STILL MATTER?

Advertising is not dead. Few products can rely on buzz alone. When used correctly, advertising can help buzz. Unfortunately, the wrong kind of advertisement can also kill buzz. Therefore, you need a sensitive advertising policy that stimulates buzz.

Advertising is needed to let networks know that a product is being launched. Print advertising is effective for reaching the opinion leaders who can generate buzz. Remember, opinion leaders are hungry for information, so they read more than average people. Advertising also reassures people that they are not alone. Milestones like selling one hundred thousand copies of a software program or book will help build awareness and let customers begin talking about your product.

It's also possible for a clever advertisement to create buzz as people talk about the commercial. Funny commercials do this best, such as the Energizer bunny and the Taco Bell chihuahua. Ads that are testimonial in nature can also stimulate buzz, if done well. They must be believable. One good example: the Saturn "real people" testimonials.

10. BUZZ IN DISTRIBUTION CHANNELS

Once upon a time, distribution channels were the only source of buzz. Retailers informed customers about what was new and exciting. While retailers may not be the only source of information for today's consumers, they still play a significant role. This is true whether the distribution channel is an online or a bricks-and-mortar retailer. As long as there is interactivity and trust between consumer and channel, buzz can result.

To create buzz about a product through a traditional retailer, work with those salespeople who interact with and are trusted by customers. This works especially well in specialty stores with a reputation for personal attention, such as bookstores and sport-specific stores.

To create online retailer buzz, look for partners who personalize the consumer's online experience. Amazon.com, for example, provides customer book reviews and recommendations. Other online retailers allow customers to chat with each other, providing a forum for buzz to generate.

A key strategy for creating buzz through a channel is to seed resellers who are trusted in their networks. For example, in 1991 the publishing company Knopf sent five thousand gift-wrapped copies of a first novel, *Damage*, to managers, buyers, and clerks at bookstores all across the country, each with a personal note from the president of Knopf. The book became a bestseller.

Other strategies to build buzz include limiting distribution, at least at first, to simulate scarcity, and using public areas like shopping malls to demonstrate products. You can also use a little mystery. This strategy worked for the creators of the board game Trivial Pursuit. The company sent selected toy store buyers single game cards in unmarked envelopes. It wasn't until the third card arrived that the buyers learned the identity of the seller and got information about the game.

11. PUTTING IT TOGETHER

You have learned what buzz is and how to go about creating it. Now it's time to put it all together by looking at one company's successful buzz campaign. The product is PowerBar, an easy-to-digest, low-fat, tasty, and nutritious snack bar designed for athletes. Invented by marathon runner Brian Maxwell in 1983, the product faced many marketing challenges. PowerBars didn't immediately become the talk of the town; spreading the word took tremendous effort.

Athletes are a competitive lot, so a snack that promised enhanced performance and endurance was a potential winner. But before sales took off, a serious marketing effort had to be undertaken. Part of the plan was easy. PowerBars are a very visible product since they are consumed in public. Once athletes started eating them, others asked what they were and how they tasted. That was a good start.

Athletes from different sports don't travel in the same circles, so the company began to seed different sports at the same time. Skiers, runners, and cyclists were treated to free samples at sporting events. Next came an offer from the company to send a friend five PowerBars for just a shipping fee. This built further buzz. Coaches and athletes were then signed up as part of the PowerBar Team Elite. They and their teams were given logo-embellished gear and products. When the American cycling team on the Tour de France ordered one thousand bars, media shots of the team chewing PowerBars created even more buzz. Today, the company sells more than $100 million worth of the bars a year.

PURPLE COW
by Seth Godin

Seth Godin has a knack for capturing his ideas in a clear and memorable phrase. *Permission marketing,* for example, was how Godin described the new world of marketing in which marketers had to do more than just push their way (without permission, if you will) into the living rooms of consumers by interrupting television programs with loud advertisements. Costly television ads can still work for major beer companies and car companies, but most businesses have to find other ways to reach their customers. The key, as Godin explained in *Permission Marketing,* was for companies to find a way to get the prospect's permission to receive a sales pitch.

The *ideavirus* is another of Godin's brilliant phrases. A virus spreads randomly and effectively with little effort. Because of the Internet, Godin argued, ideas could also spread just as widely and quickly. The key in this case was to learn how to "unleash" the ideavirus—thus the title of another of Godin's popular books, *Unleashing the Ideavirus.* In this book, Godin echoes Geoffrey Moore in pointing out the importance of the early adopters, who are the first to try out new products—only Godin calls them your "sneezers."

Which brings us to *Purple Cow,* the summary included here. *Purple Cow* has all the earmarks of a Seth Godin work: an evocative title, plenty of case studies, and some straightforward advice. The theme of the book begins with an assumption that many of the books in this anthology share: pushing your products to the customer through advertising isn't good enough to ensure a successful product. You have to find a way to get the customers to pull your product to them.

For Godin, the key is a product that "is worth making a remark about." The phrasing is key; Godin doesn't want you to make a remarkable product, he wants you to make a product that people are going to talk about. Imagine that you're driving through the countryside and, among the black and white cows, you suddenly see a purple cow. Chances are, you will mention that sighting to your friends and family.

Purple Cow is filled with short, punchy messages on why companies in any industry can create Purple Cows—and how to do it.

Seth Godin earned an MBA from Stanford University before founding his company Yoyodyne, a successful interactive direct marketing company. Yoyodyne was purchased by Yahoo in 1998. In addition to consulting and doing speaking engagements, Godin is a bestselling author of a number of books on marketing. His *Permission Marketing* spent four months on the *BusinessWeek* bestseller list; *Unleashing the Ideavirus* is the most popular e-book written (more than one million people downloaded the book); and *Purple Cow* was a *Wall Street Journal* and *New York Times* bestseller.

PURPLE COW
Transform Your Business by Being Remarkable
by Seth Godin

CONTENTS

THE SUMMARY IN BRIEF

Following the traditional rules of marketing just isn't enough anymore. In today's competitive economy, companies that want to create a successful new product must create a remarkable new product. According to bestselling author and marketing guru Seth Godin, such a product is a Purple Cow, a product or service that is worth making a remark about.

The impact of advertising in newspapers and magazines is fading—people are overwhelmed with information and have stopped paying attention to most media messages. To create Purple Cow products, Godin advises companies to stop advertising and start innovating.

Godin recommends that marketers target a niche, and he describes (through an assortment of case studies) effective ways to spread your idea to the consumers who are most likely to buy your product. Godin claims there isn't a shortage of remarkable ideas—every business has opportunities to do great things. There's a shortage of the will to execute those ideas.

THE COMPLETE SUMMARY

1. NOT ENOUGH Ps

For many years, marketers have used the five (or more) Ps as guidelines for selling their product and achieving their company's goals. The Ps include:

- Product
- Pricing
- Promotion
- Positioning
- Publicity
- Packaging
- Permission
- Pass-along

According to the popular theory, if these elements aren't all in place, the marketing message is unclear and ineffective.

Making the right marketing moves does not guarantee success, but the prevailing wisdom used to be that if your Ps were right, you had a better chance of succeeding in the marketplace.

But at a certain point in the evolution of marketing, it became clear that following the Ps just isn't enough. This book tells about a new P—Purple Cow—that is extremely important to marketers in today's fast-paced, highly competitive business environment. *Purple Cow* refers to a product or service that is different from the rest and somehow remarkable. *Purple Cow* tells about the why, the what, and the how of *remarkable*.

2. BOLDFACED WORDS AND GUTSY ASSERTIONS

Remarkable marketing is the process of building things into your product or service that are worth noticing. Not adding marketing to your product or service at the last minute, but understanding that if what you're offering isn't remarkable, it is invisible in the marketplace.

The **TV-industrial complex** refers to the symbiotic relationship between consumer demand, TV advertising, and growing companies that depend on ever-increasing spending on marketing.

The **postconsumption consumer** has run out of things to buy. Most of us have what we need, we don't want much more, and we're too busy to spend a lot of time doing research about the products or services that have been created for us.

The **marketing department** bases its efforts on an existing product, spending money to tell the target audience about its special benefits. This approach doesn't work anymore.

At this point in time, companies can no longer market directly to the masses because in today's world most products are invisible. Leading business writers have noted that over the past two decades, the dynamic of marketing has changed. The traditional approaches are now obsolete, and alternative approaches aren't a novelty—they are all we've got left.

Companies must create products and services that are remarkable—Purple Cows—and they must stop advertising and start innovating.

3. DID YOU NOTICE THE REVOLUTION?

Over the past twenty years, some people have changed the way they think about marketing. Business guru Tom Peters presented his vision of the "new marketing" with his book The Pursuit of Wow, a book that claims the only products with a future are those created by passionate people. Peters laments that, too often, big companies are scared companies, and they actually try to restrict change, including the good change that happens when people who care create something remarkable.

In their book The One to One Future, Don Peppers and Martha Rogers focus on a simple truth—that it is cheaper to keep an old customer than to make the effort to get a new one—and provide the blueprint for the entire field of customer relationship management. Peppers and Rogers conclude that there are only four kinds of people (prospects, customers, loyal customers, and former customers), and that loyal customers will usually continue to spend money on products and services they like.

In Geoff Moore's book Crossing the Chasm, he describes how new products and ideas reach different groups of people—first the innovators and early adopters, then the majority, then the laggards. Moore's premise applies to almost every product or service offered to any audience.

And in *Permission Marketing, Purple Cow* author Seth Godin outlines the public's growing attention deficit that marketers must overcome. He describes how companies win when they value the attention of their prospects and don't treat it as a disposable resource to be used and abandoned.

4. WHY YOU NEED THE PURPLE COW

Whether you are marketing a product or service to consumers or corporations, the sad truths about marketing are that:

- Most people can't buy your product—they don't have the money, don't have the time, or simply don't want it.
- If consumers don't have enough money to buy what you are selling at the price you are selling it for, you don't have a market for your product or service.
- If consumers don't have time to listen to and understand your marketing pitch, your product or service is invisible to them.
- If consumers take the time to hear your pitch but decide they don't want what you are selling, you are not going to be successful.

So Many Options

Most people who might buy your product or service will never hear about it. These days, people have so many options for getting information that they aren't easily reached by the mass media. Busy consumers ignore unwanted messages.

A remarkable idea that spreads like a virus—an "ideavirus"—is hard to spread to consumers who are satisfied. And since marketers have overwhelmed consumers with too much of everything, people are unlikely to tell a friend about a product unless they are sure the friend wants to hear about it.

This holds true for business and industrial products as well as for consumer products. People who buy for businesses—whether it is advertising, parts, service, insurance, or real estate—simply aren't as needy as they used to be. The marketers who got to them before you have a huge advantage—they are already there, and the customer is satisfied. If you want to grow your market share or launch something new, you face some daunting challenges:

- Consumers aren't as likely to have obvious, easily solved problems that your product or service will fix.
- Consumers are hard to reach because they are overwhelmed with information and will tend to ignore you.
- Satisfied customers are less likely than unsatisfied customers to tell their friends.

5. THE DEATH OF THE TV-INDUSTRIAL COMPLEX

The TV-industrial complex is dying, and that should worry us. We built a large part of our economy on this process of companies spending huge amounts on advertising to reach consumers, and now that process is going away. The death of the TV-industrial complex has caused a lot of the turmoil at our companies today.

The process is simple—find a market niche that needs to be filled; build a plant to make a product to fill that niche; buy a lot of television ads to promote the product; the ads will lead to retail distribution and sales; the sales will keep the factory busy and create profits.

A Successful Cycle

Smart companies used the profits to fund more distribution and more factories. Before long, this successful cycle built a large, profitable brand.

And as the brand became larger and larger, it commanded a higher price, which brought larger profits and more money for more TV ads. Consumers eventually believed that products "seen on TV" were of high quality, so they used television to look for products. Brands that were not advertised on television lost distribution and, ultimately, profits.

TV commercials are the most effective selling tool ever devised. A large part of America's economic success in this century is due to the fact that our companies have perfected this medium and used it extensively.

Cars, cigarettes, clothing, food—anything that was advertised well on television was changed by the medium. Marketers not only used television to promote products, but television changed the way products were created and marketed. Because of this, the marketing Ps were changed to take advantage of the dynamic between creating products and capturing consumers' attention on television.

The impact of advertising in newspapers and magazines is fading too, just like the impact of any other form of media that interrupts any form of consumer activity. Individuals and businesses have just stopped paying attention.

That's the problem. The TV-industrial complex is going away, and most marketers don't know what to do about it. Every day, companies spend millions trying to re-create the TV-industrial complex. And every day they fail.

The old rule was *"Create safe, ordinary products and combine them with great marketing."*

The new rule is *"Create remarkable products that the right people seek out."*

6. CONSIDER THE BEETLE

Remember the original Volkswagen Beetle? When it was first introduced to the public, it wasn't an immediate hit. It sold poorly until some brilliant advertising

---

COMPETING IN THE UP AND DOWN ELEVATOR MARKET

Elevators are not a typical consumer product—they can cost more than $1 million, they are usually installed when a building is constructed, and they are not very useful unless the building is over three or four stories high.

So how does an elevator company compete? Until recently, selling in the elevator business involved a lot of wining and dining clients and long-term relationships with real estate purchasing agents.

But Schindler Elevator Corp. has dramatically changed this by developing a Purple Cow product.

Waiting for an elevator that stops on every floor can be time-consuming and frustrating. The obvious solution is for a building to install more elevators to handle more passengers. But that solution is very expensive and takes time to implement.

Every Elevator Is an Express

Schindler created an exceptional solution to this problem for the Cap Gemini Co. in Times Square. When you approach the company's elevators, you key in your floor on a centralized control panel, and the panel tells you which elevator is available to take you there.

The elevator system at Cap Gemini has turned every elevator into an express—it takes a passenger immediately to his or her floor, then races back to the lobby. This Purple Cow product, implemented at a remarkably low cost, means that the building needs fewer elevators for a given number of people and passengers don't have to wait very long for a lift.

---

saved it. Because of this great TV and print ad campaign, the Beetle was profitable in the United States for more than fifteen years.

The story of the original Beetle—and how advertising made it successful—is a perfect illustration of the power of the TV-industrial complex.

A Different Story

The new Beetle is a different story. It became successful because of how it looked and how it felt to drive. It also earned good reviews from the auto industry, received great word of mouth from satisfied owners, and had a distinctive shape that appealed to car buyers. Every time the cute little Beetle drove down a street clogged by boxy SUVs, it was marketing itself.

7. THE WILL AND THE WAY

There isn't a shortage of remarkable ideas—every business has opportunities to do great things. There's a shortage of the will to execute them.

Since the old ways of doing things have become obsolete, it's actually safer to take the risk inherent in trying to create remarkable things. Your best bet is to take the steps necessary to create Purple Cows.

Takeaway Ideas

Even the best excuses, such as "We don't have the ability to find the great idea," or "We can't distinguish the great idea from the lousy ones," can be overcome by brainstorming, ideation, and creativity techniques. These can be used to find the takeaway ideas, the specific things that can be done tomorrow to start a company on its way to the Purple Cow. If you've got the will, you'll find the way.

8. IDEAS THAT SPREAD, WIN

Until an actual product or service is created, a brand or new product is nothing more than an idea. Ideas that spread rapidly—ideaviruses—are more likely to succeed than ideas that don't.

"Sneezers" are the people who launch and spread an ideavirus. These people are the experts who tell all their colleagues and friends about a new product or service that they are knowledgeable about. Every market has a few sneezers—finding and seducing these sneezers is essential to creating an ideavirus.

Capture Their Interest

To create an idea (and a product or service) that spreads, don't try to make a product for everybody, because that is a product for nobody. Since the sneezers in today's huge marketplace have too many choices and are fairly satisfied, an "everybody" product probably won't capture their interest.

To connect with the mainstream, you must target a niche instead of a huge market. In targeting a niche, you approach a segment of the mainstream and create an ideavirus so focused that it overwhelms that small section of the market and those people will respond. The sneezers in this niche are more likely to talk about your product, and, best of all, the market is small enough that just a few sneezers can spread the word to the number of people you need to create an ideavirus.

It is no accident that some products catch on and some don't. When an ideavirus happens, it is usually because all the pieces have come together and produced that result.

9. WHO'S LISTENING?

The death of the TV-industrial complex has made some people predict that all mass media will die. And because ads aren't as effective as they used to be, it is easy to conclude that ads don't work at all, and that every consumer avoids and ignores them all.

Of course, this isn't true. Ads do work—not as well as they used to, and perhaps not cost-effectively, but they do attract attention and generate sales. Targeted ads are much more cost-effective than untargeted ads, but most advertising and marketing efforts are completely untargeted. They are like hurricanes, moving across a landscape of consumers and touching everyone in the same way, regardless of who they are and what they want.

But in any given market there are still some people who are all ears—they want to hear from you. They look through the Yellow Pages, subscribe to trade magazines, and visit Web sites looking for more information. Some of these people will eventually buy.

So the big idea is this: "it is useless to advertise to anyone—except interested sneezers with influence."

Advertise at the Right Time

You must do your advertising at the right time (when these consumers are looking for help) and in the right place (where they'll find you). Advertising to one interested person is a good idea, but the real success happens when the person listening is a sneezer who will probably tell his or her friends and colleagues.

When you are not marketing your product or service to the right people, you must be investing in the Purple Cow—products, services, and techniques so useful, interesting, and noteworthy that the market will want to listen to what you have to say.

10. THE PROBLEM WITH THE COW

The problem with creating Purple Cow products is actually a problem with fear. Some folks will tell you that there are too few great ideas or that their product, industry, or company can't support a great idea. This is not true. People have a problem creating a Purple Cow product because they are afraid.

If you are remarkable, some people won't like you. Nobody gets unanimous praise, ever, and criticism always comes to those who stand out. So the timid try their best not to stand out.

A Great Opportunity

The good news is that since almost everyone else is petrified of creating a Purple Cow product, you can be remarkable with much less effort. It is just common sense that if successful new products are the ones that stand out, and most people don't want to stand out, you've got a great opportunity.

The lesson here is simple—since boring always leads to failure, boring is almost always the most risky strategy. Smart businesspeople realize this, and they work to minimize—but not eliminate—the risk from the process.

INTRODUCING THE $750 OFFICE CHAIR

Before Herman Miller got into office chairs, they were practically an invisible item. A desk chair was acquired by the purchasing or human resources department and you probably didn't even notice the difference between one desk chair and another.

The buyers of desk chairs were looking for a safe, easy choice. Chair manufacturers listened to the buyers and made safe and easy products.

When Herman Miller introduced the $750 Aeron chair in 1994, the company took a huge risk—the chair looked different, worked differently, and was very expensive. But the chair proved to be a Purple Cow product.

Sitting in the Aeron chair sent a message about who you were, and buying the chairs for your company sent a message to employees as well.

The Aeron chair story isn't a matter of inventing a gimmick as an example of the rarely achieved "viral" marketing; it's about putting the marketing investment into the product instead of into the media. Millions of Aeron chairs have been sold since its introduction, and the chair is now in the permanent collection of the Museum of Modern Art.

---

11. THE BENEFITS OF BEING THE COW

As being remarkable continues to show its incredible value in the marketplace, the rewards earned by the Purple Cow increase.

Whether you develop a revolutionary new insurance policy, record the song of the year, or write a bestselling, groundbreaking book, the money, prestige, power, and satisfaction that follow are incredible.

KRISPY KREME'S SECRET RECIPE

Many people think the soaring popularity of Krispy Kreme donuts is a recent phenomenon, but the business actually got its start in 1937 when Vernon Rudolph bought a secret yeast-raised donut recipe from a French chef from New Orleans, rented a historic building in Winston-Salem, North Carolina, and started selling Krispy Kreme donuts to local grocery stores.

Krispy Kreme has come a long way since then. In April 2000, the company held an initial public offering of common stock. Krispy Kreme opened its first international store in Canada near Toronto and will expand into other countries soon.

Krispy Kreme makes a good donut, but is it worth driving many miles to get one? Clearly, donut devotees believe it is. There is something very visceral about the obsession that donut fans feel about Krispy Kreme, and discovering and leveraging that feeling is at the heart of the company's marketing efforts. This remarkable fact is the key to Krispy Kreme's success.

Free Donuts

When a Krispy Kreme store opens in a new location, employees start by giving away thousands of donuts. The people most likely to show up for a free hot donut are those who have heard the legend of Krispy Kreme and are delighted that the company is finally in town. These people spread the word. They tell their friends and even bring them to a Krispy Kreme store. That's when Krispy Kreme works its marketing magic by dominating the donut "conversation"—they rush to create partnerships with gas stations, coffee shops, and delis to make it easy for someone to encounter their product.

If the product remains a Purple Cow, some of the newly converted Krispy Kreme fans will spread the word in a new town until the chain arrives there.

Here is the lesson: find the market niche first, and then make the remarkable product—not the other way around.

Huge Rewards

In exchange for taking the risk—the risk of failure, ridicule, or unfulfilled dreams—the creator of the Purple Cow gets a huge reward when he or she gets it right.

Once you've managed to create a truly remarkable product or service, it is important to do two things simultaneously:

Milk your Purple Cow for everything it's worth. Figure out how to extend its lifespan and profit from it as long as possible.

Create a working environment in which you have a good chance of inventing another Purple Cow in time to replace the first one when its benefits start to wane.

CUTTING INTO THE BANDAGE MARKET

When Curad wanted to challenge the Band-Aid brand for the market for adhesive bandages, most people thought it was crazy. Band-Aid was a household institution, a name so well known that it was practically generic. And the Band-Aid product was terrific. What could Curad hope to accomplish?

But Curad developed a Purple Cow product—bandages with characters printed on them. Kids, who are the largest consumers of small bandages, loved them. So did parents who wanted to make cuts and scrapes heal faster.

And of course, when the first kid with Curads wore them to school, every other kid wanted them, too.

It didn't take very long for Curad to take a piece of market share away from Band-Aid.

---

12. THE PROCESS AND THE PLAN

Is there a foolproof way to create Purple Cow products over and over again? A secret formula you can use to increase your creativity while creating a product that will meet consumers' real-life needs? Of course not.

There is, however, a process. A system that has no definite tactics but still gets results.

Go for the Edges

The process can be summed up very simply: go for the edges. Challenge yourself and your team to describe what those edges are by reviewing the other Ps—your pricing, your packaging, and so forth—and sketch out where your edges are, and where your competition is. If you don't understand this landscape, you can't go to the next step and figure out which innovations you can attempt.

For example, it would be remarkable if a health spa offered all its services for free, but without a financial model that supports that offer, the spa probably would not last very long. JetBlue, on the other hand, figured out how to get to the edge of both service and pricing with a business that was also profitable.

It's not the tactics or the plan that joins Purple Cow products together. The process a company uses to discover the fringes makes a product remarkable.

THE POSTAL SERVICE'S PURPLE COW

Because it serves a host of large, conservative customers, it is very difficult for the U.S. Postal Service to innovate. The big direct marketers have learned to thrive under the Postal Service's current system, and they don't want that system to change. Most individuals don't want to change their mailing habits, either.

Many companies are so afraid of offending consumers or appearing ridiculous that they steer far away from innovation entirely. When a committee discusses a new, different product, each well-meaning participant warns that his or her constituency might not like it. So the company sticks to products that are safe . . . and boring.

Most new-policy initiatives at the U.S. Postal Service are either ignored or rejected. But ZIP+4, the addition of four digits to the end of the customary five-digit ZIP code, was a huge success. Within a few years, the Postal Service disseminated a new idea that changed billions of address records in thousands of databases. How did they do it?

Worth the Time

First, it was a very beneficial innovation. ZIP+4 makes it much easier for marketers to target neighborhoods, and much faster and easier to deliver the mail. The product was a Purple Cow, completely changing the way customers and the Postal Service deal with bulk mail. ZIP+4 offered both dramatically increased delivery speed and a much lower cost for bulk mailers. These benefits made it worth the time it took for mailers to pay attention. The cost of ignoring the innovation would immediately affect customers' bottom line.

Second, the Postal Service spread the word to workers who are knowledgeable about technology and sensitive to pricing and speed issues. These "early adopters" were in a position to communicate the benefits to other, less astute, mailers.

The lesson here is simple: the more intransigent your market, the more crowded your marketplace, the busier your customers, the more you need the Purple Cow. Half-measures will fail. Overhauling the product by making dramatic improvements in things the right customers care about can have a big payoff.

13. THE MAGIC CYCLE OF THE COW

In this chaotic world, must your efforts to bring new ideas to the marketplace be chaotic as well? To be successful, do companies need to continually invent remarkable products for an ever-changing roster of potential customers?

The answer is no, and the reason is because many consumers don't change their roles very often. Sneezers love to talk about new products, and they are often open to hearing from marketers who repeatedly, reliably create Purple Cows. And if we respect the sneezers, they will listen.

Four Steps to Creating a Purple Cow

Take these four steps to accomplish this:

- Get permission from people you impressed the first time to alert them the next time you might have another Purple Cow.
- Work with the sneezers to make it easier for them to help your idea reach your target audience. Give them the tools and the story they will need to sell your idea.
- Once you've progressed from remarkable product to profitable business, let a different team take over. Try to create many variations of your Purple Cow product. But don't believe your own press releases—this will cause the inevitable downward slide to mediocrity. Milk your Purple Cow for all it's worth, and fast!
- Reinvest and launch another Purple Cow—to the same audience. Fail and fail and fail again. Assume that what was remarkable the first time won't be remarkable this time.

14. WHAT IT MEANS TO BE A MARKETER TODAY

If Purple Cow is now one of the Ps of marketing, it has profound implications for the enterprise: it changes the definition of marketing.

It used to be that engineering invented, manufacturing built, marketing marketed, and sales sold. There was a clear division of labor, and the president managed the whole company. The marketer got a budget and bought ads with it.

Marketing was about communicating the values of a product after it had been developed and manufactured.

The Act of Inventing the Product

That's clearly not a valid strategy in today's world, where product attributes (everything from service to design) are now at the heart of what it means to be a marketer. These days, marketing is the act of inventing the product; the effort of designing it; the craft of producing it; the art of picturing it; and the technique of selling it. So how can a Purple Cow company not be run by a marketer?

Companies that create Purple Cows—companies like JetBlue, Starbucks, Hasbro, and Poland Spring—have to be run by marketers. The CEO of JetBlue made one critical decision when the company began: he got the head of marketing involved in product design and training, and it shows. Everything JetBlue does that adds value is marketing.

Isn't the same true for a local restaurant? In a world where just about anything we need is available and satisfying, and where just about all the profit comes from the Purple Cow, we're all marketers!

If a company is failing, it is the fault of top-level management, and the problem is probably this: they're running a company, not marketing a product.

15. IS IT ABOUT PASSION?

The idea of having passion in our efforts to create remarkable new products appeals to many of us, but the skeptics among us think that passion thing is unrealistic. They don't care about passion, about the why of creating Purple Cows—they just want to do what's going to work.

And that's an important point about the Purple Cow. You don't have to like it; you don't have to be a new-product guru; you don't have to be a make-work-matter apostle. You just have to realize that nothing else is working.

Purple Cow Thinking

The well-known companies have shown that this is true. The big brands, the big successes, the profitable start-ups (big and small, worldwide and local) have mostly been about Purple Cow products and services.

You don't need passion to create a Purple Cow, and you don't need a lot of creativity. What you do need is the insight to realize that you have no other choice but to grow your business or launch your product with Purple Cow thinking. Nothing else is going to work.

16. SALT IS NOT BORING—WAYS TO BRING THE COW TO WORK

For fifty years, Morton has made salt a boring product. People at the company's headquarters would happily agree there is no chance of a Purple Cow at Morton.

The people in France who create handmade salt from seawater didn't know that. They regularly get $20 a pound for their amazing salt. A group of Hawaiians has entered the salt business as well, providing new varieties used in gourmet restaurants. And previously boring Diamond Kosher salt will earn millions of dollars in increased annual sales—because their salt tastes better on food.

Come Up with a List

Is your product more boring than salt? Probably not. So come up with a list of ten ways to change the product (not the hype) to make it appeal to a segment of your audience.

- *Think small.* One remnant of the TV-industrial complex is the need to think "mass." If it doesn't appeal to everyone, the thinking goes, it's not worth it. That's no longer true. Think of the smallest conceivable market and describe a product that overwhelms it with its "remarkability"
- *Outsource.* If the factory is giving you a hard time about jazzing up the product, go elsewhere. There are plenty of job shops that would be delighted to take on your product. After it works, the factory will probably be happy to take the product back.
- *Build and use a permission asset.* Once you have the ability to talk directly to your most loyal customers, it becomes much easier to develop and sell amazing things.
- *Copy, not from your industry, but from any other industry.* Find an industry more dull than yours, discover who's remarkable in it, and do what it did.
- *Identify a competitor who's generally regarded as "at the edges," and outdo it.* Whatever it is known for, do that thing even better.
- *Ask, "Why not?"* Almost everything you don't do is the result of fear or inertia or a historical lack of someone asking, "Why not?"

DON'T THINK PINK
by Lisa Johnson and Andrea Learned

Advertising is the most insidious form of mass media in its portrayal of wives and mothers . . . women seem to be obsessed with cleanliness, placing above-normal emphasis on whiteness, brightness and expressing a gamut of emotions at smelling the kitchen floor or the family wash."

This excerpt from a UN report on the status of women was quoted in a Soundview Executive Book Summary of 1983's *The Moving Target: What Every Market Should Know About Women* by Rena Bartos (The Free Press, 1983). The report dated from the 1970s and deplored the stereotypical portrayal of women in advertising.

Unfortunately, little has changed. For many products, gender-specific marketing as seen in television advertising continues to be stereotypical, borderline insulting, and decades behind the times. Despite the participation of most husbands in such household chores as doing laundry and cleaning the house, it is still always two pretty young moms comparing soccer T-shirts to reveal how the new and improved detergent being advertised can make even tough grass stains disappear! And beer commercials are more and more tailor-made for hormone-crazed, puerile teenage boys. (Where have you gone, Bob Uecher?)

Gender-specific marketing is still appropriate, of course, for products that are unambiguously gender-specific. But here again, marketers have shown a surprising lack of imagination in how to engage and convince women and men to buy their products—especially women, according to marketing experts Lisa Johnson and Andrea Learned. Many marketers still seem to believe that they can reach women simply by creating pastel-colored products with hearts and flowers on them.

What should marketers do differently? The principal advice given by Johnson and Learned, co-founders of the marketing consultancy ReachWomen, is encapsulated in the title of their book *Don't Think Pink*.

Don't put flowers on the package and be satisfied that you will reach women. Instead, companies can choose one of three types of marketing to speak to women consumers: visible marketing, which is clearly addressed to women; transparent marketing, which is not explicitly aimed at women but is inspired by their needs and preferences; and a hybrid of the two. Transparent marketing is illustrated by the efforts of Sherwin-Williams to make paint easier to handle through its "Twist & Pour" square plastic container. The plastic container doesn't come in pink with the label "FOR WOMEN!" on it. Everyone benefits from the lighter weight, the twist top, and the built-in side handle.

As Sherwin-Williams and other examples in the book demonstrate, creative thinking is the key to addressing the needs of those who are buying the bulk of household purchases. Thinking pink is not good enough.

After earning a degree in English from the University of Oregon, Lisa Johnson developed her marketing skills in the sporting goods industry. Over the years, she created innovative ways to research the needs and desires of women consumers—and helped companies translate that research into profitable products. In 2000, Johnson co-founded ReachWomen, a marketing consultancy specializing in marketing to women, especially those in the eighteen-to-thirty-five-year-old age group.

Andrea Learned co-founded ReachWomen with Lisa Johnson before moving to Vermont, where she is now an independent consultant, lecturer, and writer on women's marketing issues.

DON'T THINK PINK
What Really Makes Women Buy—and How to Increase Your Share of This Critical Market
by Lisa Johnson and Andrea Learned

CONTENTS

THE SUMMARY IN BRIEF

Women are making more money and more purchases than ever before and, as a result, they are an economic force that marketers need to harness. However, you can no longer "think pink" by assuming that all women are the same and all they want are pastel-colored products with hearts and flowers on them. Generational experiences, lifestyle choices, transitional events, and demographic characteristics combine to define the filters through which women make buying choices. With so much money ready to be spent, marketers cannot afford to get it wrong. By examining the different ways women think and how companies can engage women with visible and transparent marketing campaigns, the authors show marketers how to stop thinking pink and start working in partnership with women to determine what they want. Women are willing and able to help you improve your products and services. You just need to get the proper information and then present it to the appropriate consumers.

THE COMPLETE SUMMARY

1. BEYOND "THINKING PINK"

Women's roles in society and their effects on the economy have shifted greatly in the past few decades, but marketers' perceptions have not necessarily caught up. Skimping on research and working from outmoded data and stereotypes lead to pink products (pastels, flowers, or "lighter" versions of the original) that don't connect with today's savvy and empowered women.

To connect with women today, consider the following:

1. *Earning power.* Women now earn $1 trillion a year due to a shrinking wage gap, earn more advanced degrees and a larger percentage of household income than ever before, are growing in number as business owners, and, surprisingly, control 51 percent of the private wealth in the United States.
2. *Spending power.* Even greater is women's spending power, estimated at about $2 trillion a year. Women are responsible for the bulk of household purchases, and between purchasing managers and small business owners, they also control a great deal of corporate spending.
3. *Run the numbers.* Companies who have assumed that their primary market is men may be surprised to find that women are now the majority of their customers. Establish the facts about who actually buys your products.
4. *Mainstream and integrate.* Don't let knowledge about women's preferences and buying behaviors languish in the marketing department. Make sure the whole company is aware of this large and varied market.

5. *Reframe approach.* Do not assume women are a nonproductive market because you are not marketing to them successfully. Consider whether your market desires a visible campaign that is directed unquestionably toward women, a more sophisticated transparent campaign that tailors the message for women without specifically labeling the product "for women," or a hybrid campaign that combines the two.

6. *Go inside her mind.* Understand the biological, neurological, and behavioral variations between male and female brains. Women take in and retain more information when walking into a room, they are more verbal, and they seek more human connections.

7. *Segment and focus.* Today's women have been shaped by a diverse set of experiences. Don't be lulled into looking at the average income and spending of the whole group, or you will miss lucrative growth segments.

8. *Listen in new ways.* Make women your marketing partners and you will discover what they want. They are good at articulating how a product or service might work better for them.

9. *Measure ROI.* If focusing on women represents a new commitment for your company, measure return on investment (ROI) to support the business case for increased budgets, staffing power, and programming tailored to women.

10. *Carpe diem.* Companies are only beginning to understand the importance of moving away from pink thinking. Gain a competitive advantage and spur growth by leading the charge and starting now.

2. NOW YOU SEE "HER"

The two main approaches to marketing to consumers of either gender are *visible* campaigns (directly calling out "for women" or "for men") and *transparent* campaigns (delivering a product that works with a gender's information gathering and purchasing processes, but that doesn't single it out as a special group). Plus, a third or *hybrid* approach combines the two. Each option can be highly effective in reaching women in particular. The success of one approach or another depends on the product or service, the profiles of core women customers, and how they want to be reached.

Some products just demand language and imagery that are clearly directed toward women. One example of a successful visible campaign is that of the Venus razor by the Gillette Co. Wachovia used a visible campaign when it created an online retirement calculator for women that factored in their longer lives and years outside the workforce.

Hybrid Campaigns

In a hybrid campaign, the overall marketing effort might remain transparent, but certain products or elements are more visibly focused on women and their distinct needs. Home Depot's "Do It Herself" workshops promote a visible element within an overall transparent campaign.

Rejuvenating Effects toothpaste is a product that represents the hybrid approach to marketing to women. Developed as a product within Procter & Gamble's Crest line, it is promoted as the first toothpaste targeted specifically to women using the slogan "For a radiant smile, today's new beauty secret."

Beware if a visible approach, either on its own or as part of a hybrid approach, reinforces outdated stereotypes of women and their preferences for the sake of a marketing pitch, or you will turn off both men and women alike.

VISIBLY MARKETING NUTRITION FOR WOMEN

Well-executed visible marketing streamlines women's buying minds. Media coverage of nutrition and diet has increased greatly in the past decade, and everything from breakfast cereal to energy bars provides opportunities to tap into women's understanding that they need more vital nutrients, such as calcium and iron, in their diets.

It is well documented that diet is instrumental in preventing osteoporosis, heart disease, and cancer. At the same time, it is important to accommodate women's busy lives by finding quick ways to fit nutrition into their routine. Companies that talk to women early on in the development process can zero in on their concerns and create products that:

• Provide a good portion of each day's calcium requirement to prevent osteoporosis.

• Contain added nutrients and soy protein to boost protection against heart disease.

• Use promotional copy that espouses the product's essential nutrients specifically for a woman's diet.

• Maintain their established logo and brand, but possibly include a female graphic element.

• Package the product to reflect a woman's mobile life—for example, individually wrapped portions or smaller containers.

When assessing the value of a visible campaign for reaching your market, consider how connected to a woman's specific realities, such as body shape and health, your product or service may be, and how her emotions around those topics may affect her purchase. Golf clubs reengineered for a woman's smaller grip, swing, and size is a case where a visible approach is the best choice.

3. NOW YOU DON'T (SEE "HER")

Transparent marketing requires more sophistication and in-depth knowledge of your market. It requires making changes in your product and marketing that are inspired by women, but are appreciated by everyone. Though transparent marketing takes more work, it builds brand loyalty and increases sales in a way that a visible campaign can't. As more and more women realize that you pay attention to their preferences, there will be less need for the "for women" tag line. You will provide intuitive solutions and take the hassle out of buying for everyone. There is no need to be insincere, sappy, or sexist in an effort to research or use your newly found information. Women will respond to an appropriate message.

Keys to Transparent Marketing

To create a transparent campaign, you should:

1. *Narrow your focus.* Women are so diverse that you will dilute your message by trying to appeal to everyone. Determine which segment across ages, life stages, or cultures is the best fit for your product.
2. *Understand the customer community.* Intimately know what influences your customers' community. Consider the routines, thoughts, stresses, hopes, desires, and belief structures female customers encounter daily.
3. *Build customer feedback into your process.* Don't wait until a product is practically on the shelf to get feedback. Work from the beginning to market with women instead of to them.
4. *Focus on your product's context.* Have your product show up in your customer's life at key scenarios or life stages. Get it in the doctor's office or the mailbox just when the customer will need it.
5. *Understand and define your brand.* Let your brand's spirit stand out. Don't allow your brand to become bland and blend in with all the others. Capture women's attention and get the buzz started with their friends by promoting your brand's uniqueness.
6. *Be authentic.* Share your brand's strengths and weaknesses. Those you want to reach will appreciate your honesty and trust the people behind your brand.

TRANSPARENCY IN HOME IMPROVEMENT

Here is how the home improvement industry instituted transparent marketing to reflect the emergence of women as core customers:

1. *Narrow your focus.* In 2003, Lowe's found that 80 percent of women do "everyday fix-it" projects around the house. This and similar research showed that women should receive more focus from the home improvement industry.

2. *Understand the customer community.* Women do not have the time or patience to wait for husbands or handymen to fix problems. The industry did not go visibly pink, but designed innovative products and solutions that are easier for everyone to use, such as Sherwin-Williams Dutch Boy paint with its "Twist & Pour" square plastic container, twist top, built-in side handle, and no-drip spout.

3. *Build customer feedback into your process.* Large home improvement stores all offer do-it-yourself (DIY) classes. Women learn how to tile floors and companies get feedback about women's needs.

4. *Focus on your product's context.* Women are information hungry and visually oriented. Craftsman Tools targets female buyers with detailed photo displays, and Ace retail stores feature in-store libraries of how-to information on household projects.

5. *Understand and define your brand.* Home improvement has become a cool, empowering hobby and the industry's stores are now weekend destinations. Entertainment extensions like the hit TV show *Trading Spaces* and interactive how-to seminars foster that perception.

6. *Be authentic.* Women do not want to be condescended to or ignored when standing in the aisles of a local retailer. The home improvement industry has approached women as the DIYers they are and reflects a true commitment to helping them understand what to do and how to do it.

---

4. INSIDE A WOMAN'S MIND

Men and women *do* think differently. Gender-specific brain differences have a profound effect on the way information is absorbed, processed, and retained. Here are a few differences in the ways male and female brains process information:

1. *A woman's brain synergy.* Women have more dendritic connections than men and more connecting tissue, allowing them to transfer data between the brain's right and left hemispheres faster. This may be why it is easier for women to compile diverse input and come to a decision. They are also more in touch with their feelings and better able to express them. Marketers must understand

that every interaction matters, that women notice inconsistencies in messages, and that human connections are key to attracting them.

2. *A woman's observational skills.* Women can take in information on many levels, and typically absorb a much greater amount of it from their environments than men do. Give women incredible detail to absorb and digest. Your brand needs to be everywhere, including her peripheral vision.

3. *A woman's sense of discovery.* Women would rather do front-end research and then go straight to the one product that meets their needs. The prepurchase process is much more important to them than it is to men, because that's when women ask their questions and eliminate potential mistakes and time wasters. Support women's inquisitive nature, provide basic benefits and features, and plug into women's ongoing education.

4. *A woman's sense of values.* Women often incorporate their values into their shopping habits. Select messages and images that speak to your customers' values, and connect women to each other around your brand. Make improving a woman's life your brand's context: simplify her life by saving her time.

5. *A woman's communication style.* Women communicate to build bonds and forge relationships based on mutual values and interests. Avoid overautomation, focus on relationship-building opportunities (one-on-one experiences), and facilitate story sharing.

How Women Buy

Smart marketers not only know how women think, but they also know how they buy.

First, *women develop and use smart shopping skills.* Create a sales culture committed to helping consumers determine the best choice, not closing the quickest sale.

Women are constituent-driven decision makers. They set priorities according to the needs of those most dear to them, so identify ways they can support family members with purchases.

Women seek ongoing relationships and insider information. A woman's first research step is to turn to a trustworthy, unbiased source who already owns and uses the product, so provide pass-along devices (online and print) to support personal networks.

Finally, *women comparison shop.* They gather data through reading and research, so provide comparisons of your product's features against competitors.

5. SHAPING THE GENERATIONS

There are many ways to segment the women's market, but a good way to start is by considering the events that have shaped the lives of the different generations that make up the market.

The Generations

Generation	Born	Age in 2003	Estimated Population	Estimated Women Population
Y	1980 – 1997	6 – 23	74.2 million	36.2 million
X	1965 – 1979	24 – 38	62.1 million	30.8 million
Baby Boomer	1945 – 1964	39 – 58	80.2 million	40.8 million
Mature	Before 1945	59+	50.7 million	28.7 million

Generation Y Women

Generation Y grew up with the personal computer and the Internet. Gen Y women are well educated and now outnumber men in college and graduate schools. Their role models are their prosperous boomer parents, and they expect a lot from brands. The Gen Y woman's view of your brand is influenced by her characteristics: She is optimistic, technology savvy, a doer, entitled, multicultural, individualistic, education-focused, socially conscious, confused and stressed, independent yet collaborative, and entrepreneurial. She desires highly personalized offerings and appreciates opportunities for self-discovery and sharing, such as online communities.

Generation X

Though Generation Xers were once labeled slackers, they have matured and are far better described as entrepreneurial and practical. They grew up with the Vietnam War, the 1970s oil crisis, Watergate, *Roe v. Wade*, rising divorce rates, the release of the movie *Star Wars*, the PC revolution, and AIDS. Influencers that filter Gen X's views of life include a nontraditional upbringing, a gender-neutral outlook, a commitment to lifelong learning, technological savvy, self-indulgence, putting motherhood on hold, professional careers, and financial challenges.

They respond to hip humor, truthful advertising, and highly visual ads, and do research before making major purchases. They switch brands often, have environmental concerns, and prefer gender-neutral approaches.

Baby Boomers

Starting in 1996, over four million members of this group have turned age fifty, and this will continue for the next decade. These women grew up with the Cold War, the introduction of television, the Kennedy assassination, the Beatles, "the Pill," the Vietnam War, and Watergate. They went to college far more than the previous generation, and more boomer women work than women of the generations on either side of them. As they approach traditional retirement age, they don't necessarily expect to stop working. They have postponed marriage and divorced more than any previous generation.

Characteristics that affect their buying include their interests (not just their age), stress and time management, care giving, confidence and optimism, and their exercise and health. To reach them, forget senior discounts, support connectedness, promote youthful appearance, be a knowledge source, and get to the point.

Mature

Mature women span a large time frame and have diverse beliefs and experiences. Although the eighty-one million Americans over age fifty account for only 28 percent of the population, they represent 50 percent of total consumer demand, 65 percent of total net worth, and 70 percent of all personal financial assets. Their attitudes and lives were shaped by World War II, the rise of suburbia, the Korean War, and Elvis Presley.

Filters that affect their consumer behavior include selective indulgence, volunteerism and activism, embracing the Internet, and being energetic and active. To reach these women, speak to their lifestyles, not their age. They look to experts and authority figures, resent age-related adjectives, build human connection via interactivity, appreciate the personalized approach, and tap into intuition and emotion.

6. LOOKING BEYOND GENERATIONS

Beyond segmenting women by the generation they belong to, common cross-generational traits and roles in the course of their lives may carry even more weight.

Single Women

Greater career opportunity, higher divorce rates, and longer life expectancy have contributed to women living on their own for longer periods of their lives. By 2006, aggregate solo female income is estimated to reach almost $200 billion, up 20 percent from 2001. Single women are content and in control, they sometimes intentionally take on motherhood without a partner, and they have unconventional living arrangements. The filters that affect their buying include a redefinition of family, healthy lifestyles, living a spiritual journey, and empowerment. They respond to marketing messages that reflect their intelligence, honor their lifestyle choices, and affirm their self-esteem and independent spirit.

Businesswomen

Working women and female entrepreneurs wield a mighty economic influence because not only do they buy for work, but they incorporate information gathered from work purchasing in their home lives. In 2002, there were almost four million privately held 50 percent women-owned businesses generating $1.17 trillion in sales. Most working women juggle many responsibilities, so making their lives easier appeals to them.

Filters that affect businesswomen include brand loyalty, desire for customer service and training, efficient Web sites, combining personal and business buying, environmental and social responsibility, and hiring help to save time. To attract their business, promote the benefits of your product or service before price, develop products for both business and household use, offer product training, provide ways to speed through purchase, present full- and fast-service Web sites, integrate your retail experience, and fully utilize online channels.

Moms

Having children profoundly affects women's lifestyles. Their parenting styles segment mothers more than the ages of their children or traditional demographics. An average-income family will spend approximately $165,000 on a child by the time he or she reaches eighteen. Moms often choose to work even when they don't have to. Moms' buying filters are usually affected by one of two mothering styles: either traditional roles are followed and balanced with the modern need for women to be making a living, or women who did not plan their pregnancies, are perhaps unmarried, or are raising their children in a true partnership with the father innovate their child-rearing roles. No matter what kind of mothers they are, you must market to multitaskers, provide information over emotion, support their practical priorities, address their sense of balance and perspective, and educate them online.

THE FEMALE BUSINESS TRAVELER

Hotel chains are making changes to attract female business travelers, a fast-growing travel segment. Here are a few of the changes hotels have made:

• *Security.* Hotels have designed brighter lobbies, more open spaces, and tighter security to discourage intruders, because security is a primary concern of women travelers.

• *Food service.* Businesswomen actually prefer to eat in their rooms, so room layouts are more likely to accommodate meal trays, and the room service menu includes healthier and more nutritious options.

• *Design.* Hotels are being designed with a more residential feel and fewer dark and paneled decors. W Hotels host a "living room" instead of a lobby, with space for a single traveler to feel comfortable.

• *Extras.* From Wyndham's Herman Miller ergonomic work chairs and in-room Internet access to the Loews Vanderbilt Plaza Hotel's "do not forget" closet, many hotels are providing amenities for all business travelers. Others provide a technology butler for computer-related questions, in-room massage, and pet-friendly rooms.

7. CULTURAL INFLUENCERS

Another way to segment women is by ethnicity. Groups that were once thought of as minorities are now becoming emerging majorities. No matter the market, an in-culture marketing approach should be the ultimate goal. Consider cultures and dialects; variable acculturation; sensitivity to religion; and the importance of family, appearance, and language barriers.

Hispanic American Women

Between 1990 and 2000, the Hispanic population grew 58 percent and its buying power grows approximately 12 percent annually. These women have emigrated from many different countries, but no matter what their acculturation level or dialectical preferences, they generally have family and household purchases in mind. Families often include a broad range of relatives and generations, and shopping is often considered a family affair. Catholic holidays and traditions are also important. To attract this market's respect, and to reflect cultural and dialectical differences, show pulled-together fashion and makeup, remember family and children, tap into local celebrations, be online, and buy cable TV time.

Asian American Women

Asian American women come from cultures as diverse as Japan, Indonesia, and India, so they do not share the same language or religion. Their buying filters tend to revolve around community and children, and may reflect social status and roles of women in home cultures. The women are typically highly educated and often have their own businesses. Although they are very brand conscious, they are not necessarily brand loyal. To attract them, reflect the uniqueness of their different backgrounds, understand that images of success resonate, learn and honor culturally specific traditions, use familiar body types and skin colors, and don't overlook the fast-growing generation that as children immigrated to the United States with their parents.

Black Women

This emerging minority covers a broad range of dark-skinned ethnicities beyond African Americans. More black women go to college than do black men, and college-educated black women earn more money than the median for all black working men—and for all women. African American women handle more financial responsibility than women in general because they are less likely to be married.

Despite this, black women take in more than half of all children adopted by single women. Whether black women come from Africa, the Caribbean, or the United States, and whether they lived through segregation and the Civil Rights era, affect their view when making consumer purchases. To attract these women, demonstrate your commitment to their communities and church, value their lifestyles and cultural diversity, tap into their popular cultural interests, and reflect their use of media channels.

8. LEARNING CURVES AND LIFE STAGES

Life transitions such as having a baby or investing in stocks provide an excellent opportunity to build brand loyalty when there is a steep learning curve. These are the times when many new brand decisions are made.

The consumer's confidence level becomes a key issue in what she will choose to buy. Alienating either tentative or sophisticated buyers with the wrong level of information is a danger. Be certain to prepare several service levels to serve all the customers on your industry-confidence spectrum.

Tentative testers will ask for advice from friends and then do research on the Internet. Make sure that their friends are already aware of your brand and that it will be easy for newcomers to navigate your Web site and find information.

Confident consumers are interested in ways to speed through the buying process. Remove speed bumps that challenge their patience. For example, offer a "quick buy" link on your site for regular shoppers who have already given you their profile information.

To serve both ends of the confidence spectrum, ask where customers are in the buying/education process, provide a range of education, teach related skills, map key information points, and expand online options.

VALENTINE'S VARIATIONS

Asians are a diverse ethnic group with different traditions and holidays of which advertisers should be aware. One example is the different variations of St. Valentine's Day, a holiday that Americans celebrate by giving chocolates, flowers, and other presents to their loved ones.

In Japan, the holiday has been adapted as *Giri Choco,* which means "obligatory chocolate." It is a one-sided gift-giving tradition for females to buy chocolates for their boyfriend, husband, and male co-workers or classmates. One month later, on White Day, men who received the gifts must reciprocate, though with jewelry, candy, and flowers.

Korea observes the equivalent of White Day when women give men chocolate on Valentine's Day and men give women candy a month later.

Many Chinese follow the American tradition of Valentine's Day, but they also celebrate Lover's Day to commemorate a legendary love story about a young mortal cow herder and immortal weaving fairy who could not be together. On the seventh day of the seventh lunar month—the one day of the year the lovers are reunited—the Chinese will buy loved ones flowers and other gifts.

Life Transitions

Life transitions, such as going away to college, a career change, the birth of a child, or retirement, are important moments of brand reflection, consideration, and decision for customers. Therefore, they are important opportunities for marketers. People not only think about what they need, but they may reexamine how best to fulfill those needs.

Women usually make the buying decisions when navigating through change. Marketers must remember that traditional onetime events (such as marriage) are happening more often, timelines are shifting, and "mature" transitions are more frequent. For women experiencing a life transition, everything is new, including brand names, product categories, and price ranges. Marketers should help women get up to speed, tap into human relationships, create clarity through relevant associations with old experiences, group products and information into sets, become a trusted filter, and address multiple needs at once.

9. THE INTERNET-SAVVY WOMAN

Going online has become a way of life for women. To reach them, go where they already assemble. Women are 52 percent of the U.S. at-home Web population and they are online for both community and shopping.

How Do Women Use the Internet?

Women start using the Internet by experimenting with e-mail and quickly learn to incorporate e-mail and online research into their daily connections with family, friends, and businesses—making the Internet their tool and adviser.

Though women make or influence the bulk of consumer purchases in the United States today, they do not have much time to devote to traditional shopping. They are quickly becoming quite comfortable doing that online, so Web sites have to improve functionality and customer experience. With potential customers at all levels of Internet comfort, companies should address the following areas to better reach customers: connection speed, software download alternatives, navigation and viewing options, the human touch in customer service, and meeting customer needs via e-mail.

Shaping Online Views

Women's brand loyalty really hinges on both the product and the shopping experience. Success in serving women depends on meeting, if not exceeding, their expectations for an improved customer relationship. Women are so demanding of a good customer experience online that a bad experience will ruin their loyalty for the brand's offline channel as well. Because women do so much of their shopping online, it is worth it to invest some time and effort in avoiding costly mistakes.

Don't use guesswork and outdated stereotypes to decide what women want. Avoid flashy technology—women really want ease of use, solution-oriented content, and superior customer service when shopping. Don't send useless, self-serving e-mail, and don't ignore the integration of online and offline customer experiences. Also, companies must not waste the customer's time with poorly designed Web sites.

10. ONLINE RESEARCH

Because so many women are already online for research and shopping, work with them to learn more about what they want as consumers. To discover their true requirements, values, and preferences, you must:

- Sit back and observe. To learn about what attracts women online and keeps them there, look at popular Web sites like Dailycandy.com for ideas about hip and happening shopping and events, and Tickle.com for ideas about women's entertainment needs.
- Ask and see (through their eyes). Companies should use online polls, quizzes, surveys, feedback, promotions, and e-mail advisory boards to gather information about purchasing behaviors and customer needs.

When conducting online research, do pose questions in a fun, conversational tone; make it simple to sign in and get started; know the incentives that will inspire responses; express appreciation for participation; keep initial surveys or interactions brief; and use e-mail addresses only for your originally stated purpose. Don't ask for too much personal information; make your questions stiff or clinical; use e-mail addresses for spam; or abuse respondents' generosity by requesting feedback too often.

11. ENLISTING WOMEN AS YOUR MARKETING PARTNERS

If you ask them the right questions, women have an incredible ability to help you solve brand challenges for the products and services they purchase. Ask women and then listen to them carefully early in the development process of products, packaging, and marketing. Instead of using traditional focus groups, try having conversations in relaxed atmospheres; use a live talk-show format; tap into existing meetings of women's groups, such as book clubs, walking groups, or investment clubs; perform virtual listening by sharing online; ask industry insiders; get feedback; and review data.

Tips for joining conversations with women include:

- Encourage storytelling. Women use the context of stories to share vital information about the things that brands need to know.
- Use all your senses to listen. Pay attention to the energy level in the room and the conversation's content.
- Support the conversation through environment and context. Fun and relevant environments can do wonders to support authentic conversations.

- *Look at her holistically.* Women often view products and services as part of a solution or improvement that they will incorporate into their lives.
- *Use your best listeners.* When conducting research and listening to women, send marketers to listen to women who understand and enjoy the market, and who are clear on the objectives of your brand.

The biggest advances in learning from the conversations of women will come as companies use streamlined internal communication systems, such as an intranet and e-mail, to make the ongoing feedback from women available throughout their organizations in real time.

THE DISCIPLINE OF
MARKET LEADERS

by Michael Treacy and Fred Wiersema

What makes a good business book? The first answer is that the book presents something new, a new insight or a new methodology that is pertinent to the needs of businesspeople today. The second answer is that the book organizes or captures what people already know intuitively or from experience but have not seen presented in a cohesive, understandable way.

The subject of the next summary, *The Discipline of Market Leaders,* doesn't give the feeling that a revolutionary new insight has been revealed. What authors Michael Treacy and Fred Wiersema have done brilliantly In this bestseller is to organize all the intuitive reflections and observations about today's competitive world and about the needs and desires of today's consumers into one simple but insightful framework.

This simple framework begins with the premise that when customers buy their products, they focus on one of three types of value: operational excellence, product leadership, or customer intimacy. The authors call these the three "value disciplines."

The thesis of *The Discipline of Market Leaders* is that successful companies choose one of these value disciplines and become the best in that value discipline. These companies focus on either low prices, dependability, and convenience (operational excellence), the highest-performing products in their industry (product leadership), or close relationships with, and total solutions for, their customers (customer intimacy). While maintaining this intense focus on one value discipline, companies must also meet market expectations in the other disciplines; customer intimacy companies, for example, must be able to deliver good products or services at reasonable prices.

Beyond the framework, the authors offer their readers guidance on how to choose the value discipline that is most appropriate for their companies, and how to implement that value discipline.

Michael Treacy received an engineering degree from the University of Toronto and a Ph.D. from the MIT Sloan School of Management. Formerly a professor of management at MIT and a partner at CSC Index, an international management consultancy, Treacy is now chief strategist at GE3, a consulting firm he founded. In addition to *The Discipline of Market Leaders,* Treacy also wrote the bestseller *Double Digit Growth,* published in 2003.

Originally from the Netherlands, Fred Wiersema earned a Ph.D. from Harvard Business School and was a senior partner with CSC Index. He is the founder of The Customer Strategy Group LLC and the author of *Customer Intimacy,* a follow-up to *The Discipline of Market Leaders,* and *The New Market Leaders.*

THE DISCIPLINE OF MARKET LEADERS
Choose Your Customers, Narrow Your Focus, Dominate Your Market
by Michael Treacy and Fred Wiersema

CONTENTS

THE SUMMARY IN BRIEF

Why are some companies so much better at serving their customers than others? Why, for example, can Wal-Mart continue to offer the absolute lowest prices while prices everywhere else are climbing? Why is great coffee available for a dollar at Starbucks but not at airport concession stands that still sell instant coffee from jars? Why can you get patient help from a Home Depot clerk when you're buying a $2.70 box of screws, but you can't get help from IBM's direct-order service when you're buying a $2,700 computer?

The answer: focus.

Market leaders don't try to be everything to everyone. They know that different customers place greater value on different things. Some customers want price and convenience. Others are looking for state-of-the-art products. Others are looking for partners and solutions.

The market leaders are the ones who have chosen to excel in one of the customer "value disciplines": best cost, best product, or best solution. It's not as easy as it sounds. Focus means knowing:

- Which customer value discipline to choose.
- How to design your entire organization around one particular customer value while still maintaining appropriate standards in the other areas of customer value.
- How to offer better value year after year to avoid losing your leadership.

In this summary you'll meet market leaders who became the best in their value discipline. You'll discover how they did it. You'll learn how to turn your company into a market leader for your industry.

And, maybe, you'll finally understand why Lands' End can remember your last order and family members' sizes while American Express still tries to get you to join—even when you've been a member for ten years.

THE COMPLETE SUMMARY
1. CUSTOMERS WANT DIFFERENT KINDS OF VALUE

Despite the extraordinary number of diverse companies and industries, all customers fall into one of only three different categories.

For one category of customers, the most important value of a product is its performance. There's a limit to how much they will pay, of course, but price is not the most important consideration.

For a second category of customers, the most important value is personalized service and advice. Once again, price is a consideration (no one wants to overpay), but it's not the driving force behind their choice of product or service. They prefer to pay a little more to receive better attention.

For a third category of customers, the cost of a product is the primary consideration. Total cost begins with price but doesn't end there. Customers don't want to pay a very low price initially only to have the product cost them in the long run because of constant repairs. The total cost refers to how much customers will pay for the entire time that they own the product. Thus, dependability is as much a component of low cost as is initial price.

In sum, value for different customers means different things. The question for business is how to excel at fulfilling the value expectations of all of the different customers.

The answer: don't try.

The New Rules of Competition

Different customer-value offerings demand different operational processes, different priorities, and different resources. It is therefore impossible for any one company, no matter how large, to commit operations and strategy to more than one value offering. Choose one, and design your company so that it is committed to providing that value.

On the other hand, you must maintain an appropriate level of customer value in the other value dimensions, or the value you have chosen will be sabotaged. Product performance, for example, can't be completely ignored just because you excel at offering purchasing advice. Home Depot goes to great lengths to help customers choose the right hammer. But if the hammer breaks two days later, that helpful advice means nothing.

Likewise, the highest product performance is useless without some consideration of price. The fanciest computers in the world won't get off store shelves if customers can't afford them.

Another danger once you've achieved excellence in a value offering is the temptation to rest on your laurels. To keep your leadership, continuously improve your performance in your chosen customer value.

These are the new rules of competition:

- Provide the best offering by committing to one customer value.
- Design the entire operations of your company to fulfill that commitment.
- Maintain appropriate standards in the other values.
- Improve year after year.

CUSTOMER VALUE VS. CORE COMPETENCE

Focusing on one type of customer value is not the same as focusing on core competencies. Two companies can use the same competencies in very different ways.

Both Honda and Briggs & Stratton have core competencies in small engines. Briggs & Stratton chooses to focus on delivering the lowest-priced engines. Honda focuses instead on offering innovative products. This allows Honda to break into a broad range of different markets, from motorcycles to cars to generators.

2. WHAT IS A VALUE DISCIPLINE?

A company's ability to fulfill the expectations of customers is called its "value discipline." The three value disciplines correspond to the three different types of customer expectations. Market leaders beat the competition by focusing on one of three value disciplines: operational excellence, product leadership, and customer intimacy.

■ **Operational Excellence.** The first value discipline is *operational excellence*. Operationally excellent companies fulfill the expectations of customers who demand the best total cost from their products. To achieve the best total cost for their customers, operationally excellent companies must provide low prices, dependability, and convenience. These companies are not product or service innovators, nor do they cultivate one-to-one relationships with their customers.

The key strength of operationally excellent companies is that they execute well. Their manufacturing, delivery, and service systems are kept running smoothly to ensure convenience and the lowest prices. McDonald's is a prototypical operationally excellent company.

VALUE DISCIPLINES TRANSCEND INDUSTRIES

When describing value disciplines, the industries in which companies compete are irrelevant. Customer-intimate companies will have the same characteristics and goals whether or not they are in the same industry.

For example, Home Depot sells screws to do-it-yourselfers, while Cable & Wireless sells international telecommunications to businesses. The two companies have different products, customers, distribution channels, suppliers, and all of the other traditional business components.

But they share value disciplines, and as a result they have similar operational priorities and strategic goals. They seek, for example, to understand and know the customer before trying to sell a product. And they will take a short-term "hit" (e.g., offering something free) in return for a long-term relationship.

Companies in different industries sharing value disciplines have more in common than companies in the same industry with different value disciplines. The systems and corporate culture of Nordstrom and Wal-Mart, for example, are very different despite both being large retail chains.

■ **Product Leadership.** The second value discipline is *product leadership*. Product leaders offer customers the highest-performing products in their industry. They are continuously innovating, leading their industries in establishing and then redefining the state of the art. At the same time, they seek to offer competitive pricing levels.

The key strengths of product leaders are invention, product development, and market exploitation. They know how to make something new, and they know how to sell it. (The ability to make innovation salable is a driving force behind the rise to dominance of product leaders from Japan.) Sony, whose groundbreaking products include the Walkman and the minicamcorder, exemplifies the product leader.

■ **Customer Intimacy.** The third value discipline is *customer intimacy.* Customer-intimate companies develop close relationships with their customers and seek to offer total solutions to their problems. Personalized service and advice are the key components of this value discipline.

A customer-intimate company won't have the best or highest-performing products. But it will ensure that customers get exactly everything they want and need. Roadway Logistics Systems, which takes on responsibilities such as warehousing and freight management on behalf of its clients, is one example of a customer-intimate company.

WHY CHOOSE?

Y ou might think that your company doesn't need to choose one value discipline over another. You might insist, "We're good at all three disciplines."

Look again. Companies that aim at all three disciplines don't excel. They are merely mediocre across the board. Your company may be competent. It may still be active in its industry. But is it offering anything—product, price, service— better than everyone else in the industry?

The Operating Model

To succeed in a value discipline, you must design the company so that all of its inner workings—operating processes, business structure, management systems, and culture—are coordinated and focused on fulfilling the chosen customer value.

These inner workings, called "operating models," differ with each value discipline. Operationally excellent companies design their operations to ensure dependability in product supply and hassle-free customer service.

Product leaders' operating systems center around invention (bureaucratic processes, for example, are eliminated to encourage innovation), product development, and market exploitation. The processes of customer-intimate companies give employees freedom to adapt to customer needs and requests, and resources to implement solutions.

3. THE DISCIPLINE OF OPERATIONAL EXCELLENCE: OFFER THE BEST TOTAL COST DEAL

Operationally excellent companies offer customers one thing: the lowest possible cost of a product.

For traditional operationally excellent companies, best cost meant lowest price—finding a way to manufacture and distribute a product cheaper in order to sell it cheaper. Today, offering the lowest cost is more complex.

FORD: PIONEER OF OPERATIONAL EXCELLENCE

Henry Ford can be considered the father of operational excellence. His company had only one purpose: delivering an acceptable product at the lowest price.

Ford established an underlying principle still applicable today: variety kills efficiency. Everything at the Ford Motor Company was controlled, standardized, and proceduralized. Standard parts and standard procedures reduced costs and eliminated mistakes. As for customer-tailored products, Henry Ford said it best: "You can choose any color you want, as long as it's black."

Tangible and Intangible Costs

The total cost of a product cannot be measured solely at the time of purchase. It must include the cost to the customer during the life of the product. A cheap product that breaks the next day costs more than a more expensive product that lasts a year.

Taking a defective product to be repaired, or buying a new product, not only costs the customer money. It also costs the customer time. Although intangible, the loss of time adds to the total cost of a product. Customers may feel that they are getting a better deal by paying a little more for an item that takes less time to purchase or doesn't require return trips to the store.

Convenience—the delivery of quick, dependable service—is a related intangible item. Customers don't believe aggravation offsets any reduction in price.

The Transaction Environment

Customers of operationally excellent companies want to buy products at the lowest price quickly and conveniently. All of the internal processes and corporate attitudes—the operating model—should be geared to offering flawless transactions.

For example, streamline the customer transaction process. Eliminate time-consuming processes, such as filling out forms, during the purchase of the product or service. Hertz, for example, makes sure all required processes are handled before or after you pick up your car. The result: no more lines.

Vertical vs. Virtual Integration

Supply and distribution systems are very important to operationally competent companies. Henry Ford ensured efficiency by vertical integration—controlling through ownership the entire manufacturing-to-sales process.

THE AT&T UNIVERSAL CARD

AT&T burst onto the crowded credit card scene in March 1990. In two years, its Universal Card Services business unit turned a profit—way ahead of schedule. And today it is the second-largest banking card in the United States.

AT&T succeeded by following the tenets of an operationally competent company.

First, when the card was introduced, its price was lower than that of any other card on the market. Not only was it free, but it also boasted low interest rates.

Second, AT&T ensured no-hassle service. Customers were angry with other cards for poor service that included surly phone representatives, lengthy and often inaccurate processes for standard changes such as change of address, and complicated procedures for the replacement of stolen cards.

AT&T streamlined the process for handling customer inquiries. Cards to new customers were in the mail in three days. And customer service representatives were trained to treat problems such as change of address immediately by phone.

The key to good service: standard operating procedures practiced over and over again by employees. Every situation has a standard procedure with which every company employee is familiar.

But AT&T hasn't stood still. It is constantly improving and polishing those operating procedures to cut costs for itself and cut hassle for its customers.

Today, companies don't usually own suppliers but work with them as partners. The pioneers of these types of supplier relationships were Wal-Mart and one of its principal suppliers, Procter & Gamble. Product flows between P&G and Wal-Mart more smoothly than between internal departments of many companies. Purchase authorizations, receipt notifications, and other intracompany red tape have been eliminated. The result: smoother distribution, greater dependability, and lower prices.

4. THE DISCIPLINE OF PRODUCT LEADERSHIP: TURN INVENTION INTO BREAKTHROUGH PRODUCT

Product leaders are inventive companies. They bring to the market a product or service never offered before. And then they go back to their offices and start trying to invent something even better.

Product performance is the key value that customers expect from product leaders.

Performance can be measured in utilitarian terms. High-performance products fulfill a task in the most efficient manner. The Sony Walkman, for example, does not offer the best sound or the nicest look. But it allows people to listen to music while doing something outdoors, such as jogging.

Performance can also be measured in terms of gratification. Swatches, for example, are not any more efficient at telling time than ordinary watches. But their design turned a utilitarian tool into a fashion statement.

DON'T FAKE IT

Product leaders don't tinker with a product, such as redesigning the package, and then declare that it's "new and improved." Consumers aren't fooled.

Nabisco repackaged its Oreo cookie line to include mini Oreos, Double Stuff Oreos, larger and smaller packs of Oreos, and seasonal packs of Oreos. Consumers reacted indifferently.

When Nabisco finally introduced a truly new cookie, the SnackWell line of "healthy" cookies, it became the bestselling cookie in America.

Vision: A Target for Dreams

How do product leaders operate? While operationally excellent companies emphasize procedures, product leaders emphasize the imagination. They'll worry about pricing or distribution issues later. First on the agenda: dreaming up a new, better-performing product.

The term *dreaming* can be misleading, since it connotes something elusive, never to be fulfilled. Product leaders shun this airy attitude. They are not interested in dreams; they are interested in products. Dreaming is useless without the ability to turn those dreams into reality.

Product leaders harness aimless dreaming by setting ambitious but clear targets. They use a process called right-to-left thinking. First they imagine something. Then they work backwards to find out how to achieve what was imagined. Product leaders, in other words, begin with a vision and then try to turn that vision into reality.

Product-Leader People

The talent to imagine an ideal and the ability to turn that ideal into reality are the attributes of people at product-leading companies. The combination is not always easy to find. Product leaders search the world's leading universities seeking technically competent people who are also creative and versatile.

And they must be able to work in teams. Today, innovation is no longer the domain of lonely inventors working in dimly lit labs. Manufacturable and marketable products usually emerge from cross-functional teams made up of gifted but idiosyncratic people.

To keep their people on track toward a new development, managers of product-leading companies:

1. Organize the work in sets of clear challenges. They put milestones on the path to success so that employees have cause for celebration on the way.
2. Don't create business structures that oppress. Heavy bureaucracy doesn't lend itself to invention. Product leaders break people up into teams or clusters.
3. Emphasize cross-functional procedures in the later stages of product development. Product leaders don't want to discover too late that an engineer's design can't be manufactured, or that it's not what customers wanted. The answer: coordinated efforts involving the research and development, production, and marketing departments to catch potential problems.

INTEL INSIDE: STORY OF A PRODUCT LEADER

Intel has one mission: outwit the competition year after year by introducing microprocessors more advanced than any currently on the market.

The success of past years means that Intel is in effect constantly trying to outperform its own products. Its current bestselling Pentium chip (glitches notwithstanding) is an improvement on its fourth-generation 486 chip, which itself improved on its third-generation 386 chip.

Another key to Intel's success is targeted innovation. Intel's people aren't just left to dream in any direction they want. Their job is to create machines that will solve the problems of the future.

"When people talk about classic innovation, I always think of 3M," says Gerry Parker, general manager of Intel's Technology and Manufacturing Group. "People at 3M are geared to invent one crazy thing after another. We are essentially innovating to solve a very specific problem, not just any problem. We're not a think tank of innovation for its own sake. We're making a product."

---

5. THE DISCIPLINE OF CUSTOMER INTIMACY: BECOME YOUR CUSTOMER'S PARTNER

Customer-intimate companies don't offer their customers the very latest in product innovations. Nor do they offer the lowest prices. Customer-intimate companies go beyond product and price to offer the best total solutions to their customers' problems. In the end, these solutions offer a better value for the customer than lower prices or fancier products.

For example, if customers do not know how to use the product effectively, or lack skills necessary to achieve optimal results in their industries, the value of low-priced or advanced products will be eroded.

Typically, customer-intimate companies help customers get the most from their products.

They begin by offering a range of services from hands-on help to education. Customer-intimate retailers such as Home Depot and Nordstrom have knowledgeable and caring salespeople who patiently work with customers to ensure that their purchases fulfill their needs and expectations.

Customer-intimate service companies offer personalized service solutions and customize products to meet unique customer needs. Cable & Wireless offers telecommunications service features for its small business clients that can't be obtained from MCI.

Business Partners

When possible, customer-intimate companies go further by becoming deeply involved in the customer's business processes. Cott Corporation, for example, makes soda for retailers to sell under their own labels. However, Cott does not only provide the beverage. It also provides know-how and experience to help retailers manage, market, and sell all of their private-label products.

The most intimate of the customer-intimate companies will take on personal responsibilities for certain aspects of their customer's business. Baxter International, for example, supplies medical equipment for hospitals. Rather than simply trying to sell equipment on a transaction basis, Baxter becomes a hospital's supply manager. Taking full responsibility for coordinating inventory and logistics, Baxter ensures that the supply of equipment to the hospital is dependable and cost-efficient.

The main requirement for customer-intimate companies to be successful is that they have a thorough knowledge of their customer's business, including its business processes. These companies are experts not only in the manufacture of their products, but in the use of their products in the customer's business area.

Cott Corporation, for example, not only knows about the manufacturing and bottling of soda, but also is an expert in supermarket management.

AIRBORNE EXPRESS: FLYING HIGH

Airborne Express isn't the biggest overnight express company. UPS and Federal Express are bigger. But despite the intense competition from its two large and highly competent rivals, Airborne Express is the fastest-growing company in the industry.

The secret of its success: unlike the other two, Airborne Express has chosen to focus on offering customer-tailored service. Federal Express, an operationally excellent company, promises to "absolutely, positively" get your package to its destination on time. And it delivers on its promise.

But Airborne Express goes beyond this promise. It will work with its customers to design a schedule—no matter how demanding—and then will create a delivery system that fits the requirements of that schedule.

For example, Xerox needed delivery times across the U.S. that ranged from 8 A.M. to 9:30 A.M. Airborne Express instituted a system that responds to Xerox's needs and more, allowing, for example, overnight shipment on very short notice.

The system tailor-made for Xerox includes coding containers that carry Xerox material and coding the beepers of drivers so they know when a Xerox delivery is involved. Drivers then prioritize their route so that the Xerox delivery comes first.

Airborne Express is able to offer such service without shortchanging other customers by limiting its customer base. Again, focus is key. Airborne Express doesn't try to outdo Federal Express or UPS in home delivery. It has specifically targeted a limited number of large business customers to maintain a high volume of business from a narrow network of delivery locations.

Customer-Intimate People

Customer-intimate companies require decentralized organizations with empowered employees. The strength of these companies is their flexibility to respond and adapt their product or service offerings to the customer's needs.

Employees have to be multitalented, ready to jump in when needed. And these aren't just the customer-service and sales people. For a customer-intimate company to succeed, the entire organization, including all service and product units, must be geared toward customer response.

6. THREE STEPS TO CHOOSING A VALUE DISCIPLINE

Which value discipline best fits the strengths of your business and the expectations of your customers?

To choose the right value discipline, you must answer three questions:

1. *Where does the company stand and why?* This is more than a simple competitive-positioning question. Go beyond market share and find out where you stand on delivering each of the three dimensions of value.

    What dimensions of value do your customers care most about? How important are the secondary dimensions of value? How do you compare with your competitors in providing value in all three dimensions of value? Why do you fall short of the value leaders in each dimension of value?

2. *How could the company change to become a market leader?* You have to balance what's important to the customer with which dimension of value your company can best compete in.

WATCH OUT FOR BIASES

Before you and your management team embark on discussions to choose a value discipline, be aware that past habits can bias the search for innovative change.

• Don't cut short the brainstorming process. Spend enough time allowing any and all ideas to float before shifting the process to more concrete evaluations

• Don't underestimate competitors that look different or have different styles of operation. Today's strange can become tomorrow's standard.

• Don't pursue multiple markets and values through one business unit. Each unit should be geared to one specific value discipline.

• Don't avoid tough questions just to be a team player.

Look at the value leaders in your industry. Would it be possible for you to match the operating systems they have put in place to achieve their leadership position? The choice begins to take shape as you determine which value dimension can be realistically accomplished by your operation.

Think innovatively of how you can change your operation to fulfill the customer's needs in each of the value dimensions. Then make a short list of options showing how you can provide value in each.

3. *Which discipline should we choose?* Take the options you created and give them to "tiger teams" for evaluation. The job of the tiger teams—small teams of high

performers—is to determine what operating systems would need to be in place to implement each of the strategic options.

SAVING KIDDIEVILLE

Child World, a chain of 160 stores, recently went bankrupt. The reason: no clear value discipline. Could Child World have been saved? To answer that question, imagine a nationwide chain of toy stores called Kiddieville.

Kiddieville's in trouble. It mimics Toys "R" Us with large, high-volume stores, but it's not big enough to be able to offer the low prices. It tried to expand its product range to related items such as diapers and to upgrade its stores with better displays and nicer signs. The result: higher overhead but stagnant sales.

Then Kiddieville decides to choose a value discipline.

Following the three steps outlined above, Kiddieville first takes stock of its position in the market. Competitors Wal-Mart and Toys "R" Us are operationally excellent companies offering low prices and convenient shopping. Disney and Warner Brothers are product leaders, while FAO Schwarz is a customer-intimate store.

Kiddieville managers then discuss realistic options to make Kiddieville competitive. Could it ever compete with Wal-Mart and Toys "R" Us on price? Probably not. But could it build more convenient stores or offer total solutions for birthdays and holidays?

Managers consider options and then hand a few to tiger teams for detailed evaluation.

In the end, Kiddieville could decide to become a leader in a specific product range—preschool toys, for example. The new emphasis would be on smaller stores, less volume, but the opportunity to sell unique merchandise.

This is just one of several solutions. So about Child World . . .

If the operating systems are put in place for the suggested value dimensions, will the value your company offers be higher than the value provided by current market leaders? What is the potential market for these value dimensions? How much would it cost for the company to change operating systems to match the requirements of the potential value dimension? What are the critical success factors for providing market-leading value in those dimensions?

Once the tiger teams have returned with their reports, the time has come for senior management to make the final decision. The choice of a value discipline is a fundamental, strategic choice affecting your company's organization structure, management systems, business processes, and culture.

Only by choosing explicitly in favor of one value discipline will you be able to rise above mediocrity to achieve market leadership.

7. CAREFUL: THE COPYCATS ARE WATCHING

When you've reached the top, when you've become a market leader, you become a target for your competitors. If you rest on your laurels, you will be toppled. The reason: business is a copycat world.

Nothing in business stays proprietary. Successful products, processes, technologies, and strategies can, and will, be copied. The only way to stay above the pack is to improve your performance continuously. You should be your best competitor.

For example, if you are an operationally excellent company, reduce your prices and create even more hassle-free services. If you are a customer-intimate company, seek better solutions for your customers than the ones you now offer. If you are a product leader, try to render your own products obsolete.

Each type of value-discipline leader faces different types of challenges that must be met to keep its leadership.

DON'T FORGET OTHER VALUE DISCIPLINES

It is important to concentrate on one value discipline. At the same time, improve your performance in the other disciplines. If not, the gap between you and the competition in these secondary disciplines will become so great that it will eliminate any value advantage from your primary discipline.

Apple Computer led the market in its chosen value discipline, product leadership. However, it started losing market share when its performance in another discipline, price, didn't match market expectations. It has since made improvements that reduced prices significantly.

Operational excellence depends on efficient systems. These systems include assets such as information systems, distribution networks, and equipment. The challenge for operationally excellent companies is to focus on improving the right assets for the future.

American Airlines' high tech SABRE division was vastly successful in streamlining the airline's standard operating procedures. But it paid no attention to its core assets of planes and hub infrastructure, which are now expensive ball-and-chains compared with Southwest Airlines' smaller-scale core assets.

THE CUSTOMER: FIRST, LAST, AND ALWAYS

No matter what value dimension you choose for your company, the underlying principle for all remains the same: the customer comes first, last, and always. This is not only a boardroom belief. In market-leading companies, every employee passionately believes that serving the customer is his or her most important function.

The "customer credo" is manifested in different ways for different value disciplines.

In operationally excellent companies, employees fulfill customer expectations by being totally dependable. If Federal Express has promised delivery by 10 A.M., each employee will do the maximum to ensure that promise is kept—down to the truck driver who travels through a blizzard to get the package on a plane.

In product-leading companies, employees want to dazzle the customer with the newest and best products. Employees know that innovation for innovation's sake is not sufficient. They are seeking innovation that will attract buyers.

In customer-intimate companies, the customer credo is more obvious. The company is a customer's partner and takes responsibility in the success of the customer's business. Employees will do whatever it takes for customers to get the most out of the products or services they buy.

Whatever the value discipline of the company, employees must constantly seek ways to improve value to their customers. This attitude, called "customer advocacy," is present in all market-leading companies.

The challenge for product-leading companies is to realize when customer attitudes and desires that led to previously successful products have changed. In other words, it may not be enough to render your product obsolete with a better, more efficient model. There comes a time when the assumptions behind those earlier successes have to be retired.

General Motors, for example, had been very successful making roomy, large-engined cars. It returned to the market with even roomier cars and larger engines. However, the product no longer fit customers' tastes. GM lost its market leadership until it changed tack. It is now becoming a product leader once again.

Customer-intimate companies face a similar challenge. Their groundbreaking service of yesterday can become today's standard. If every company now offers the same services that they developed, customers will be asking for something different.

Like product leaders, customer-intimate companies must be aware of changing tastes.

IBM was untouchable in the services it could provide its customers. But when responsibility for information systems shifted from information-technology specialists to line managers and financial executives, IBM was unable to communicate with them. The new clientele went elsewhere.

RENOVATE BEFORE YOU INNOVATE

by Sergio Zyman

Sergio Zyman is just as well known for his marketing prowess as head of marketing for Coke as he is known for what could be called The Great Marketing Mistake: New Coke. There is hardly a business book on marketing or developing products for customers that can resist mentioning the disastrous decision to change Coca-Cola's traditional formula for one that more closely resembled rival Pepsi's. Of course, Zyman also receives great credit for immediately recognizing the disaster and turning it into an advantage with the label Classic Coke.

After his bestseller, *The End of Marketing as We Know It,* in which Zyman argued that slick and fancy ads served no purpose if they didn't get the customers to buy more products, and its follow-up *The End of Advertising as We Know It,* Zyman addresses the issue of New Coke in *Renovate Before You Innovate.* The major mistake that he and Coke made with the New Coke attempt was to innovate when there was no need to innovate. Customers were not unhappy with the taste of Coke, so why change it? On the other hand, that does not mean that a company should rest on its laurels. On the contrary, companies should always be looking to renovate the offering—in other words, don't look to do new things, look to do more of what makes your products successful in the first place.

Zyman explains that the first step is to understand the value equation—the sources of the value that you bring to customers. Core competencies is just one part of the equation. Assets and infrastructure are also key components of the value equation. But perhaps the most important element is the company's core essence—that which defines you as a company and a brand. The core essence of Starbucks, for example, is to offer a great coffee experience.

In the age of innovation, Zyman once again presents a contrarian view—and offers the examples and case studies to back it up.

Sergio Zyman is the founder of the Zyman Group, a leading marketing strategy firm, and the former chief marketing officer of The Coca-Cola Company. He has also worked for PepsiCo and Procter & Gamble. A sought-after speaker, Zyman is the author of the bestseller *The End of Marketing as We Know It,* as well as *The End of Advertising as We Know It* and *Building Brandwidth.* A native of Mexico City, Zyman holds an Executive MBA from Harvard University.

RENOVATE BEFORE YOU INNOVATE
Why Doing the *New* Thing Might *Not* Be the *Right* Thing
by Sergio Zyman with Armin A. Brott

CONTENTS

THE SUMMARY IN BRIEF

Obsession with innovation is a current business fad. Many companies rely too heavily on innovation to solve their problems, and they attempt to start over with something fresh to revive old and tired businesses. Innovation sounds great. But it is often the lazy approach to marketing, and it typically doesn't work.

So what's the solution? Sergio Zyman preaches the power of renovation to accelerate and sustain top-line growth. It starts with recapturing the essence of your existing brands, products, and core competencies and doing more of the things that made your business great in the first place. It includes redefining your competitive space and creating preference for your business. In the end, it provides the most compelling customer experience.

Renovate Before You Innovate will challenge conventional business wisdom, facilitate smarter business decisions, and help companies "sell more stuff to more people more often for more money more efficiently."

THE COMPLETE SUMMARY

1. OBSESSION WITH INNOVATION

While innovation and risk taking can be critically important elements of some companies' strategy, for most companies, it simply isn't the right way to drive organic growth. What should you do instead? In a word, *renovate*. This means no longer doing *different* things with existing assets and competencies, but doing better things with them instead. It means reengaging with your customers by using your relationship with them to provide the products and services they truly want. Renovation is starting with what you can sell and then seeing whether you can deliver it. There is, however, a big difference between what companies should do and what they actually end up doing.

Core Competencies vs. Core Essence

Your core competencies are not simply a list of your products or services. They are based on four distinct factors: *knowledge* (what you know and what you've learned), *experience* (what you've been through), *resources* (what you have), and *people* (what you do and how you do it). These competencies are the things you're good at—the things you know how to do better than anyone else.

Core essence is somewhat more abstract. It's who you really are as a company or brand. It's the relationship customers and noncustomers alike have with your brand; it's what your brand stands for in their hearts and minds and the promises your brand makes to consumers. Your core essence is critical in determining where you can go as a business—if you try to extend your brand beyond your core essence, customers will not cooperate.

Champions at Leveraging Core Essence

If you succeed in leveraging your core competencies, core essence, and assets and infrastructure (the three elements of the value equation), you'll be able to grow your business successfully. Consider Starbucks Coffee, whose core competencies are building stores, motivating people, and sourcing the best coffee in the world. Its core essence is providing a great coffee experience. Likewise, grilling food is the core competency of Outback Steakhouses; its essence is Australia; and its new chain of seafood restaurants, Fishbone (which is modeled on Outback), is a great success.

Businesses that pursue an innovation strategy generally identify new growth opportunities that enable them to leverage their core competencies and assets. They embrace a philosophy of "Let's start with what we can build and see if we can sell it." Companies that rely on renovation, conversely, start with their core essence and identify new growth opportunities that are consistent with what consumers have shown they're willing to buy. The philosophy of renovation is "Let's find out what we can sell and see whether we can make it."

NEW COKE: A FAILED INNOVATION

Sergio Zyman knows the downfalls of trying to grow strictly through innovation—he was the manager of one of the great innovation busts of the twentieth century—New Coke. The New Coke formula was foisted upon the market in response to Pepsi's constant repositioning of original Coke's brand through such schemes as the Pepsi Challenge taste tests. Rather than challenge Pepsi on its brand's value proposition (giving consumers a reason to drink Coke), Coke decided to make its product taste more like Pepsi.

It was a disaster. After only seventy-seven days, Coca-Cola brought old Coke back to the market (this time as Coca-Cola Classic). It reconnected with its customers, deepened its relationship with them, and, in the process, increased sales. In that regard, Coca-Cola was lucky; corporate graveyards are littered with organizations that innovated themselves right out of business.

Common Pitfalls

Most companies that consider innovation make one or more of these major mistakes:

- They focus on leveraging their core competencies instead of their core essence. A critical part of being able to leverage the three elements of the value equation is having a firm grasp of what they are. Getting the right competencies is easy—if you don't know how to do something, hire someone who does. Getting a new core essence, on the other hand, is virtually impossible.
- They pursue creativity at any cost and treat all new ideas as potentially equal. The push to "think outside the box" often masks a hidden agenda that comes from higher up in the organization: Do something—anything—with idle capacity or underused assets. Unfortunately, the side effects of this approach can be precarious. Money is often thrown at bad ideas as well as good ones. The resulting products often confuse customers who find no real benefit in them. These questionable products wind up taking up precious shelf space that could be dedicated to more useful items.
- They limit their innovations to only new products, forgetting that innovation is about creating new value for customers, consumers, and the business. When it comes to identifying organic growth opportunities, an amazingly large percentage of companies are one-trick ponies, focusing only on coming up with new products, excluding anything

else. Even worse, the emphasis is clearly on quantity over quality. Such a narrow approach can do more harm than good in many ways, including possible damage to existing brand equity and customer frustration.

- *They grow horizontally rather than vertically.* Trying to grow a business through innovation means spreading resources horizontally, developing new brands, new customers, and new directions. It's a tremendously risky and expensive path to take.
- *They try to innovate by acquiring other companies rather than growing organically.* Acquiring another company or brand is the Hail Mary pass of innovation—a desperate, last-ditch attempt to get out of trouble. As with the Hail Mary pass, there's a good chance things will go in exactly the opposite direction from the way they were supposed to go.

2. RENOVATE INSTEAD

The most important of the three elements of your value equation is your core essence. Many people confuse core essence with jingles, logos, or advertising slogans. In fact, however, true core essence is the most powerful, compelling attribute of your brand. The core essence of Windows, for example, is "user-friendly"; for Crest toothpaste, it's "fights cavities"; for Pepsi, it's "revolution, choice, and change."

Core essence is expressed and supported by everything your company does—it is the seed from which your corporation evolves. Without one, you simply cannot grow, rendering you vulnerable to the impulse to flit from one idea to another, never building an organization that will be able to endure over the long haul.

Customers Decide

The most important thing to remember, however, is that what you say is your core essence is completely irrelevant. It is what consumers and customers think that counts. In fact, there's often a big disconnect between what you think your core essence is and what is actually on the minds of consumers. This leaves you with one choice if you want to leverage your core essence—you need to hit the street and start asking people questions about three things that they perceive about your company and your brand:

- *Emotional benefits*—how your product makes them feel.
- *Functional benefits*—elements in the minds of customers that make your brand superior to your competitors'.
- *Attributes*—things that affect the functional and/or emotional benefits, even though they aren't benefits themselves.

Doing this kind of research will enable you to see your company the way consumers do. Once you've determined your core essence, you will be able to use that knowledge to renovate every aspect of your business and start generating, evaluating, and developing organic growth opportunities.

Is Your Company a Business or a Franchise?

Whether your business is a franchise depends on whether your business is truly in a position to grow beyond what you're doing now. A business can grow, but only in its defined area. A franchise, conversely, can expand far beyond its perceived area of expertise. Being a franchise enables a company to redefine its competitive frame, broaden its market, redefine its basis of competition, and leverage its unique expertise.

Being a franchise gives you some very powerful advantages that your competition doesn't have. Becoming a franchise isn't a question of just deciding to do it and flipping a switch. You must have at least one of the following:

- *Attitude.* If you want to be great, you have to want to be great, conducting your business as if you know you're great.
- *Value.* Leverage your commitment to value to move into other areas where you can provide that value.
- *Experience.* Do not be afraid to expand your experience beyond your perceived boundaries, if the opportunity is a good one for you and consumers.
- *Expertise.* Explore new avenues by leveraging your expertise in your existing field. (See "Nike Leverages Its Expertise.")

From Business to Franchise through TACOS

Businesses become franchises by continually renovating. It's only by renovating that you will learn the kind of information about your customers, your company, your market, and your competitors that you will need to grow and expand. You can evaluate your prospects for turning your business into a franchise by using the TACOS formula:

$$\text{Trademark} + \text{Area} + \text{Customer Offer} = \text{Success}$$

- *Trademark* is a manifestation of your core essence—your unique selling proposition, or what you offer that no one else does.
- *Area* is where you place your trademark—one of the major factors in determining the trademark's relevance.

- *Customer offer* is your product or service. What you're able to offer your customers is going to be a function of your trademark and where you place it.
- *Success* is what results when all the TACO ingredients have fit together perfectly. Your trademark has to be properly placed in an area where it doesn't overwhelm or get lost, and you have to offer your customers something relevant that capitalizes on your expertise in other areas.

Key Components

A truly effective business renovation involves overhauling these key components of your business:

- The way you think.
- Your destination.
- Your competitive frame.
- Your segmentation, or how you think about customers.
- Your customers' brand experience.

3. RENOVATE YOUR THINKING

The process of renovating begins with renovating your mindset and the way you think about a number of basic business and marketing ideas. Developing a renovation mentality involves several steps:

- Training yourself to think like the challenger (or aggressor) and not the champion (or leader).
- Committing before you even start to measure the results of every single dollar you spend on marketing.
- Getting the idea of giving price concessions out of your head right now.

Aggressors vs. Leaders

The leader is the big player in the market—cautious, cumbersome, and content to kick back and rest on his laurels, never changing a thing about his business or approach. The aggressor is the new kid on the block, or one who has been successful in another area and is trying to make inroads into a new market. He is fast, smart, and hungry and he has nothing to lose.

Big players in existing markets cannot get complacent. The only way to stay alive is to keep renovating, remain true to the business's core essence, and keep doing better and more relevant things with existing assets.

WHEN LEADERS ARE FORCED TO FOLLOW

The differences between leaders and aggressors are illustrated in the following examples:

- Diet and caffeine-free soft drinks were not introduced by Coke.
- Overnight package delivery was not introduced by the U.S. Postal Service.
- Online mapping was not introduced by Rand McNally.
- Cell phones were not introduced by AT&T.

Not one of these innovations was developed by an industry leader, but each one forever changed its industry. Had the leaders listed above been the ones to introduce these things, they would have been renovations—extensions of an existing brand. None of that ever happened, though, because these companies were asleep at the wheel.

Make Marketing More Effective

Customer loyalty is one of the most perishable commodities in the world. There is a critical moment in every transaction, when the choice comes down to your brand or a competitor's, and the customer must decide whether you have provided a compelling reason to buy your product. If you have, you'll make the sale; if you haven't, you'll see the customer's back as he or she walks away from you.

Reminding people why you're great is always important, but there are two situations that nearly every company finds itself in at one point or another:

1. *You're under assault by aggressors and it's getting increasingly harder to stay afloat.* In this case, you must redefine your positioning against these competitors in a way that not only differentiates, but also creates preference. You must know what your core essence is, who your customers are, why they buy from you when they do, and why they go to certain competitors when they don't.
2. *You're an also-ran in a stagnant category.* In this case, you must give current customers a reason to buy from you more often by offering them value instead of just a product or service.

Measurements Count

The purpose of marketing is to drive sales, and every dollar you spend on marketing should generate measurable results. You must have a plan to measure the results of your marketing activities before you put them in place. In other words, you have to create control markets and build in measurement criteria up front. Ask yourself these three questions:

- How much are we spending on marketing?
- What exactly are we spending it on?
- What are we getting in return for our investment?

If you know the answers to these questions, you will ultimately sell more products to more people, more often and more efficiently. Your overall goal must be to maximize the returns generated by your marketing investments. Know exactly how much you're spending on each specific marketing activity. Then, when you have a handle on spending, you'll be able to determine the return each activity generates. Once you have that information, you'll be able to focus your efforts on the activities—or combination of activities—that produce the best returns, instead of wasting money on things that don't work.

The Traps of Inefficient Marketing

Most companies rarely focus their efforts like this; instead, they fall into one of the following traps:

- They don't track what they do, nor do they measure the amounts they invest.
- They rarely use consistent metrics to link activities, investments, and sales.
- They rarely measure systematically the volume of response generated from any specific activity.
- They neglect to take a structured approach linking marketing investments with brand objectives.

What they should be doing is the following:

1. Change the way they think.
2. Break down their overall marketing budget and determine exactly how much they spend on each marketing element.
3. Calculate how much of their sales are being driven by each individual marketing element.
4. Determine the net profitability of those elements, resulting in a clear picture of the efficiency of each.
5. Focus their efforts on the things that generate the highest return.
6. Dump the things that lose money or bring in little profit.

NIKE LEVERAGES ITS EXPERTISE

Nike has used its expertise in athletic shoes to get into new markets and attract new customers. It started off in a relatively small sector—making shoes for runners—but expanded into offering products for sports performance, such as water bottles, running shorts, and other gear. After that, it expanded into an even bigger sector—overall performance products. Finally, it raised the bar by venturing into any area that values accomplishment—Just Do It.

Don't Slash Prices

Everything you do communicates something about your brand to your customers and prospective customers. Even your prices communicate something about your business, and can be an important part of your marketing strategy. Most companies, however, fail to manage their prices at all. Prices tend to go one way—down. Think long and hard about lowering them, even temporarily. Temporary price breaks tend to become permanent. Your competitors will see your lower prices and drop theirs; once they do this, you'll have to lower yours again to stay ahead of them. It's a downward spiral that leads to decreased profits.

4. RENOVATE YOUR BUSINESS DESTINATION

Take a deep breath and think honestly about your current circumstances and everything—good and bad—that you're facing. Be honest with yourself—don't try to convince yourself that your business is headed in one direction when it is really going the opposite way. Determine, also, what obstacles you're facing. Once you have those things down, you can determine how to get where you want to be.

The Destination Statement

The first step is to come up with a destination statement, which articulates where you want to end up as a business. You need to articulate how you want the consumer to think, feel, and act in relation to your company and brand. The statement must also express the outcome you want to achieve in the marketplace—where you want to be, as opposed to where you are currently.

The best destination statements address these questions:

- How do we define our business? What business do we want to be in on a long-term basis?
- Who are our target customers? Who should we sell to, directly and indirectly, now and in the future?

- What do we want them to think? What attributes and benefits will customers ascribe to our brand?
- What do we want them to feel? What intangible, higher-order benefits and attributes do we deliver?
- How do we want them to act? What do we want them to do as a result of their feelings and thoughts?
- What do we want as a result? How will our company benefit from all this over the long term?

"Dimensionalizing" Your Destination

Your destination (as well as the statement that articulates it) must be specific enough to guide the decisions you make, painting a clear picture—for everyone who directly or indirectly encounters the end consumer—of who you are, what you believe, where you're going, and what drives you on the journey. It must also lay out clearly—from the perspective of consumers—how they interact with you, how they think about you, how they feel about you, and the role you play in their lives.

What's in It for the Customer?

A clearly defined destination leads to more effective business objectives, guides the development of marketing strategies, and ultimately drives success in the marketplace. The real goal of destination planning and articulating a concise destination is this: having a clear destination will clarify what your value proposition is and how to improve it.

Your value proposition is the catalyst that propels your brand and business to their destination. All that matters is what your brand means to your target customer and, in turn, how the customer acts on that meaning. What gives your brand meaning is your answer to the customer's most important question—"What's in it for me?" Your answer to that question is your value proposition.

Your value proposition must operate on the three levels of perception customers have about your company and your brand, as mentioned earlier: emotional benefits, functional benefits, and product attributes. Put another way, your value proposition must have the power to move consumers up the value chain.

5. RENOVATE YOUR COMPETITIVE FRAME

When most people think of their competition, they think only of their industry rivals, other companies in the same category, or other companies that offer similar products and services. That, however, is only part of the story.

Your real competition is the entire set of viable alternatives to your product that compete for your customers' money and time. This is your competitive frame, and it includes many things that you might never have considered.

COKE IN RUSSIA

One great example of a competitive frame can be seen in Coke's first foray into the Russian market. The company spent much time researching its competitors, and what it found was shocking Coke's biggest competitor wasn't Pepsi, or some regional cola, or even vodka. Coke's biggest competitor was the city bus. Many Russian consumers simply did not have enough disposable income to buy a Coke *and* take a bus home from work, so they had to choose one or the other.

Rather than being able to compete on taste and refreshment, as they had in other markets, Coke had to convince Russian consumers that it was a good value for the money, and that when it came down to a choice between a Coke and a McDonald's hamburger or a candy bar or a magazine or some other nonessential item, Coke was the best—and most satisfying—investment.

Defining Your Frame

How you define your competitive frame will have a direct impact on the size of the opportunity, the diversity of consumers and competition, and the benefits you'll need to offer in order to compete effectively. Defining a narrow competitive frame may seem safe, but it's usually a big mistake. The broader your definition (assuming it's consistent with your core essence), the more purchase occasions and the greater wallet share you will capture.

Some companies have enough equity and relevance that they can expand their franchise into completely new categories. These companies might not look like your competitors right now, but they could be back to claim your business tomorrow.

How Are You Different?

By definition, every brand is very different from a commodity (a good product or service that is perceived to be undifferentiated from other similar products or services). Typically, the only determinant of a commodity's value is price. Quality is assumed to be identical, unless you tell consumers otherwise and give them a compelling reason to pay more.

Differentiation, on the other hand, is where value is created, and is what separates you from the pack. The driving philosophy here is the belief that customers do not buy sameness. The only way to build brand equity and drive sales volume is through offering consumers relevant emotional benefits.

SMALL BUSINESSES AND COMPETITIVE FRAMING

While it might seem that a discussion of competitive framing could be applicable only to large companies, it applies to small companies, as well. If, for example, you run a neighborhood pizza restaurant, you might define your competitors as "other local pizza restaurants." However, when a chain like Domino's Pizza enters your market, you will suddenly be faced with huge competition with regard to time and convenience, even if you make a better pizza. You're also competing against cheap frozen pizzas in grocery stores; high-end pizza parlors and their frozen pies; make-your-own pizza products like Boboli pizza crusts; as well as local Chinese, Thai, and Italian restaurants. When the Super Bowl comes around, you'll be going head-to-head against chips and dip, too.

Bottom line: Run your business aggressively to take on a variety of competitors, or you'll rapidly lose sales.

---

6. RENOVATE YOUR SEGMENTATION

The objective of segmentation is to group markets, customers, or consumers in order to maximize profit. Traditionally, it's done by dividing consumers into neat, predictable demographic, psychographic, or behavior-specific groups. The assumption for each is identical: that everyone in each group will behave the same way—reading the same magazines, watching the same TV shows, eating in the same kinds of restaurants, and so on. When you segment your market using these traditional methods, you get segments that are:

- *Meaningful and mutually exclusive.* Each segment should be different enough from the others that it is unique. Plus, each customer should belong to only one segment.
- *Measurable.* Each segment should be clearly definable and have a quantifiable market share.
- *Substantial.* Each segment must be able to produce enough volume and profit to justify an investment in new offerings or marketing strategies.
- *Attainable and actionable.* You must be able to design a separate value proposition for each segment, and you must be able to reach that segment in order to sell to it.

Demand-Based Segmentation

These factors are not enough to help you achieve volume growth. If you want growth, you have to allocate your resources to the segments that produce the highest profits. What you need is a completely different approach to segmentation, one that enables you to segment your market based on the values, attitudes, and behaviors that shape demand, as well as the attributes, and benefits that will increase that demand. Such an approach is called demand-based segmentation, and it incorporates these three steps:

1. Identify your most valuable customers.
2. Segment the opportunity.
3. Segment the occasion.

Identify Your Most Valuable Customers

Demand-based segmentation is about giving existing customers a reason to buy more. Roughly 80 percent of your business comes from 20 percent of your customers. You'll get that 20 percent to buy more by segmenting those existing customers based on their usage. Create an ideal customer profile and conduct the requisite research to help you segment customers by their attitude toward your company. Such attitudinal segmentation might look something like this:

- Hard opposition—the unconvertible loyalists of your competition. You can write these people off.
- Soft opposition—the consumers who are currently not in your brand franchise, but aren't loyal to any one competitor. Winning them over will be hard and expensive.
- Undecided—those with no allegiances to speak of. You can probably win these consumers' business with price promoting, but you cannot win their loyalty.
- Soft support—those who like your brand and occasionally use it, but not often enough. Moving them to greater loyalty is efficient and highly effective in building profitability.
- Hard support—the consumers who are your strong loyalists. They'll keep buying from you even if they have to pay a premium to do so.

Segment the Opportunity

Segment consumers based on their response to specific benefits, products, services, promotions, and other inducements. Demand-based segmentation defines the marketing levers that are the most effective and that you can use to target and sell to each segment. In other words, it makes segmentation actionable, enabling you to forecast increases in usage by influencing the perceptions of the brand and products used, considering the following questions:

- What specific products and/or services will increase consumption?
- What is the probability of increased usage due to specific products?
- What amount of increased usage can be expected?

This segmentation will produce a framework of opportunities rather than a structure of the market. As such, it will guide all marketing strategies.

Segment the Occasion

There are two particular occasions that deserve special discussion:

1. *Purchase occasions.* Growth in this area comes from penetrating additional places where the decision to make a purchase is made. Penetrating additional purchase occasions helps you differentiate from competitors.
2. *Communication occasions.* Many companies also miss opportunities to understand the many ways they have to communicate with customers. Thinking outside the normal methods of communication can help you reach more consumers, as well as sell more to those customers who already buy from you.

7. RENOVATE YOUR CUSTOMERS' BRAND EXPERIENCE

Even though you might think you're selling a product or a service, you're actually selling an experience. That experience is often the only significant thing that separates you from your competitors. In most cases, experiences have little to do with the products themselves, no matter how hard the companies that offer them try to make a connection. Harley-Davidson motorcycles, for example, are not the most comfortable, fastest, best-designed bikes on the market. That's not what matters, though. The reason people buy a "Hog" is for the Harley experience—"ride to live, live to ride"; wind in your hair, American classic, and so on.

The real reason products in and of themselves have become almost afterthoughts is because technology has advanced to the point where nearly any company can "copycat" a product and have it on store shelves in a ridiculous amount of time.

The 9/11 Factor

The big question is why experience has become the new basis of competition in so many categories. In 2001, consumer research found that after 9/11, consumers started placing much more emphasis on family and relationships. Recent research found that, although 9/11 has become a less painful memory, there are some lingering effects. Consumers indicated that, on any given day, if they had to choose between making more money and taking things a little easier, they'd go with easier. The brands and products they find most appealing are the ones that make their time more enjoyable, not the ones that save them money.

Time, it seems, has become a kind of new currency, and its scarcity has made consumers more conscious, discriminating, and aware of the "present tense" than ever before. Product benefits and attributes are simply no longer enough. Today's consumers want experiences—experiences they can feel and touch, experiences that will change their emotions, their attitudes, and maybe even their lives.

Being aware of this shift is great news for your company. Being able to compete on the basis of experiences expands your competitive frame and gives you more opportunities to deliver value and differentiate yourself from competitors.

GIBSON REACHES OUT WITH *THE PASSION*

Churches are not usually the first locations that leap to mind when you think about places to advertise movies. Mel Gibson, however, saved millions of marketing dollars for his film *The Passion of the Christ* by doing advance screenings at churches, distributing 250,000 promotional DVDs, and conducting three hundred *Passion* "summit meetings" with clergy and other religious officials and laymen. Before the movie was even released, churches had reserved $10 million worth of seats.

Thanks in part to a combination of these alternative communication occasions, *The Passion of the Christ* generated $125.2 million in its first five days, rivaled only by two other films: *The Lord of the Rings: The Return of the King* and *Star Wars: Episode I*. Both of those films spent considerably more on advertising.

Service-Based Experience

Experiences can sometimes be service based. Any company, large or small, can provide a similar level of service-based experience. The only rule is that every single employee—from the CEO on down—must know and fully support the company's core essence and business destination, with no exceptions.

Overall, the experience you offer is likely to be a combination of product attributes, service, retail environment, and every other point of contact you have with consumers—your advertising, promotion, marketing, PR, and sponsorships. It also includes your Web site, packaging, and employment policies; how your receptionist answers the phone; and how your top executives behave at parties.

The only way to build loyal customers is to deliver experiences that create value beyond mere satisfaction. Consumers are looking for experiences that complement their lifestyle and brands that say something about their aspirations.

Index